ISRAEL
vs. IRAN

Related Titles from Potomac Books

*Does Israel Have a Future? The Case
for a Post-Zionist State*—Constance Hilliard

*Transforming America's Israel Lobby: The Limits of Its Power
and the Potential for Change*—Dan Fleshler

Axis of Unity: Venezuela, Iran & the Threat to America—Sean Goforth

*Iran's Revolutionary Guard: The Threat That Grows
While America Sleeps*—Steven O'Hern

ISRAEL vs. IRAN

The Shadow War

YAAKOV KATZ | YOAZ HENDEL

Potomac Books
Washington, D.C.

Library of Congress Cataloging-in-Publication Data
Katz, Yaakov, 1979-
  [Yisra'el neged Iran. English]
  Israel vs. Iran : the shadow war / Yaakov Katz and Yoaz Hendel.
    p. cm.
  Includes bibliographical references and index.
  ISBN 978-1-59797-668-8 (hardcover edition: alk. paper)
  ISBN 978-1-59797-886-6 (electronic edition)
  1. Espionage, Israeli. 2. Israel—Relations—Iran. 3. Iran—Relations—Israel. 4. Nuclear weapons—Iran. 5. National security—Middle East. I. Hendel, Yoaz. II. Title. III. Title: Israel versus Iran.
  UB271.I8H4513 2012
  327.125694055—dc23

                                                                2011045394

Printed in the United States of America on acid-free paper that meets the American National Standards Institute Z39-48 Standard.

Potomac Books, Inc.
22841 Quicksilver Drive
Dulles, Virginia 20166

First Edition

10 9 8 7 6 5 4 3 2 1

Yaakov dedicates this book to the lovely
and beautiful Katz women:

Chaya, Atara, Miki, and Rachel.

Yoaz dedicates this book to the beloved "shadows"
who watch over him:

Shiri, Tavor, and Be'eri.

In these troubled times, our families remain our source of hope.

Contents

Preface

Our work on this book began after a conversation we had in the winter of 2009. It was a few weeks after Israel's successful Operation Cast Lead against Hamas in the Gaza Strip and the two of us were driving back to Jerusalem from a press conference with the Israel Defense Forces (IDF) about the Iranian-Hamas relationship.

We discussed what we had learned in the briefing. One of us mentioned that the growing axis between Gaza and Tehran was only the tip of the iceberg. It was then that this book was born.

Our objective was to explore Iran's growing influence and presence along Israel's borders, particularly via Hamas in the Gaza Strip and Hezbollah in Lebanon. Our focus was on the period from the end of the Second Lebanon War in 2006 until today. As we mention numerous times throughout this book, the 2006 war against Hezbollah was really a war against Iran, as was the operation in Gaza in 2009. Iran's pursuit of nuclear weapons adds a new dimension to the ongoing war.

Over the years, the Israeli military has been a focus of our attention in various ways. We are both IDF veterans and continue to serve in the reserves. Professionally, we write daily about the IDF and its various operations, about intelligence assessments, and about Israel's overall strategic standing in the Middle East. Our jobs have allowed us not only to report on Israel but also to watch it from the front lines and to become a part of the story. The Palestinian terrorist campaign against Israel throughout the Second Intifada, beginning in 2000; Israel's unilateral withdrawal from the Gaza Strip in 2005; the Second Lebanon War in 2006;

and Operation Cast Lead in the Gaza Strip in 2009 are only some of the major events we have had the opportunity to be a part of.

We truly owe this book to the hundreds of people—many of whom are still in active service in the Israeli and American defense establishments and intelligence agencies—who agreed to meet with us and share their stories and insights. Most of the people we interviewed asked for anonymity, a request that we have respected.

Readers are justified for being suspicious of anonymous sources. As reporters we have tried our best to use the names of our sources whenever we could. In today's world, though, particularly in Israel and particularly when talking about issues of national security and intelligence, off-the-record conversations are the bread and butter of any military reporter. As Israelis we are also bound by our country's rules of censorship. Although Israel is a democracy and has complete freedom of the press, military censors need to approve content when it comes to issues of national security first. We found the censors to be tough but fair, and we appreciate their level of professionalism.

Yaakov is indebted to the *Jerusalem Post*, where he has worked for nearly a decade. Every day the paper gives him the opportunity to tell the story of the Israeli military. He particularly thanks David Horovitz, the former editor in chief of the *Post* who has served as a mentor and friend, and to the paper's current editor, Steve Linde.

Yoaz would like to thank the Begin-Sadat Center for Strategic Studies at Bar-Ilan University for serving as a place for academic growth.

A special thank you goes to our editor, Hilary Claggett. She was as excited about the book as we were from the beginning, and we appreciate her enthusiasm.

We also thank Yakov Rand, who assisted us in translating many parts of this book, as well as Yaakov Katz's mother, Debbie Katz, for taking the time to read the book as a work in progress. Their important insights and comments made this work what you see today. We also thank Paul Packer for his assistance in helping us gain access to a remarkable story, one of many we are fortunate to be able to tell in these pages.

Last, but not least, we owe a profound debt of gratitude to our families. Without their support, this book would not have been possible.

INTRODUCTION

Jerusalem is at once the city where everything began and, according to doomsday prophesies, the place where everything will come to an end.

A short drive from Jerusalem's Old City, which is home to some of the most sacred Jewish, Christian, and Muslim sites in the world and has seen centuries of bloodshed, is a museum meant to remind the world of what evil can do. It is called Yad Vashem, Hebrew for "memorial and name." The State of Israel in 1953 chose the mountain atop which Yad Vashem is located, surrounded by hills with tall, dark-green pine trees and by expanses of modern housing in southern Jerusalem, as the location to safeguard the memory of the six million Jews whom the Nazis killed during the Holocaust.

Similar to the Tomb of the Unknown Soldier in Washington, D.C., or Turkey's mausoleum of Mustafa Kemal Atatürk, Yad Vashem is where all visiting dignitaries come to pay their respects and lay a wreath.

Perched on the edge of a cliff and facing a forest to the south of Jerusalem is a cattle car, one of the thousands that the Nazis used to transport Jews to their deaths at concentration camps across Europe. Looking down at the valley beyond the car, one sees a collection of dozens of slab stones, each engraved with the name of a Jewish community in Europe that was destroyed during the Holocaust. On the other side one can look out to the newly rebuilt Jerusalem and see the apartment buildings made of Jerusalem stone.

In January 2010, on the eve of International Holocaust Remembrance Day, Israeli prime minister Binyamin Netanyahu visited Yad Vashem for the opening of an exhibit that displayed the original blueprints of the Auschwitz-Birkenau

Nazi death camp. Netanyahu issued a warning to the world of the looming threat Iran posed to the State of Israel. He cautioned that while Iranian president Mahmoud Ahmadinejad spoke only about his desire to destroy Israel, the day would come when he would aspire to destroy the rest of the world as well.

"There is evil in the world; if it is not stopped, it spreads," Netanyahu said. "There are new calls for the extermination of the Jewish State. This is certainly our concern, but it is not only our concern."[1]

Speaking about Iran at Yad Vashem helped Netanyahu make his point. He had said on numerous previous occasions that the Islamic Republic of Iran is the reincarnation of Germany under Nazi rule in the 1930s, and that its pursuit of nuclear weapons could potentially lead to a second Jewish Holocaust.

A few years earlier, in 2006, at a conference of Jewish organizations in Los Angeles, Netanyahu had been even more explicit in making the comparison. "It's 1938 and Iran is Germany. And Iran is racing to arm itself with atomic bombs," Netanyahu told delegates at the annual United Jewish Communities General Assembly. "Believe him and stop him. . . . This is what we must do. Everything else pales before this."[2]

Despite the rhetoric, Israel under Netanyahu's leadership in 2012 was preparing for two realistic options—either to come to terms with a nuclear Iran or to attempt a military strike aimed at destroying the Islamic Republic's nuclear facilities. This ostensible contradiction is understood with great clarity in Jerusalem, where the Israeli government in 2012 was completing the construction of a massive bunker that would be used to keep the government and parliament safe in the event of a nuclear attack. Fitted with air purification systems, offices, conference rooms, and the most advanced communications technology in the world, the bunker is supposed to enable Israeli leaders to continue running the country even at a time of nuclear war.

Twenty minutes north of the bunker is Beit Zecharia, a pastoral town located on a mountain. According to foreign reports, outside in the nearby caves and fields is an Israeli Air Force (IAF) base where Israel stores its Jericho class long-range ballistic missiles armed with nuclear warheads.[3] The base and the purported nuclear arsenal would be used to prevent a nuclear attack on Israel from ever happening. In the middle of both sites is Yad Vashem, a reminder of what is really at stake.

Netanyahu's selection of Yad Vashem as the place to deliver his speech, juxtaposing the threat to Israel from Iran and the consequences for Jews of the

Holocaust, made sense for Israel. As the leader of Israel, Netanyahu, who again made this comparison a number of times in 2012, wanted to make it clear that the country would not allow Iran to become a nuclear power.

For similar reasons in 2008 the head of the IAF, Maj. Gen. Eliezer Shkedy, approached Lt. Col. Moti Habakuk, the head of his branch's history department, with a strange request.[4] A few years earlier, in addition to Shkedy's work as commander of the IAF, then prime minister Ariel Sharon asked him to serve as the officer in charge of the IDF's new Iran Command. His responsibilities were quite obvious—preparing Israel's long and strategic arm of F-15 and F-16 fighter jets for potentially flying the distance to attack and destroy Iran's nuclear program.

This task was not simply another job for a man like Shkedy. The son of Holocaust survivors, Shkedy was deputy commander of the air force when F-15 fighter jets flew over Auschwitz in 2003. He often gave a photograph of the trio of planes flying right above the death camp's gates to his subordinates or visiting dignitaries and foreign military officers. On the photos Shkedy would write, "To remember and never forget that we can only rely on ourselves."

When Shkedy asked Habakuk to write a research paper in 2008 comparing public remarks that Adolf Hitler made in the 1920s and 1930s to those Ahmadinejad had made since his rise to power in 2005, the head of the history department readily agreed. The results of the research were shocking, with both leaders voicing similar declarations regarding the Jewish nation, Zionism, and race.

Here is one example. In 1922 Hitler said, "If I am ever really in power, the destruction of the Jews will be my first and most important job." In 2005 at a conference called "A World without Zionism," Ahmadinejad said, "Israel must be wiped off the map." Shortly thereafter he said, "The Zionist regime is a decaying and crumbling tree that will fall with a storm."

For Shkedy the conclusion was clear. Ahmadinejad could not be allowed to continue developing nuclear weapons, and the IAF's fighter jets would need to be ready to prevent a repeat of what his parents had experienced more than sixty years earlier.

In Israel, the Iranians' rhetoric and ideology leave no room for confusion. Netanyahu, along with several cabinet ministers and IDF generals, views Iran as the reincarnation of Nazi Germany and Iran's nuclear bomb as the equivalent of the gas chambers and crematoriums.

The prime minister's visit to Yad Vashem in January 2010 occurred only a few weeks before the United Nations (UN) Security Council was scheduled to debate a new round of sanctions against Iran, which had rejected several generous offers from the West to suspend its enrichment of uranium but allowing it to retain its nuclear energy capability. Netanyahu's message was quite clear: if the sanctions were not passed, Israel did not plan on sitting back and tolerating the global community's inaction. It was preparing its own solutions as well.

During his election campaign in late 2008, Netanyahu often spoke about Iran. In closed-door meetings he dismissed the Palestinian peace process as a nuisance that he planned to deal with but would not put at the center of his diplomatic agenda. Instead, he would focus on Iran and how to stop its nuclear drive. Thus, Netanyahu was slightly taken by surprise on his first visit as the newly elected prime minister to President Barack Obama's White House in May 2009. During their two-hour discussion, Obama, only five months after taking office, preferred to concentrate solely on the Palestinian peace process while Netanyahu had expected Iran to top the meeting's agenda.

The disagreement between the two leaders was quite evident. While Obama tried to persuade Netanyahu to make peace with the Palestinians and pave the way for the creation of a broad pan-Arab coalition against Iran, Netanyahu argued both that Iran was preventing peace by supporting Harakat al-Muqawama al-Islamiya (the Islamic Resistance Movement, or Hamas) and that if Iran were neutralized, a Palestinian state would no longer be a dream but would instead become a reality.[5] For Netanyahu, Iran is without a doubt an "existential threat," but the same cannot be said of the rest of his cabinet. Defense Minister Ehud Barak, for example, shared his view in a widely publicized interview in the Israeli press in September 2009: "I am not among those who believe Iran is an existential issue for Israel. Israel is strong, I don't see anyone who could pose an existential threat."[6] A top IDF general who is involved in operational planning seconded Barak's opinion. "Israel has over seven million people," the general said in 2010. "If two million people are killed, does this spell the end of our existence? I don't think so."[7]

Other Israeli cabinet ministers, however, take a more hard-core approach. Vice Prime Minister and Minister of Strategic Affairs Moshe Ya'alon—who also served as a former chief of staff of the IDF—said in February 2010 that Iran's ultimate goal was to be an existential threat to Israel. Ya'alon pointed not only to Iran's pursuit of nuclear weapons but also to its unbelievably widespread support for terrorist organizations in the Middle East, primarily Hezbollah in Lebanon and Hamas and Islamic Jihad in the Gaza Strip. "We saw seventy years ago the horrific ramifications of ignoring an impending threat," Ya'alon said. "The free world cannot ignore history."[8]

But even those who do not believe that Iran poses an existential threat to Israel find the prospect of a nuclear Iran alarming. It's not only the nuclear threat to Israel that worries the entire Israeli establishment but also the possibility of a nuclear arms race in the Middle East. While Israel might be leading the world in its warnings regarding the inherent dangers in Iran's success in developing a nuclear capability, it is not the only country that feels genuinely threatened.

In November 2010 WikiLeaks, an organization run by Julian Assange, made public hundreds of secret cables that American diplomats based throughout the Middle East and the Persian Gulf had sent. Some of the leaders of these Arab countries were quoted as begging the United States to attack Iran. Saudi king Abdullah, for example, was quoted in one cable from 2009 as saying that the United States needed to attack Iran and "cut off the head of the snake."[9]

A year later King Hamad bin Isa al-Khalifa, the ruler of Bahrain, met with commander of the U.S. Central Command (CENTCOM) Gen. David Petraeus and urged the Americans to take action against Iran's nuclear program. "That program must be stopped," King Hamad was quoted as saying. "The danger of letting it go on is greater than the danger of stopping it."[10]

Bahrain, a small but rich island country in the Persian Gulf, could possibly be one of the first countries to fall under the growing Shiite web if Iran succeeds in obtaining nuclear power. While the regime in Bahrain is Sunni, the majority of the Bahraini people are Shiite, and Iran is already suspected of meddling inside the country and trying to undermine the ruling family. While the presence of the U.S. Navy's Fifth Fleet in the country has served as a deterrent to prevent any destabilization, protests broke out in 2011 in an effort to topple the regime.

WikiLeaks also provided insight into Israel's shadow war against Iran. In August 2007 Undersecretary of State for Political Affairs Nicholas Burns traveled to Tel Aviv for meetings with top Israeli officials. One of them was the Mossad chief at the time, Meir Dagan, who is credited with leading Israel's efforts to deny Iran a nuclear capability.[11] (Dagan stepped down from his post in January 2011.) During the meeting Dagan spelled out his plan for stopping Iran. The main strategy was to seek increased UN-imposed sanctions to prevent the know-how and nuclear-related technologies from reaching Iran and to support Iranian opposition and student groups that could potentially overthrow the Islamic regime. Last, Dagan spoke about "covert measures," though he was not willing to say more.

Dagan's plan to stop Iran rested mainly on the regional fears that its nuclear program has already set off. Other countries in the region are also conducting nuclear research. If any of them succeed in obtaining full-fledged nuclear weapons technology, the already volatile Middle East will become even more dangerous.

Egypt, which views itself as a regional superpower, will not sit idly by if Iran develops nuclear weapons. This stance was made clear during French president Nicolas Sarkozy's visit to Cairo in 2007, during which he offered Egypt assistance in developing civilian nuclear technology.[12]

Saudi Arabia, Iran's greatest adversary in the region, will also be forced to act if Iran becomes nuclear, as will Turkey, which is also a regional power broker. In 2010 Turkey passed a bill in parliament that paved the way for the construction of three nuclear reactors by 2020. Jordan and the United Arab Emirates in 2010 also looked into nuclear power for energy purposes.[13]

The upheavals that swept across the Middle East in 2011—known as the Arab Spring—underscored for Israel the importance in stopping Iran and these other regimes from obtaining nuclear weapons. While the prospect of nuclear weapons in the hands of Egypt or the House of Saud is not a comforting thought, it becomes even more frightening considering the realistic possibility of hostile Islamists overthrowing these weaker governments. The Muslim Brotherhood's victory in parliamentary elections in Egypt in late 2011 was all the proof Israel needed to confirm its fears.

Furthermore, a nuclear-armed Iran would have a negative impact on Israel's military options in the event of a future conflict. Imagine the following scenario: An Israeli soldier is abducted in a cross-border attack by Hezbollah in Lebanon or Hamas in the Gaza Strip. Israel would likely want to respond but would have few offensive options as it faced an emboldened group of proxies that have the backing of Iran, which could threaten Israel with a nuclear attack for invading Lebanon or the Gaza Strip.

The possibility that Iran would provide a nuclear device to one of its terrorist proxies also contributes to the Israeli leaders' fear that foreign investors will flee Israel, along with many Israelis.[14] In one poll, 27 percent of Israelis said they would consider leaving if Iran went nuclear. Their departure could spell the failure of Zionism to create a Jewish refuge. Instead, Jews will look to the Diaspora as a more trustworthy option for both their personal and collective survival.[15]

While Iran poses an existential threat to Israel, Israel will not be the only country that is threatened if Iran obtains nuclear weapons. While Ahmadinejad's and Supreme Leader Ayatollah Ali Khamenei's anti-Israel rhetoric makes it seem as if Iran is only an Israeli problem, in reality he and his violent and radical regime are a threat to the entire world. Consider the results of a running poll that each year asks Americans which country poses the greatest threat to the United States. In 1990 only 6 percent of Americans perceived Iran as the greatest threat, while Russia led with 32 percent. In 2006 Iran overtook Iraq and was perceived as the greatest threat to U.S. security by 27 percent of those polled, followed by China with 20 percent. Russia was way behind, with only 3 percent.[16] Iran continued to hold first place in ongoing polls taken through 2010.[17]

Another way to arrive at this conclusion is by analyzing Iran's missile program, which we will discuss at length in chapter 2. The Iranians are currently engaged in one of the most intensive missile program in the world, developing constantly increasing ranges. Iran's missile arsenal consists of both short-range tactical rockets such as the Zelzal (Earthquake)—dozens of which were transferred to Hezbollah before the 2006 war—and ballistic missiles, such as the BM25, that can reach all the way to Europe. They have also developed the Shahab/Ashura/Sajil missile array, which allows Iran to project its power not only over the entire Middle East but also into six European Union countries: Poland, Slovakia, Romania, Hungary, Bulgaria, and Greece.[18] If Iran were intending to threaten Israel alone, why would the Iranians need missiles with such long ranges?

The answer might be found in the speech Ahmadinejad gave during the UN General Assembly on September 25, 2009. Instead of seeking to reassure delegates that Iran's nuclear intentions were purely civilian and not military, he took advantage of his official visit to the United States—which the Iranian Revolution dubbed the Great Satan in 1979—to embark on a discourse about the wonders of the Twelfth Imam. (Devout Shiite Muslims hold the Twelfth Imam, also known as the Mahdi, to be a direct descendant of the Prophet Mohammed, who went into hiding in the ninth century at age five and has not been seen since. The Mahdi, these followers believe, will only return to this world after a period of war and bloodshed—what some might call the Apocalypse—and will then lead the world into an era of stability and peace. As mayor of Tehran, Ahmadinejad secretly instructed the city council in 2004 to build a grand avenue in the city center that the Mahdi would use one day after his reappearance. As president, he allocated $17 million for a mosque closely associated with the Mahdi in the city of Jamkaran.)

In a speech in which he intended to prove that Western dominance over the world had come to an end, Ahmadinejad told the UN, "The promised destiny for mankind is the establishment of the humane pure life. There will come a time when justice will prevail across the globe. . . . These will all come true under the rule of the Perfect Man, the last Divine Source on earth, the Mahdi, an offspring of the Prophet of Islam, who will re-emerge."[19]

The combination of his radical ideology and his pursuit of nuclear weapons has left the Israeli leadership without any doubts that Ahmadinejad is not only the enemy of Israel but also of the entire Western world, including the United States and Europe.

Iran's influence is felt throughout the entire Middle East. To maintain this influence, Iran uses proxies: Muqtada al-Sadr's Shiite Mahdi Army in Iraq, the Muslim Brotherhood in Jordan, the Alawite regime in Syria, Hezbollah in Lebanon and Gaza, and Islamic Jihad, Hamas, and other radical Palestinian groups in the West Bank and Gaza. By working through proxies, Iran achieves maximum instability with minimum responsibility. And Ahmadinejad has reason to believe his mission to destroy Israel and defeat the West is on track. Like radical Islamists before him, Ahmadinejad gains inspiration from the U.S. withdrawal from Lebanon in 1984, the Soviet defeat in Afghanistan in 1989, the Israeli withdrawal from Lebanon in 2000, the Spanish pullout from Iraq in 2004, and the Israeli unilateral disengagement from the Gaza Strip in the summer of 2005.

Iran has also had several role models, chief among them North Korea, which helps Iran believe that it will ultimately prevail. Although the world cried out against North Korea's nuclear developments, it did little to stop Kim Jong-il from obtaining a nuclear weapon. Sanctions, UN Security Council resolutions, and direct diplomacy all failed to stop Pyongyang's pursuit of the bomb. The world's failure in North Korea's case without a doubt motivated Iran to pursue its own nuclear program.

In early 2012, the possibility of an Israeli strike against Iran appeared to be growing even as the world imposed, for the first time, some of the toughest sanctions ever against Iran's energy sector and banking system. A parade of American officials, including Secretary of Defense Leon Panetta, chairman of the joint chiefs Gen. Martin Dempsey, and National Security Adviser Tom Donilon, came to Israel in an effort to persuade the government to hold off its attack. They all returned without a clear commitment from Israel that it would wait.

Behind the flurry of activity was the opening of the Fordow facility near the Iranian city of Qom, where the regime planned to begin the higher-level enrichment of uranium. The Israelis argued that the Iranians were fortifying their facilities to the point that if they waited too long—what Barak coined the entry into the "immunity zone"—a strike might no longer be viable.

On the surface, it is not obvious that Israel and Iran are enemies. The countries do not share a border, but they do share a rich history as two of the only non-Arab countries in the greater Middle East. Diplomatic ties between Israel and Iran were initiated immediately after the establishment of the Jewish state in 1948 under Israel's first prime minister, David Ben-Gurion, and lasted until Ayatollah Ruhollah Khomeini came to power in 1979, turning Iran from one of Israel's closest friends into its fiercest enemy. Israel's undeclared war with Iran began in the 1980s, when Iran founded Hezbollah; it has grown to even greater proportions since the Second Lebanon War in 2006, as have Hamas and Islamic Jihad in the Gaza Strip, also with Iranian assistance.

The Israeli-termed "terror summit" in Damascus in February 2010 involving Ahmadinejad, Syrian president Bashar Assad, and Hezbollah leader Sheikh Sayyid Hassan Nasrallah was a stark reminder for Israel of what it is up against in the region, how all its enemies work in tandem, and the type of retaliation it will likely face if it decides to attack Iran. By 2012, Israel had enjoyed over five years of quiet since the end of the Second Lebanon War, with Hezbollah appearing to be deterred from attacking Israel—demonstrated best by its refusal to fire rockets into Israel during Operation Cast Lead despite requests from Hamas. However, Israel's earlier failure to destroy Hezbollah in 2006 and its sometimes poor showing on the battlefield during the war led other countries and terrorist groups—primarily Iran, Syria, and Hamas—to believe that they, too, could take on the once-perceived invincible IDF.

On the surface, diplomats at the United Nations and in Western capitals across the globe lead the efforts to thwart Iran's bid to obtain a nuclear weapon. But undercover, the intelligence agencies of most Western countries—led by Israel's Mossad and the Central Intelligence Agency (CIA) of the United States— are operating in the darkest shadows to stop the ayatollahs.

This book chronicles Israel's quest—in its shadow war with Iran—to restore its deterrent capabilities, which include assassinations around the world, the bombing of a Syrian reactor, and other remarkably effective military and covert operations. But to do so we need to go to the beginning, to the summer of 2006.

1

THE WAKE-UP CALL

In mid-July 2006 on an army base in northern Israel, a faint twilight enabled soldiers of the Egoz Reconnaissance Unit—the special unit of the Israel Defense Forces (IDF) for guerrilla warfare—to observe their commander as he discreetly conversed with the unit's squad leaders. Occasionally the officers would glance over their shoulders at the group of impatient soldiers who stood with their heavy gear on their backs and loaded rifles in their hands.

The young soldiers' faces were covered in camouflage paint and their eyes sparkled at the mere thought of the operation ahead and the chance to join the Second Lebanon War and defend their country against Hezbollah, the Iranian-backed Shiite guerrilla group in Lebanon. Most of the Egoz soldiers had combat experience from operations against the Palestinian terror infrastructure in the West Bank and Gaza Strip, but for all of them, this operation represented their first foray into war and into Lebanon.

The IDF was rife with rumors of the secret passageways that Hezbollah had built following Israel's withdrawal from Lebanon in 2000 and of the advanced Russian-made antitank missiles and the Iranian-supplied surveillance equipment it had acquired. But in Egoz, the unit members had remained calm.

Already during the first few days of Israel's ground offensive in 2006, the soldiers clearly saw that this operation was different from any previous one they had known and that this time they lacked the security that the IDF's heavily fortified Merkava (Chariot) had provided during the Second Intifada. Prior to the conflict, the pride of Israel's military industries had become a preferred target in Lebanon. On July 12, for example, the day Hezbollah kidnapped Israeli reservists Eldad Regev and Ehud Goldwasser, it also successfully destroyed a Merkava Mark-3 tank. The combination of the kidnapping and the loss of the tank and its four crew members was enough to create the shock needed to force Israeli prime minister Ehud Olmert's hand and send the country to war, its first in almost a quarter century.

From the start, it was clear that the first soldiers who would enter Lebanon on foot would be from the Egoz unit, which was subordinate to the IDF's Northern Command. Despite the years of quiet along the northern border, Egoz still trained on rocky and mountainous terrains modeled after southern Lebanon, where Hezbollah had established its bases, deployed its rocket launchers, and dug its trenches. Though the soldiers complained about what they thought was "useless" training, their experience in this terrain was believed to give them an edge in fighting against Hezbollah.

Egoz had existed as a Special Forces unit since 1956, but it had been disbanded and reformed several times in the ensuing decades. The idea of resurrecting Egoz for contemporary antiguerrilla warfare first surfaced in the IDF in the early 1990s, while Israel still maintained the Security Zone—created in 1982—in southern Lebanon. Every few months, infantry and tank brigades alternated guarding the borderline military posts. Hezbollah constantly improved its tactics, and every few weeks soldiers encountered Hezbollah guerrillas. In most cases the IDF soldiers killed the Hezbollah fighters, but between 1982 and 2000 more than five hundred of the IDF's soldiers were killed in Lebanon.[1] For a country of seven million residents, in which nearly every young person is a soldier, the death toll had an enormous effect on the national sentiment toward the IDF's continued presence in the Israeli Security Zone.

When Hezbollah began shelling the borderline posts with mortars, the IDF decided to change its tactics and to fight Hezbollah while using Hezbollah's own methods. The task of reassembling Egoz was assigned in 1995 to a young officer from the navy, Lt. Col. Erez Zuckerman. An amateur farmer and avid horse enthusiast whose reputation preceded him from his years of commanding covert and dangerous operations in Shayetet (Flotilla) 13 (the Israeli equivalent of the U.S. Navy SEALs), Zuckerman brought a small team of commandos with him and obtained approval from the chief of staff to begin assembling squads from the rest of the IDF's Special Forces.[2]

Six months after Zuckerman received his mandate, the new Egoz unit was operational and was sent into Lebanon on its first mission in 1995. The legend in

the Shayetet was that the "terrorists followed Zuckerman," and on his first foray
into Lebanon, to an area generally considered free of terrorists, a fully armed
Hezbollah cell attacked the unit. Zuckerman stormed first, killing the terrorists.
After a second successful encounter several weeks later, Egoz had established a
reputation as a fierce new opponent to Hezbollah in southern Lebanon. Its capabilities as an elite and specialized unit became an undisputed fact.

At the beginning of the ground incursion in 2006, the Egoz soldiers moved
quickly. While Egoz was crossing the border, a unit from the Paratroopers Brigade was making its way to Maroun al-Ras, a Lebanese village that, according
to the Directorate of Military Intelligence (also known as Aman), was home to
Hezbollah's top regional command center. (Aman provides intelligence to the
IDF's tacticians and serves as the government's adviser on intelligence affairs.)
The paratroopers had been assigned the mission the same morning of Egoz's mission, and by noon they had already deployed along the border on the outskirts of
the Israeli village of Avivim.

The briefings had been conducted within the companies, because the unit
commander had not had time to brief all of his soldiers together. The operation
was simple: take control of the eastern side of the village, enter one of the structures deemed safe based on aerial photographs, and then, using firepower, conquer the village. After six years of fighting inside Palestinian towns in the West
Bank and Gaza Strip, IDF soldiers were supposed to be experts at taking over
civilian homes and stationing themselves inside. Therefore, when planning the
mission, they naturally looked for the largest, strongest house in the soon-to-
become battlefield.

Major Erez,[3] the deputy commander of the unit, recounted in an interview
after the battle:

> The only dangers we were thinking about were mortar shells and close
> firefights. We had sharpshooters and firepower strong enough to over-
> come such encounters, and at no point were we afraid of moving forward.
> Soldiers from Aman, who were sent along to assist, did not reveal every-
> thing they knew so as not to expose their sources, and this is how we
> went in to battle; we did not take into account Hezbollah's anti-tank mis-
> siles and surveillance capabilities. We understood very soon after setting
> out on the mission that we had severe operational problems; although we
> crossed the border quietly, a few hundred meters into Lebanon we noticed

a group of UN soldiers watching us. The direction of our movement and our objective were obvious to the UN and, therefore, to Hezbollah as well.

The outcome of that single battle seemed later to have been almost preordained. Four soldiers were killed, including a company commander. Thus began the IDF's ground war in Lebanon.

A week after the failed mission and back in Israel, the reserve soldiers looked through the kit bags they had received at call-up centers. They were shocked to find outdated equipment in all the wrong sizes. The cartridges were rusty and did not fit into their rifles. The combat vests reminded them of old photos from the 1967 Six-Day War, and the helmets were filled with cobwebs. It was a far cry from what they had remembered from their regular mandatory service. Having their orders changed daily added to their frustration with the country's top military and political echelons.

Ten days after the UN-brokered cease-fire went into effect on August 14 and ended the thirty-four days of fighting, hundreds of young men and women gathered in Jerusalem's Rose Park. Sandwiched between the Knesset (Israel's parliament) and the Supreme Court, the Rose Park has seen its fair share of demonstrations against political decisions, tax hikes, and even security failures. Now, the fighters from Lebanon had their turn.

The two men who organized the protest, Roni Zweigenbaum and Assaf Davidoff, were part of the Alexandroni Brigade. During the war they had been sent to fight in the western sector of southern Lebanon, a pastoral area with an amazing view of the Mediterranean Sea. Although Zweigenbaum and Davidoff's unit suffered severe shortages of combat equipment supplies (as did many other units), they went into battle filled with motivation. However, when their division commander had trouble sending in convoys to replenish their dwindling supplies and provisions, the soldiers were forced to find food in the field. They broke into convenience stores and homes, and in many cases they left behind cash as compensation.

When the reservists returned to Israel they heard that Brig. Gen. Gal Hirsch, the commander of the Ninety-first Division, had publicly criticized their actions.[4] For these reservists, who had left everything to fight for their country, this condemnation was too much. As far as Zweigenbaum and Davidoff were concerned, by protesting in front of the Knesset they were continuing to serve their country.

At the entrance to the protest tent they had set up near the Knesset, the reservists had petitions calling for the resignation of Prime Minister Olmert and

Defense Minister Amir Peretz. Protesters blamed the IDF generals and political leaders for losing the war and would later claim that the war was plagued by a constant sense of hesitation, as though someone or something had been holding back the IDF from fighting the way it had in its previous wars in 1967 and 1973. They felt that their commanders were not utilizing the resources at their disposal and had little or no dedication to the mission or to the soldiers. Stories of battalion commanders turning around and returning to Israel after entering Lebanon were not uncommon. The feeling was one of overall disappointment.

The Israeli and foreign press covered the demonstration extensively, and the patriotic sentiment that had characterized the newspapers' early coverage of the fighting was replaced with competing analyses and descriptions of the war's failures. Some focused on the IDF's mismanagement. Others concentrated on Olmert and Peretz and their political paralysis. Either way, many understood that something needed to change. Further, because the demonstration was not led by Israel's liberal Left or an antiwar group but by Israel's "finest"—the reservists—the protest could not be ignored.

Despite his own misgivings but with the support of members from Kadima, his political party, Olmert appointed retired judge Eliyahu Winograd to chair a commission of inquiry into the war. The prestigious panel—whose members also included two former generals, a legal expert, and a world-renowned political science professor—published the testimonies it heard and its conclusions in the panel's final report, which sent shock waves through the Israeli government and the IDF's top command. It implicated each person linked to the war. No one escaped criticism. Most of those involved found themselves out of the military in a short period, some resigned, and others were denied promotions. For instance, over the course of the Second Lebanon War, Zuckerman had been promoted to brigadier general but took responsibility for his division, which had fought poorly, and resigned. Thus, Lebanon had heralded the beginning and the end of Zuckerman's military career.

Defense Minister Peretz, leader of the left-wing Labor Party, resigned. Ehud Barak, a former chief of staff, defense minister, and prime minister in 2007, replaced him. Only Olmert stayed in office, that is, until scandals unrelated to the war prompted his resignation as well.[5]

While the war had caused damage to Israel's reputation and significantly weakened its deterrence, it had also, inadvertently, shocked the ayatollahs in Tehran.

The Iranian Revolutionary Guard Corps (IRGC) had not supported Hezbollah leader Sheikh Hassan Nasrallah for so many years and had not invested so much money, so many hours of training, and so much weaponry for him to throw it all away by kidnapping two reservists and forcing Israel into a war. Hezbollah was supposed to be Iran's backup doomsday weapon, the sword hovering over Israel's head in the event that the latter would decide to attack Iran's nuclear facilities.

In Iran, the group responsible for training Hezbollah is called the al-Quds (Jerusalem) Force. Consisting of a few thousand fighters, the force was established in the 1990s to help export the Islamic Revolution beyond Iran's borders. To do this work, the force sets up educational systems and cultural programs to promote Islamic ideals. It also strives to subvert pro-Western and moderate Arab countries such as Egypt, which in April 2009 uncovered a major Iranian and Hezbollah plot to strike at popular tourist spots. (Israel's Mossad—the national intelligence agency responsible for espionage overseas and equivalent of the Central Intelligence Agency [CIA]—provided the intelligence information that Egypt used to thwart the attacks.[6]) The force's best-known role, though, is in establishing armed terrorist groups such as Islamic Jihad and Hezbollah and providing them with funding, training, and weaponry. In 2012, al-Quds Force was operating in Syria supplying the embattled President Assad with financial and military assistance in a bid to defeat the opposition and remain in power.

The Iranians had expected Nasrallah to be discreet and to give Israel the impression that it had much to lose if it were to antagonize Hezbollah's Iranian patron. In the months following the war, IRGC officers closely accompanied Nasrallah. Analysts in the Israeli defense establishment viewed their presence as an expression of Iran's disappointment and lack of faith in the Hezbollah chief, implying that a responsible adult from Iran was now required to supervise Nasrallah. This reality brought the Hezbollah leader to confess in a televised interview shortly after the war that had he known how Israel would react to the kidnapping of Regev and Goldwasser, he never would have chosen to go ahead with it.

While the Second Lebanon War harmed Israel, it also damaged Iran's deterrence capabilities. In the summer of 2006 everything was brought out in the open, and the worst and most-feared scenario had occurred, as Israel had gone to war against Hezbollah and emerged intact, albeit with several scratches.[7] Nasrallah put on a show to make it seem as if the Arab forces were finally successful in stinging the Zionist enemy, but in fact he had single-handedly ruined the Lebanese summer tourist season and brought destruction to a large portion of southern Lebanon and Beirut. Even more important was the role Nasrallah played in waking the IDF from its deep slumber. Had it not been for the 165 casualties and the 2,628 wounded—IDF soldiers and Israeli civilians—one might be forgiven for saying that the Hezbollah contributed to Israel's rebuilding its military might. This small war, although poorly managed, ultimately served as a wake-up call for Israel and led to the recognition that the IDF quickly needed to improve and prepare itself for the big war against Iran that loomed on the horizon.

This Lebanon war also represented the first time that Israel found itself fighting against not only Hezbollah but also Iran, which had been meddling in Lebanese political affairs for decades but not publicly. The fighting in southern Lebanon uncovered Iranian weaponry, surveillance equipment, money, and motivational paraphernalia.

Shortly after Israel withdrew from Lebanon in 2000, al-Quds Force had begun sending in thousands of missiles of various ranges, including the short-range Katyusha and the long-range Zelzal and Fajr (Dawn) rockets. Some of the shipments came by sea; others arrived by air and land via Syria.

The Iranians also trained hundreds of Hezbollah fighters, as demonstrated by the story of Ali Suleiman. Skinny and soft-spoken, Suleiman's appearance was deceiving. The IDF had captured the twenty-two-year-old Shiite from southern Lebanon in the village of Ayta a-Shab in the middle of the 2006 war.

When Aman interrogated him in Israel, Suleiman described how he had joined Hezbollah in 2000 and undergone two months of basic training as well as religious and ideological indoctrination in Hezbollah's stronghold in the Bekaa Valley in northern Lebanon. There he learned basic tactical skills: how to handle explosives, how to use communication devices, and how to fire antitank missiles. Suleiman said that in 2003 he boarded a bus in the valley that drove him and about forty-five other new Hezbollah recruits to Damascus. There, they went to an airport and, without passports, boarded a plane bound for Iran.

In Iran, Suleiman underwent IRGC-run additional training in military bases right outside Tehran. On July 12, 2006, Suleiman commanded an antitank cell that participated in the attack on an IDF convoy during which Regev and Goldwasser were abducted, setting off a month of fighting between Israel and the guerrilla group. Suleiman presented one example of the way the Iranian-Hezbollah axis worked. Thus the 2006 war represented not only a struggle against a terrorist group in Lebanon but also Israel's first taste of war against Iran.

For years the IDF had succeeded in areas where others had not. It had overcome threats and challenges that the Western world had considered unsolvable. Suicide bombers, female terrorists, and the Palestinians' national aspirations for independence had necessitated innovative methods of warfare, which the Israelis developed and perfected while paying a hard price.

In September 2000, under the leadership of Yasser Arafat, the al-Aqsa (Second) Intifada erupted. Palestinian terror increased, partly as the result of direct orders from Arafat himself. The intifada reached its peak during the horrifying month of March 2002, when on Passover eve a suicide bomber entered the Park Hotel in Netanya and blew himself up, killing thirty Israelis. Prime minister Ariel Sharon felt that a line had been crossed and gave the IDF the green light to launch Operation Defensive Shield, the decisive battle against Palestinian terrorism.

For the first time since the Oslo Accords had been signed in 1993, the IDF entered all of the Palestinian territory, arrested terror operatives, and fought a war that some in Israel would later refer to as "mowing the terror lawn." The terrorist organizations continued to carry out attacks, although with limited success owing to the IDF's operational freedom within every single Palestinian city, no matter how dense or narrow. The impossible had occurred, and the IDF had succeeded in suppressing Palestinian terror and their ability to kill Jews at any cost.

Foreign military officers began flocking to Israel to learn about the IDF's newly invented model of warfare, which included a mix of urban fighting, special operations, and targeted killings. From a distance, the IDF's successes seemed almost historic. As summarized by Maj. Gen. Tal Russo (in 2012 the head of the IDF Southern Command), the military had fought against a terrorist organization and was successful in temporarily defeating it while using surgical means.[8]

But in Israel almost no one spoke about the source of the terror, about the Iranian oil revenues that fueled a large part of terrorist activities against Israel, or about the orders terrorists received from headquarters in Damascus, Tehran, and Beirut to keep on fighting. Iranian fingerprints were virtually everywhere: on the weapons, on the explosives, and even on the large sums of money that were transferred to the territories to finance Hamas and Islamic Jihad's activities. The surveillance equipment, computer systems, night visions goggles, and mortar shells came almost exclusively from Iran. Furthermore, the Palestinian terrorist organizations were becoming increasingly similar to Hezbollah, Iran's contractors from the north. While the terrorists themselves were Palestinian, their orders came from Iran.

Inside closed conference rooms, the heads of Israel's intelligence agencies were well aware of Iran's involvement. On the outside, however, the army spoke in general terms and took pride in Israel's success in fighting the Palestinians, even though its success was limited in the larger scheme of things. Other nations saw Israel as a country that had fought a small war against a terrorist organization, and won. They overlooked Iran's role and the notion that even in small wars a stronger player is always in the background, imposing its will on the smaller groups doing the fighting. The IDF began holding seminars on what it called limited warfare or low-intensity conflicts to process and study the lessons learned from the war against Palestinian terrorism.[9] In the IDF National Defense College, instructors spoke about the inevitable change in the character of wars and presented studies showing that more than 70 percent of all wars fought after the end of the Cold War had been small, asymmetrical conflicts between countries with large powerful armies, like Israel, and non-state organizations with virtually no conventional military capabilities, such as Hamas or Hezbollah.

The United States under the George W. Bush administration was at the same time developing its own methods for confronting the urban warfare its forces encountered on the streets of Kabul and Baghdad. Senior IDF officers who were sent to study at military academies in the United States compared notes with their American counterparts and helped Israel fine-tune its own new operational doctrine.

The IDF's basic assumption was that another conventional war similar to the 1973 Yom Kippur War in the Middle East, a war fought between two countries of similar strength while using traditional weapons, was no longer possible. They deemed the chances of Israeli tanks on one side of the Golan Heights one day facing Syrian tanks on the other side as almost nonexistent. The wars Israel had fought since the 1980s instead had been against countries and organizations that preferred to fight without a clear battlefield. Since signing the peace agreement with Egypt, the chances for war on the southern front had also significantly decreased. Even though a war with Iran was certainly perceived as a possibility, the probability that ground troops, tanks, or artillery would be used was deemed impossible without a mutual border. As a result, Israel was left with only two clear fronts—in Lebanon and the Gaza Strip, against Iranian proxies.

In the West Bank, Israel still fought the war against Palestinian terror on a small scale, but the enemy's strength was diminishing as time went on. Hezbollah was a different story. Israeli intelligence was aware that under Iran's auspices,

Hezbollah was accumulating great power in Lebanon. However, in this case the Israelis also assumed, incorrectly, that a pragmatic approach and the political process the movement was undergoing inside Lebanon would curb Hezbollah's desire to break the status quo and attack Israel. Senior Israeli defense officials referred to Hezbollah not as a terrorist group but as an organization. This terminology ultimately led them to miscalculate the movement's capabilities and the methods that the IDF should prepare to use in a future war against it.

Leading up to the 1990s the IDF faced three types of challenges. The first and most complex came from Iran and Iraq, both considered "third circle threats," in reference to their distance from Israel. The "second circle" included the countries bordering Israel, and the "first circle" meant the internal Palestinian terror. Over the years, though, the latter challenge effectively disappeared, and Israel found itself facing terror from Lebanon and the Gaza Strip. The U.S. invasion of Iraq essentially neutralized one of the third circle threats as well. Only in 2007 would the IDF, recognizing the possibility of an American withdrawal, identify Iraq as a potential future threat. IDF decision makers concluded, meanwhile, that the army should invest its time and resources in fighting the limited war in the West Bank and Gaza and no longer make training its soldiers on how to capture a Syrian military post a top priority.

This direction came at a time when the entire army was busy conducting arrest operations and putting up roadblocks to catch Palestinian terrorists. In 2004 Avi Dichter, head of Israel's Shin Bet Security Agency (the domestic security agency responsible for gathering intelligence on Palestinian terror groups in the West Bank and Gaza Strip), compared the war on terrorism to emptying a barrel with a teaspoon. Although a seemingly Sisyphean task, Dichter claimed that every barrel has a bottom. The IDF had sent all its troops to conduct routine missions in Judea, Samaria, and Gaza and to serve as Dichter's tens of thousands of "teaspoons," working fervently to empty the "barrel of terror."

In short, the IDF scrapped training for conventional war. It kept tank personnel busy guarding bases and putting up roadblocks. It trained infantry soldiers exclusively for urban warfare. The IDF also enlisted reserve units—Prime Minister David Ben-Gurion, Israel's first premier, had called them the IDF's backbone—to "empty the terror barrel." Instead of training during their annual month of service, they spent time patrolling fences or manning watchtowers. The IDF's experience and capabilities in the war on terrorism improved tremendously, but at the same time its ability to fight a real war deteriorated. Although the terror had never posed an existential threat to Israel, it had made the lives of its citizens unbearable, and the Israeli government was determined to eradicate it.

As the "lawn mowing" and counterterror operations took up more and more of the IDF's time and effort, some officers in the military tried to outline what the next war would look like. They assumed that the next war either would be similar to the type of operations they were carrying out in the territories or would be fought in the air against Iran with the deployment of few ground forces. They concluded that the IDF no longer had any reason to invest resources in training for the conventional wars that they believed no longer existed.

The Operational Theory Research Institute (OTRI), founded in 1994 and located next to the National Defense College just north of Tel Aviv, led the army's search for new military theories. Brig. Gen. Shimon Naveh and Brig. Gen. Dov Tamari, both talented officers and extremely knowledgeable in military theory, headed the OTRI. To define the complexities of modern warfare, Naveh and Tamari introduced a theoretical, academic rhetoric into the military discourse. Instead of speaking in black-and-white terms such as "conquer," "withdrawal," and "defense," the instructors at the institute taught cadets about new military objectives such as shaping the enemy's psyche and perception.[10]

The OTRI derived these new terms from what the IDF perceived as its immediate threat, or the terror and guerrilla warfare in Lebanon and the Palestinian territories, which, although sponsored by Iran, seemed far from presenting a conventional threat to Israel. This new way of thinking, however, ignored other short- and long-term threats, particularly Iran's influence over the region. The IDF's new master operational strategy was based on the theories taught at the institute and on other principles adopted from foreign militaries, primarily the U.S. armed forces. The IDF approved the new approach a mere three months before the Second Lebanon War started.

The first principle of the new strategy changed the army's combat priorities, placing more emphasis on standoff firepower and less on mobilized troops and ground maneuvers.[11] In other words, whereas in past wars the focus was on gaining control over enemy territory, the new approach called for first heavily bombing the enemy and then sending in only a small ground force of mainly infantry troops. The idea was to limit the high number of Israeli casualties and thereby avoid fomenting national sentiment against the war. This principle was demonstrated primarily when the IDF increased the Israeli Air Force's size at the expense of providing the Ground Forces Command with more tanks and armored personnel carriers.

This move made a great deal of sense when put into the Iranian context. The IAF and Israel Navy are the IDF's "long arms" and would be necessary for attacking a far-off country like Iran. This change in policy, however, slowly deteriorated the IDF's ground forces, diminishing its capability to fight traditional wars against traditional enemies. Another sign of the change in perception was the appointment of Maj. Gen. Dan Halutz, a fighter pilot and former chief of the IAF who had never commanded an infantry force, to the post of IDF chief of staff in 2005. Halutz himself had articulated the basic concept of the new military doctrine in a lecture he gave in January 2001 at the National Defense College. "Land forces should never be deployed as long as a viable alternative exists," Halutz argued. "This approach requires us to discard a number of anachronistic assumptions: first, that victory means territory. Victory should be defined as achieving a strategic objective, not necessarily territory. . . . Winning is a matter of perception and air strikes significantly affect the enemy's perception."[12]

In practice, applying this principle meant reallocating Israel's defense budget. Between 2002 and 2005 the total budget of the land forces was slashed by 25 percent as the IAF's budget grew. This change stemmed from the IDF's updated view that "classical" maneuvering over land should only be a complementary tactic for decisive air strikes.

The second principle of the new strategy changed the IDF's definition of "victory." The new definition relied heavily on former U.S. secretary of state Henry Kissinger's famous axiom from the Vietnam War era that guerrilla organizations "win if they do not lose." Since Israel could not afford to lose against the growing Muslim fundamentalist threat, the IDF changed its objective and no longer spoke of victory in territorial terms but rather spoke about hitting valuable targets with heavy firepower and precision munitions with the main goal of altering the enemy's perception of Israel and boosting the IDF's deterrence. Victory, IDF officers would say, was not absolute and not obtained by a knockout punch. It was instead achieved in points. This updated strategy was one reason why the IDF hesitated to call up reserve forces when the Second Lebanon War started. When Halutz finally decided to issue the call-up, after years during which the reservists were considered unnecessary, it was necessary to refresh, retrain, and rebuild the land forces.

The change to the IDF's doctrine began on August 15, the day after the UN-brokered cease-fire restored quiet to Israel's northern border. As the Winograd Commission was appointed, the IDF began its own housecleaning and assigned officers to dozens of committees to examine the army's actions during the war. But before the officers accepted their new appointments, the IDF top brass already clearly saw that the operational doctrine adopted before the war had failed. Even had Iran not been a factor and had not supported Hezbollah and other terrorist groups, Israel could not endure a situation in which it failed to defeat its enemy decisively in a military campaign. This understanding was at the foundation of Israel's existence: a strong army was needed to survive in the volatile Middle East.

In changing the operational doctrine, many of its supporters had to go as well. Brigadier General Hirsch, commander of the Ninety-first Division from the region where Goldwasser and Regev were kidnapped, had been deeply influenced during his time at the OTRI. Hirsch claimed that the institute and its faculty had changed his life. He had been seriously wounded in action while serving as chief intelligence officer for the Judea and Samaria Division during the Second Intifada and had spent his free time studying Dr. Naveh's new theories at the institute during his long rehabilitation. Later, following the internal IDF report that prompted his premature resignation, Hirsch claimed that the institute's enemies—those who could not handle its critical approach and profound military thinking—had decided to target him as well.

A few months following the war, the drumbeat of criticism of the IDF's performance refused to stop. The IDF chief of General Staff Lieutenant General Halutz decided to address his officers. For two days the Israeli military's top brass convened for the first time at an air force base in the center of the country to discuss the findings of the army's internal inquiries and its plans for the future. By then, Halutz had already decided to resign. The only question was when, since he believed he was the right man to repair the failures the war had exposed in order to prevent them from recurring in the future.

At the end of the two-day session Halutz called a press conference in his office. He hinted that in his opinion, he was not to blame for the failures of the war, but he believed that the media and the Israeli public were out to get him. Halutz instead faulted the containment policy that the IDF had employed in the north during the six years between its withdrawal from Lebanon and the 2006 war. The policy was aimed at keeping conflict with Hezbollah on a low flame even at the price of knowingly allowing the erosion of Israel's deterrence capabilities. Halutz explained that the IDF had become accustomed to the mode of operation in the territories and the routine patrols and had removed its focus from the threats growing in the north. It seemed as though he finally had understood what he should have known long before the war started. Halutz also admitted that the ground forces had not been adequately prepared. Neither the operational commands nor its goals, he said, were clear enough. Maybe the IDF should have prepared for a ground offensive, he admitted, adding that an earlier call-up of reservists would have allowed them some time to train before being sent into Lebanon.

Just a few weeks later Halutz turned in his resignation and was replaced by Lt. Gen. Gabi Ashkenazi, a former deputy chief of staff and commander of the Northern Command who had competed with Halutz for the top post in 2005. Ashkenazi was serving as director general of the Ministry of Defense during the war and had bitten his tongue when he observed the military's mishandling of Hezbollah. The day after he took office in February 2007, Ashkenazi had already formulated a plan for reconstructing the army. First, though, he had to decide what type of army he wanted to build. "An army has to always be in [one of] two different positions—either fighting a war or preparing for one," Ashkenazi said as he took office.[13] He gave orders to the IDF to prepare for a conventional war and to derive from that type of training the necessary skills to succeed in low-intensity conflicts as well.

This directive meant that he was returning the IDF to its old training format of conquering territory, training for war with Syria, and refocusing to use its infantry, armored, engineering, and artillery forces more effectively and to work with assistance from the IAF and navy. The real issue was interoperability—that is, getting all of the IDF's different branches to work together, to speak the same professional language, and to understand how to help each other. While the IDF continued to invest in the IAF, particularly because of the looming nuclear threat from Iran, it concentrated on the ground forces. Reverting to the old strategy did not eliminate the challenges the army faced, but at least now Israel's senior officers knew that at the end of the lengthy process the IDF would be more professional and better trained.

During the reevaluation, the IDF also brainstormed about what the next war would look like. They knew it was only a matter of time before tensions at the border flared up again. Already, a few months after the Second Lebanon War ended, IDF surveillance teams began spotting Hezbollah guerrillas along the border, although this time they dressed in civilian clothing and drove Land Rover jeeps and Mercedes sedans. Sometimes they would roll down a window, lift a long-lens camera, and snap a few pictures of an IDF outpost on the other side of the border before driving away. Other times they would get out of their vehicles and stroll along the border, right next to positions manned by Lebanese Armed Forces (LAF) and the United Nations Interim Force in Lebanon (UNIFIL).

Although the men didn't wear Hezbollah uniforms, the IDF had no doubt that they belonged to the guerrilla group. On rare occasions the IDF cameras that lined the border would catch a familiar face. Aman officers then ran the face through databases of known Hezbollah operatives and commanders stored on IDF computers. These Hezbollah operatives were not alone. On some tours they would take groups of foreigners with them, and sometimes members of the IRGC, Hezbollah's main benefactor, accompanied them.

The reality along the Israeli-Lebanese border in 2012 was that while Hezbollah no longer maintained overt military positions along the border as it did before the war, it still maintained a presence there. According to Israel, Hezbollah's positions grew stronger every day. Israel estimated that Hezbollah in 2012 had somewhere between 50,000–60,000 rockets of various ranges that could reach almost anywhere within the State of Israel, from Kiryat Shmona in the north to Tel Aviv in the center of the country and all the way to Dimona in the south, home to Israel's nuclear reactor.

But Hezbollah seemed to show more restraint. One way the IDF arrived at this conclusion was by analyzing the Lebanese Shiite group's behavior during Operation Cast Lead, which the IDF waged against Hamas in the Gaza Strip in January 2009.

Previously, during Operation Defensive Shield in 2002, when the IDF took up positions in all the major cities in the West Bank, Hezbollah had fired six hundred rockets and mortars as well as three hundred antitank missiles into Israel. In total, fourteen Israelis were injured. In comparison, during Cast Lead, when IDF troops swept into the Gaza Strip, Hezbollah did not fire even a single rocket.

This realization led to an understanding in the IDF's Northern Command that although Hezbollah was rebuilding its military capabilities and might have more rockets than it did before the Second Lebanon War, it was extremely restrained, possibly more than ever. This observation did not mean, however, that war would not break out once again. Indeed, Israel believed that ultimately war with Hezbollah would erupt again, either in an isolated conflict sparked by a cross-border kidnapping attack as in 2006 or as part of Iran's retaliation following an Israeli strike against its nuclear facilities.

As noted, Iran was unhappy with Hezbollah's attack on July 12, 2006. During the month-long war in 2006, Israel destroyed more than 90 percent of the long-range missiles Iran had delivered to Hezbollah. The IDF also caused extensive damage to the group's infrastructure—built with Iranian money—in the bombing campaign against the Beirut neighborhood of Dahiya, a closed-off compound in the Lebanese capital that is only accessible to card-carrying Hezbollah members.

In Israel the assessment was that in a new war with Hezbollah the IDF would face the same challenges it had in 2006 although to a larger extent. For instance, in 2006 Hezbollah had fired an average of 150 rockets a day. In a future conflict that number would likely triple. The Israelis also thought that Hezbollah would fire triple the number of advanced antitank missiles at IDF tanks and would wield its newfound antiaircraft weapons, which were believed to be capable of severely impairing the IAF's flights over Lebanon.

As with Hamas in the Gaza Strip, Hezbollah in southern Lebanon also relied heavily on protection from the civilian population. It used civilians as human shields and hid its rockets in residences and its command centers on the first floor of ten-story apartment buildings. This two-point strategy was aimed at deterring Israel from attacking these targets, which would cause high numbers of civilian casualties, and at bringing harsh international criticism against Israel if it decided to attack regardless.

A demonstration of Hezbollah's weaponry being embedded within the civilian population came in July 2009, when a Hezbollah arms cache accidentally exploded in the southern Lebanese village of Khirbet Selm, twelve miles north of the border with Israel. The cache was hidden inside a home and contained dozens of 122mm Katyusha rockets and high-powered machine guns.[14] Seizing the public diplomacy opportunity, the IDF, which had known that the home was being used as a weapons storehouse, immediately dispatched an IAF drone to hover above the home in which the cache had been hidden. The IDF's video, later released to the media, showed dozens of holes in the roof that IDF ballistics experts said were the size of 122mm Katyusha rockets. A previous drone had captured additional footage of the same area several months before the explosion. It showed several senior Hezbollah operatives entering an underground tunnel near the house and popping out of the ground half a mile away, demonstrating the group's use of underground tunnels to move its forces and weapons undetected.

In October 2009 another home exploded in the southern Lebanese village of Tayr Filsay. Located about twenty miles north of the border with Israel, the home belonged to Abdul Nasser Issa, a low-level Hezbollah operative. This time, too, the IAF dispatched a drone that filmed Hezbollah operatives removing long-range missiles from the residence and loading them onto a truck. The drone then followed the truck as the operatives drove to a nearby village and unloaded the weaponry at another home.

These instances are simply two reported examples of Hezbollah using civilian homes for weapons storage, and according to Israel's Northern Command, by 2010 Hezbollah already had thousands of similar arms caches scattered throughout the 160 villages in southern Lebanon. The homes were connected to tunnels that could allow guerrilla fighters to move between battlefields and surprise Israeli forces.

Meanwhile, Aman collected information on potential targets for a future war with Hezbollah, but for the most part it kept the information to itself. Then in July 2010, as the evidence was mounting, the IDF's Northern Command decided that despite the risk, it was time to send Hezbollah a message. On a sunny summer morning, Israeli military correspondents were invited to IDF Northern Command headquarters in the city of Safed. If not for the soldiers walking the gravel paths among the stone buildings, the base resembled a typical vacation village. Inside the briefing room, the command's chief intelligence officer approached the podium and began a slideshow.

The first slide was a satellite picture of the Lebanese village of al-Khiam, located a few miles north of the border with Israel. The rest of the slides showed extensive footage—videos and maps of homes that Hezbollah had taken over and used to store weapons caches and to establish command and control centers—as well as the location of improvised explosive devices (IEDs), some of which weighed up to half a ton and had been hidden inside the village. In the maps, Hezbollah weapons caches were shown approximately 150 feet from schools and hospitals. Storage and command centers were located in most cases inside or adjacent to Lebanese civilian homes.

Hezbollah, the officer said, was believed to have a force of about thirty thousand guerrilla fighters throughout southern Lebanon in comparison to a little less than fifteen thousand in 2006. The fighters' main objective, he continued, was to prevent an Israeli ground invasion, but they were also responsible for operating Hezbollah's extensive missile array of more than forty thousand rockets and missiles, which would allow them to strike at any point within Israel.

The IDF's decision to declassify the intelligence information entailed an element of risk, particularly the possibility that Hezbollah would see what the IDF knew and decide to hide its assets elsewhere. However, the IDF felt it had more to gain diplomatically than lose in releasing the information. By showing the world that the Lebanese guerrilla group was storing its military infrastructure in homes and near schools, Israel intended to establish a legitimate reason for the devastation it would likely cause in Lebanon in a future war.

In December 2010, WikiLeaks revealed an American diplomatic cable that showed that Lebanese government officials were actually working against Hezbollah. In the cable, which originated in the U.S. Embassy in Beirut, Lebanese defense minister Elias Murr was accused of advising the Israeli Air Force on which targets to attack during the 2006 war. In another cable, a top Saudi official is quoted as suggesting the revolutionary idea of Arab countries establishing a force similar to that of the North Atlantic Treaty Organization (NATO) to intervene in Lebanon and confront Hezbollah.[15]

In the beginning of 2011 tensions again rose along Israel's border with Lebanon when Hezbollah opted to topple the Lebanese government before the United Nations published its findings about the 2005 assassination of former Lebanese prime minister Rafik Hariri. While the disarray appeared to be contained in Lebanon, the IDF raised its level of alert, fearing that political instability in Beirut could eventually lead to rocket fire on Israeli cities.

To deal with the growing threat, the IDF built special training centers for infantry troops to prepare them for a combination of urban and guerrilla warfare. One example was a replica of a Hezbollah nature reserve, or a forestry area where the group had dug bunkers and deployed rocket launchers to train IDF troops. The Engineering Corps also built an urban warfare training center at its base in the Negev Desert. It resembled a regular Palestinian village, only with tunnels, secret passageways, and booby-trapped homes. After the IDF understood that Hezbollah was no longer deploying its rockets from open fields but from homes, in 2007 the IDF also had built new urban warfare centers—consisting of mock Lebanese villages—that were connected to the replica of the nature reserve.

"During the Second Lebanon War, our biggest challenge was the nature reserves that Hezbollah had created in the open and has used to strike at our forces and launch rockets," a top officer from the Northern Command said in 2009.[16] "Now, the challenge will be to fight against Hezbollah in an urban setting and then to move through the tunnels into the forest."

The IDF needed to ensure that Hezbollah's goal of using the civilian infrastructure to deter an Israeli attack would not work. As a result, immediately following the war and despite international condemnation, the IAF continued to fly over Lebanon, to keep an eye on weapons shipments, and to watch where they went. By 2009, the IDF had already added thousands of new targets to its target bank.

One of the reasons for increasing the targets had to do with the political change that took place in Lebanon. During the war, Israel avoided striking Lebanese government targets and infrastructure because at the time it was willing to make a distinction between the Lebanese government and Hezbollah, which was holding it hostage. In 2009, though, Hezbollah joined the Lebanese coalition government, and ten ministerial positions went to the March 8 Alliance whose members were part of Hezbollah and the Amal Movement.

"If before, we related to Hezbollah as a militia on the side, today it has become the real Lebanese army," Israeli prime minister Binyamin Netanyahu said a month after the establishment of the new Lebanese government. "Hezbollah has supplanted the Lebanese army as the significant force. It is arming itself and organizing itself like a regular army. The Lebanese government and Hezbollah are growing interconnected, and they will share joint responsibility for any attack on Israel."[17]

Maj. Gen. Gadi Eizenkot, head of Israel's Northern Command, went even further, saying that the IDF's plan for a future war would be based on the Dahiya Doctrine, in reference to Hezbollah's stronghold in Beirut that the IAF flattened with smart bombs during the 2006 war. "What happened in the Dahiya neighborhood of Beirut in 2006 will happen in every village from which Israel is fired on," Eizenkot said. "We will apply disproportionate force on [that village] and cause great damage and destruction there. From our standpoint, these are not civilian villages, they are military bases."[18] As another member of the IDF's General Staff said with regard to Hezbollah: "I am not jealous of the enemy that attacks us."[19]

The IDF Operations Directorate, which is based in the military's heavily fortified underground command center known by its Hebrew name Bor (Pit), has drawn up plans for a future war with Hezbollah. Located in Tel Aviv's Kirya Tower—the IDF's version of the Pentagon—the Bor is accessed through a large steel door that is sealed shut in the event of a nonconventional attack. In front a big sign reminds visitors, before entering, to remove the batteries from their cell phones to prevent eavesdropping.

The stairs seem almost endless. On one floor there is a door with a sign "Northern Front—Syria" where operations officers pore over maps and plans pertaining to a future war with Israel's neighbor to the north. Down the hall are similar signs for Lebanon and Gaza. Down another two flights of stairs is the chief of staff's conference room, where the IDF's top brass meets almost weekly for highly classified discussions and reviews operational plans. The room is quite bare except for a U-shaped table and a wall lined with plasma TV screens, video cameras, and pictures from previous meetings held in the room that covered the unilateral withdrawal from Gaza in the summer of 2005, the Second Lebanon War, and Operation Cast Lead in the Gaza Strip in 2009.

Three years after the 2006 war, a top IDF general stood in the chief of staff's conference room and pointed to a map of Israel, Lebanon, and Syria that was projected on a screen at the front of the room. The general pushed a button, and the map filled with hundreds of small dots in different colors. "The war we face is a collage war," the general explained. "If until now our wars had a clear form, as we move farther away from the Second Lebanon War we understand that the next war will have a different character than previous wars."

In a future war against an organization such as Hezbollah or Hamas, the general said while pointing to the different-colored dots, IDF commanders will encounter aspects of guerrilla, terror, and conventional warfare. In other words, a commander invading Lebanon will face antitank missiles (conventional), kidnapping attempts (terror), and underground tunnels (guerrilla).

Then the general showed an aerial picture of a Lebanese refugee camp. The houses were extremely close to one another and had almost no room to pass between them. "This is what our war looks like today, gentlemen," he said. "Long-range rocket attacks against our cities, ambushes from within homes, state-of-the-art intelligence, and all within a complex combat surrounding."

The general's message was best illustrated in a secret military film. Taken from an unmanned aerial vehicle (UAV), the film showed two armed terrorists identified as Hamas operatives walking in a narrow alley between two small buildings. All around them were children. The armed men placed what looked like two pipes on the ground and ran into one of the structures. A few minutes later one of the pipes—a missile—was launched into Israel. The IAF destroyed the second pipe before it could be launched. The commingling of children, terrorists, and rocket launchers in an urban setting clearly demonstrated the challenge the IDF faced.

"So what solution are you proposing?" asked one of the senior participants in the discussion.

"We are working on a combination of time and space," the general explained. "Israel will need to work to move the war as quickly (time) as possible to the enemy's strategic centers (space). The solution is to combine standoff firepower against selected targets with a preplanned ground offensive by tanks, infantry, and engineering corps."

At least once a month in the year following the war a disagreement would erupt in the Bor's conference room among the top generals over the significance of Eizenkot's Dahiya Doctrine and whether it should be used again in a future conflict. Most believed it should.[20] Those who opposed the doctrine argued that owing to the makeup of Hezbollah it would be almost impossible to deal it a fatal blow. Unlike fighting against a conventional military, they claimed, the organization did not revolve around one center of gravity, which, if destroyed, would end the war. For example, during the 1973 Yom Kippur War, Israel's retaking the Suez Canal from Egypt was a clear sign that Egypt had lost the war.

The results of the 2006 war, and the discovery that Hezbollah had far superior military hardware than expected, forced Israel to turn its focus not only to Lebanon but also to the sources of Hezbollah's weaponry—Iran and Syria.

When Hafez al-Assad was president of Syria, he often made Hezbollah secretary-general Hassan Nasrallah wait seven hours in the hallway before letting him into his office. Assad also gave Hezbollah rockets that had only a twelve-mile range. Once Assad's son Bashar became president in 2000, Nasrallah received an open pass to the presidential palace and was given permission to take back to Lebanon whatever he wanted, even long-range rockets.

Another development since the 2006 war was Iran's decision to solidify its control over its Lebanese proxy. Although manifested in several ways, it was demonstrated primarily within the chain of command and by Tehran's deployment of dozens of IRGC officers to command Hezbollah fighting units in Lebanon.

News of Iranian discontent with Nasrallah began to surface following the 2006 war. Several reports in the Arab press claimed that Iranian supreme leader Ayatollah Ali Khamenei had ousted Sheikh Nasrallah from his post.[21] While these reports were later refuted, they demonstrated Iran's frustration with Hezbollah. This dissatisfaction led to Iran's instituting a number of structural changes to the guerrilla group's hierarchy, under which Nasrallah had to seek Iranian permission prior to conducting certain operations.

"Sheikh Hassan Nasrallah's authority is somewhat restricted, and whenever he pops his head out of a bunker he sees an Iranian on top of him," a top IDF officer from the Northern Command confirmed in 2009. "Nowadays, most of the control over the group is from Iran."[22]

Iran's control was also evidenced in its refusal to allow one person to replace Imad Mughniyeh, the legendary Hezbollah military chief who was killed in a meticulously planned car bombing—attributed to the Mossad—in Damascus in February 2008. Mughniyeh was perceived to have too much power since he was the liaison to the Revolutionary Guards, Hamas, and Islamic Jihad; had been in charge of Hezbollah's military arm; and commanded the guerrilla group's extensive international infrastructure and terror cells. So instead of appointing a single successor, the Iranians split up Mughniyeh's responsibilities among a few men. The idea was not to give one person too much power and responsibility. In 2011 IDF intelligence claimed that Iran had cut Hezbollah's budget by more than 40 percent, a move that led to more tension between the two. Nevertheless, Hezbollah knew that it could not make a move without a green light from Tehran.

Following the war, Hezbollah's weaponry came from a number of sources, mostly Iran and Syria. In November 2009 Israeli Navy commandos seized the MV *Francop*, a cargo ship that was carrying hundreds of tons of weaponry—including long-range rockets—from Iran to Lebanon. The shipments also sometimes came by air, and planes were said to land rather frequently at Beirut International Airport loaded with weaponry and explosives. While some of the planes originated in Iran and Syria, others came directly from those Eastern European and Southeast Asian countries that manufacture the antitank missiles and Katyusha rockets upon which Hezbollah forces depend. As Israeli intelligence discovered as early as 2007, whatever weapons Iran and Syria had, Hezbollah could have as well.

The operational impact of Hezbollah's weapons was significant. In a future conflict, Israel Navy ships will likely have to patrol the Lebanese coast from greater distances than in the past war. Although still flying over Lebanon to collect intelligence, in 2007 the IAF began doing so at higher altitudes out of fear that Syria had transferred to the group advanced Russian-made antiaircraft systems. In April 2010 came the real surprise: Syria had indeed transferred Scud missiles to Hezbollah. In December 2010 WikiLeaks published a cable that U.S. assistant secretary of state for Near Eastern affairs Jeffrey Feltman wrote warning that Syria was planning to transfer Scud-class ballistic missiles, to Hezbollah in Lebanon.[23] Despite the U.S. government's protest and Assad's denial of having any knowledge about such shipments, Syria provided the missile to Hezbollah. Although the Israeli government reportedly considered bombing the convoy as it crossed from Syria into Lebanon, it backed down at the last moment because of American pressure.[24]

"We need to remember," cautioned one senior Israeli defense official, "that the Lebanese-Syrian border is completely open and it is just a seven-hour drive from Damascus to the Hezbollah stronghold in the Bekaa Valley."[25] However, while the possibility for an isolated Israeli-Hezbollah war exists, the more likely scenario—owing to the group's political restraint—is that the next flare-up along the border will have more to do with Iran than with Lebanon. Further, on the one hand, should Israel decide to attack Iran's nuclear facilities, Hezbollah most definitely will be activated as part of the retaliation, and the Israeli home front will feel the brunt of the group's Iranian-supplied 50,000-plus missiles. On the other hand, should Israel not attack, the possibility of war with Hezbollah still increases, for the guerrilla group will feel more confident to take risks with the nuclear backing it has from Tehran. Either way, Israel's war with Iran had already begun.

2

TECHNOLOGY AND TRAINING

In 1953, five years after the State of Israel was established, Prime Minister David Ben-Gurion took a vacation from his work in Jerusalem to think about a serious issue—how to ensure the continued survival of the Jewish state. Ben-Gurion was bothered by the basic question of how Israel, a tiny country surrounded by hostile Arab nations that openly called for its destruction, could continue to exist.

A few weeks later he returned to the prime minister's office with a paper titled "The Doctrine of Defense and the State of Armed Forces," which, with some minor changes, continues to serve as one of the principal documents that form Israel's defense doctrine. One of the tenets of Ben-Gurion's paper is that since Israel would always be inferior in size and numbers to the Arab world, it needed to develop a strong qualitative military edge.[1]

Ben-Gurion's rationale was quite simple. While Israel can't have more soldiers than Syria does, it can have better-trained ones; while it can't have more tanks than Egypt does, it can have more advanced ones; and while it might have the same type of F-15s and F-16s that Saudi Arabia and Egypt have, Israel's aircraft will be equipped with smart bombs, specially designed armaments, and advanced electronic warfare (EW) systems.

Israel achieved this goal through an unparalleled investment in defense and with the billions of dollars Israel receives annually from the United States in foreign military aid. The Second Lebanon War and the growing challenge Israel faces from Iran and its pursuit of nuclear power continue to reinforce Ben-Gurion's defense doctrine. A year after the war, the United States and Israel signed a ten-year memorandum of understanding (MOU) under which Israel was to receive

$30 billion in foreign military financing. "We look at this region and we see that a secure and strong Israel is in the interest of the United States," Undersecretary of State for Political Affairs Nicholas Burns said in a press conference following the signing of the MOU in Jerusalem. "The Middle East is more dangerous today than it was 10, 20 year [sic] ago. . . . The regional dangers seem only to increase as Iran develops nuclear technologies and along with Syria supports organizations like Hamas, Hizbullah and the Islamic Jihad."[2]

However, maintaining the qualitative edge has become more and more difficult in light of the growing threats from Iran and Syria directly, as well as from Hezbollah and Hamas. The challenge is multiplied since in many conflicts—particularly when going against Hamas and Hezbollah, which hide behind civilian infrastructure—Israel's military edge is not demonstrated as clearly as it would be in a conventional war.

In recent years, Israel has purchased its large platforms—missile ships, fighter jets, transport aircraft, attack helicopters—from the United States. The one exception is the IDF's main battle tank, the Merkava, said to be the most advanced in the world and the best protected. While Israel has relied heavily on U.S. assistance, it has developed one of the strongest defense industries in the world. In 2010 Israel came in fourth place—after the United States, Russia, and France—in worldwide defense sales, which reached $7.5 billion.[3]

Following the war in 2006 and the discovery that antitank missiles can penetrate the infantry's old-model armored personnel carriers, the IDF took the hull of the Merkava and developed the Namer (pronounced "nah-MER," or Hebrew for tiger), a new, better-protected, and completely digitalized transport vehicle for infantry troops. In addition, Israeli defense industries also developed active protection systems for the Namer and the Merkava and installed them on the vehicles in mid-2009. The Haifa-based Rafael Advanced Defense Systems Ltd. makes one such system, the Trophy, which creates a hemispheric protective zone around armored vehicles. When its advanced radar system detects and tracks a threat, Trophy then counters it with a cloud of countermeasures that intercepts the antitank missile.

While refraining from developing such large platforms as fighter jets, over the years Israeli defense companies have become world leaders in the development of unmanned aerial vehicles, mini satellites, radar systems, and smart weapons. In 2010, for example, five NATO member countries—Germany, Australia, France, Spain, and Canada—all flew Israeli-made UAVs in Afghanistan.[4] Another demonstration of Israeli technology was provided on June 7, 2006, when a pair of American F-16 fighter jets dropped two half-ton bombs on a safe house in the Iraqi city of Baqubah, killing Abu Musab al-Zarqawi, head of al Qaeda in Iraq, who was responsible for the deaths of hundreds of Americans and Iraqis. The F-16s carried an assortment of munitions, including laser- and satellite-guided missiles. But what enabled the precision strike was the LITENING targeting pod hanging from the aircraft's belly. Made by Rafael, the LITENING is one of the most advanced targeting pods in the world. Using a variety of sensors, it enables pilots to fly at high altitudes and miles from their targets and still hit them with maximum accuracy.

Israeli defense inventions have also had civilian applications. When swallowed, Given Imaging's miniature camera in a capsule can transmit pictures of the small intestine. The idea behind this life-saving device came to a missile scientist who took part in the development of the three-thousand-pound Popeye missile, which was designed to accurately hit a target, through a window, from standoff positions of up to sixty miles away and uses a miniature camera for guidance. Now the same camera that ensures accurate missile strikes is used today to save lives as well.[5]

The story of Haim Eshed demonstrates Israel's growing status as a defense superpower. In 2010 Eshed was wrapping up almost a decade as head of the Israeli military space program, but his involvement began more than thirty years earlier. In 1979 Eshed was a young colonel in the IDF's Aman, which was in a frenzy following the signing of the Egypt-Israel Peace Treaty. The question on everyone's mind was how Israel would monitor Egyptian military forces following its planned withdrawal from the Sinai Peninsula. Eshed approached the head of Aman at the time, Maj. Gen. Yehoshua Saguy, and dropped a bombshell.

"Israel needs to establish an independent satellite capability," Eshed said.[6] As he later explained, "I understood that with peace at our doorstep we would no longer be able to fly over the Sinai to collect intelligence and that if we wanted to know what was happening there, the only way would be from above, from satellites."

Eshed was already a hero in the IDF. In 1967 he was awarded the chief of staff's Medal of Valor for developing a system that is still top secret. As head of Aman's Research and Development Division, Eshed wrote a proposal that made its way to Defense Minister Ezer Weizman and finally to Prime Minister Menachem Begin, who in 1980 approved the funding for the project.

"I have no doubt that part of Israel's readiness to move forward with the withdrawal was the knowledge that we had the ability to indigenously develop a satellite," Eshed recalled. It took almost a decade, but Israel's first satellite, called Ofek-1 (*ofek* is Hebrew for "horizon"), was launched into space September 19, 1988, gaining Israel membership in the exclusive club of nations with independent satellite-launching capabilities. The club includes the United States, Russia, France, Japan, China, India, and the United Kingdom, and in 2009 added a new member, Iran.

"When we started the program there was something rude about it," Eshed recalls. "We were a small country that had just been established, and we were seeking to develop a capability that at the time only the world's superpowers really had—the United States and the USSR [Union of Soviet Socialist Republics]." But that didn't stop Eshed, and in the thirty years since its first step into space, Israel has launched fifteen satellites.

One of the most impressive Israeli satellite launches took place in June 2008 in India. Unlike Israel's other spy satellites from the Ofek and Eros series, the satellite launched—called TecSAR—is one of a handful in the world that uses advanced radar technology instead of a camera. This technology enabled the satellite to create high-resolution images of objects on the ground in any weather conditions—including fog and clouds—something the Ofek and Eros satellites could not do.

By the mid-2000s, though, Israeli satellites were rarely looking down on Egypt. Most of the time, they kept their cameras zoomed in on Iran, Syria, and Lebanon. Iran's Omid ("hope" in Farsi) satellite was launched in 2009 in honor of the thirtieth anniversary of the Islamic Revolution. Iranian state television showed footage at an unidentified location in Iran of what it said was the nighttime liftoff of the rocket carrying the satellite. The U.S. military, meanwhile, had detected the rocket launch.

Iran had long held the goal of developing a space program, generating unease among world leaders who were already concerned about its nuclear and ballistic missile programs. Their primary concern is not with the satellite's capabilities, which were limited, but with the missile that carried the device into space. The Iranians' ability to put a satellite in space means they also are able to put a nuclear warhead wherever they want in the world.

"You need specific and added energy when firing a satellite that weighs between thirty and fifty kilograms [roughly sixty and one hundred pounds] into space," explained Professor Isaac Ben-Israel, a former head of the IDF's research and development directorate who worked closely with Eshed. "The equivalent within the atmosphere is firing a ballistic missile with a nuclear warhead that weighs one ton all the way to Western Europe."[7]

Israel's current investments in military platforms are split between offensive and defensive systems. The country decided to order the fifth-generation stealth Joint Strike Fighter—also known as the F-35—which would provide the IAF with the ability to fly undetected in enemy territory. At the same time it is developing advanced missile defense systems to protect the State of Israel against enemy missiles.

Former IAF commander Maj. Gen. Ido Nehushtan, who stepped down after a four-year term in April 2012, has said that the IAF looks at the Middle East through a pair of multifocal glasses. Through one lens Nehushtan sees the threats close to home, such as Hezbollah and Hamas, and through the other lens he sees the threats that are far away, like Iran. All of these threats make up what Nehushtan calls a radical "axis of evil" in the Middle East: led by Iran, it comprises Syria, Hezbollah in Lebanon, and Hamas and Islamic Jihad in the Gaza Strip. Because of the close relationship between members of this radical axis and the possibility that one will come to another's rescue, IAF pilots need to know how to fly the same day on three separate fronts: Gaza, Lebanon, and Iran. "The entire axis creates different challenges for the IAF and requires us to be ready for different fronts and different types of fighting without knowing what will happen first. This requires us to be ready all the time for every possible scenario," Nehushtan explained.[8]

A U.S. Air Force "strike package" usually consists of several waves of specialized aircraft, each with a distinct mission. One wave traditionally neutralizes enemy aircraft and clears a flight corridor. The second wave is tasked with suppressing enemy surface-to-air missiles to enable operational freedom. Another wave entails refueling tankers, airborne warning and control systems (AWACS), and EW planes that jam enemy radar stations. The final wave consists of the bombers and strikers.

The IAF is built completely differently. Having a limited number of aircraft, it relies on each and every one to be capable of flying various missions. While the F-15s and F-16s—the backbone of the IAF's strike fleet—may have been developed for particular purposes, both are expected to fly operations close to and far away from home, as required.[9]

From the beginning, Israeli leaders understood the importance of developing a strong air force that would be unparalleled in the region. In all of Israel's wars, the IAF played a major role, sometimes serving as the tipping point between victory and defeat. As a result, and understanding that their forces are inferior, Israel's enemies have spent recent years creating offensive capabilities that can bypass and undermine the IAF. Lacking sufficient finances and the infrastructure to establish and maintain an air force, the Syrians, Iranians, and their terror proxies of Hamas and Hezbollah have equipped themselves instead with missiles and rockets to reach Israel without the need for planes. (In contrast, the IAF's annual budget, which is classified, includes a couple of billion dollars simply for routine maintenance, fuel, and flight hours. Force building and procurement, such as for new planes, can reach several additional hundreds of millions of dollars a year.[10]) Adding to the IAF's potency are the close relationships its top brass has cultivated with Aman, the Shin Bet, and the Mossad.

During the Second Lebanon War, for example, close cooperation among the agencies materialized in Operation Specific Gravity, later described as the most dazzling thirty-four minutes of the war. On the first night of the war, IAF fighter jets swept across Lebanon and in a little more than half an hour wiped out most of the guerrilla group's Iranian-supplied long-range missiles and launchers. Because Israel's intelligence agencies provided precise intelligence and well-trained IAF pilots perfectly executed their strikes, the IAF hit more than ninety targets.[11] Those first thirty-four minutes were characteristic of the IAF's overall contribution to the month-long war. By comparison, in the Gulf War in 1991 the U.S. Air Force only succeeded in locating and destroying launchers in eight instances.[12] The IAF again repeated its success during Operation Cast Lead in the Gaza Strip in January 2009. After the launchers fired rockets, the aircraft monitoring the skies above identified their locations, and the IAF knocked out hundreds of Kassam and Katyusha rocket launchers.

Following the war in 2006, Israel's enemies began investing in advanced and mostly Russian-made antiaircraft systems with the objective of impairing the IAF's operational freedom. "We see that militaries in the north are investing in building up and upgrading their military capabilities to be able to counter the IAF," Nehushtan said in the same interview. "The process of increasing military capabilities among Israel's enemies is not stagnating but is continuously moving forward. . . . There are ways to deal with this and we cannot stand still."

The different members of the radical axis also closely cooperate in the development and production of these weapons, according to Israel's Aman. Hamas and Hezbollah representatives regularly attend weapons tests in Syria and Iran, and on occasion engineers and scientists from North Korea join them. Each member of the axis has a role. The engineering work is usually done in Iran, the production is split between Iran and Syria, and the weapons are then exported to Hezbollah and Hamas.[13] In September 2007, for example, dozens of Syrian military officers and Iranian engineers had been killed in an explosion at a secret Syrian military facility in the city of Aleppo (Halab in Arabic) as they were trying to mount a chemical warhead with mustard gas on a Scud-C missile.[14] Syrian opposition sources also later claimed that Syrian intelligence and the Iranian Revolutionary Guard Corps in the Aleppo facility supervised the manufacture of car bombs that were used in anti-Coalition attacks in Iraq.

While known to have a fairly advanced chemical and biological weapons program, Syria is also investing, for the first time since the 1980s, in advanced aircraft. In 2009 it ordered close to twenty MiG-29 fighter jets from Russia and advanced antiaircraft systems, such as the Pantsir/SA-22 and the SA-X-17, with ranges of up to about twenty-five miles.[15] Iran is also investing unprecedented amounts of money in antiaircraft systems, with the main emphasis being put on the Russian-made S-300, to defend its strategic nuclear installations. Despite the postelection unrest in Iran in June 2009, President Mahmoud Ahmadinejad flew to Moscow and pressured the Kremlin to deliver the system, which the Iranians feel could make or break an Israeli airstrike on the Islamic Republic's nuclear installations.[16] One of the most advanced multi-target antiaircraft missile systems in the world, the S-300 has a reported ability to track up to a hundred targets simultaneously while engaging up to twelve at the same time. As of early 2012 Iran had yet to obtain the system, even though, according to Israeli intelligence, it has sent teams to Russia to study it and train on it.

In Israel there are two schools of thought regarding the severity of the S-300 threat. Some agree with IAF commander Nehushtan, who said: "We need to make every effort to stop this system from getting to places where the IAF needs to operate or may need to operate in the future."[17] Other officials are less concerned and claim that if and when the S-300 is delivered to Iran, Israel will be able to develop an EW system to neutralize it. An example of this capability was demonstrated in 2007 when the IAF used EW systems to penetrate Syrian air defenses, believed to have been the most dense and comprehensive in the region, and bombed a Syrian nuclear reactor. "You need this kind of capability. You're not being responsible if you're not dealing with it. And if you can build this kind of capability, the sky's the limit," said Pinhas Buchris, then the director general of Israel's Ministry of Defense, about EW systems.[18]

In addition to EW systems that fighter jets carry, in 2006 Israel took receipt of several U.S.-manufactured Gulfstream G-550 business jets, and Israel Aerospace Industries (IAI) outfitted them with some of the most advanced network invasion, EW, and signals intelligence (SIGINT) gathering systems. It also turned one of the planes into an AWACS to support future long-range operations.

Electronic warfare technology is the most sensitive system an air force can use. "Even the closest of allies don't share EW technology," explained a senior Israeli defense official involved in such matters and claimed that Israel is today one of the world leaders in developing EW and radar systems.

Meanwhile, Hezbollah and Hamas are also believed to have obtained an antiaircraft capability, though on a much smaller scale. They use mostly shoulder-fired surface-to-air missiles such as Strela-2/SA-7s, which are believed to have a range of about five kilometers. To counter them, IAF helicopters flying over the Gaza Strip shoot off decoy flares every few seconds. Hezbollah also may have more advanced systems, such as the SA-8, a truck-mounted system with a range of dozens of kilometers. "We operate under the assumption that whatever is in Iranian and Syrian hands is likely in Hezbollah hands as well," explained a senior Aman officer.[19]

The IAF's response to the major improvements in air defense systems among its enemies is threefold: procure new stealth-enabled fighter jets, increase training, and prepare personnel mentally. While the IAF has had several midair accidents that have led to the loss of life in recent years, the last time an aircraft was shot down was during the Second Lebanon War, when a Hezbollah antitank missile hit a transport helicopter landing troops in southern Lebanon. Five soldiers died, including the only female casualty of the war, Sgt. Maj. Keren Tendler (Res.). A flight technician, Tendler was the first female soldier to die in an Israeli war since 1973.

The last time the enemy captured a pilot was in 1986 when navigator Ron Arad parachuted into Lebanon. His whereabouts are unknown to this day, despite unprecedented Israeli efforts to recover even the smallest piece of information about him. The fate of a kidnapped soldier or a captured downed pilot is not taken lightly in Israel, where governments have over the years released hundreds of convicted terrorists in controversial swaps for soldiers, some alive and others dead. If Iran were ever to capture a number of Israeli pilots, the Islamic Republic would have a strategic psychological weapon that it could use effectively against Israel.[20]

Therefore, in order to prepare pilots for possible captivity, the IAF decided in late 2009 to begin increasing pilots' mental training with an emphasis on survival skills. In addition, to counter the increasing surface-to-air missile threat, that same year the IAF started to use a specially designed virtual training system so its pilots could practice evading heat-seeking missiles. Until then, the IAF trained its pilots against antiaircraft missiles by activating its own air defense system and having a Hawk missile hypothetically lock on to the training fighter jets. Now, with the new virtual trainer, the pilot lifts off, flies in Israeli airspace, and in the helmet's heads-up display sees missiles being fired. If the plane is hit, the pilot sees a sign indicating that the plane has been "destroyed."

"A pilot needs to know that he will not always return home," explained an IAF base commander, whose pilots participated in the strike against the Syrian reactor in 2007. "We are sharpening this message since we need to know how to live with this threat."[21]

In the face of this growing threat, by 2016 Israel also plans to begin taking receipt of a first squadron of F-35s. Manufactured by Lockheed Martin in Fort Worth, Texas, the F-35 is a stealth fighter jet whose radar signature is reportedly similar to a small bird's. "This plane will significantly boost Israel's deterrence," explained a former IAF commander. "It will give Israel the ability to fly anywhere it wants undetected—including downtown Tehran—without our enemies even knowing we are there."

Nehushtan compares the anticipated arrival of the F-35 in Israel to the delivery of Israel's first batch of F-15s in 1976, making Israel the first country outside the United States to receive them. At the time, the fourth-generation F-15 was one of the most advanced aircraft in the world and superior to the Russian planes that were being exported to the Middle East, such as the MiG-21s that formed the backbone of Egypt's fleet. "The moment the plane arrived it boosted Israel's deterrence in face of the air forces that were against us," explained Nehushtan. "A plane that is advanced and is of a new generation [like the F-35] has strategic significance and boosts our deterrence. It is therefore important that we are the first in the Middle East to get it."[22]

But this strategy appeared to be undermined in 2011, this time by Israel's closest friend—the United States. While Israel will begin receiving at least twenty F-35s sometime around 2016, other countries in the region are also arming themselves at an alarming pace. In late 2010, Barack Obama's administration unveiled unprecedented plans to sell Saudi Arabia $60 billion worth of the most advanced military platforms, including some eighty-four F-15 fighter jets, seventy Black Hawk helicopters, and sixty Apache attack helicopters. Egypt was also purchasing new F-16 fighter jets from the same block as the latest Israeli F-16Is, known as the Sufa (Storm). Israel, for its part, told the Pentagon that it understands the importance of selling advanced military platforms to moderate Arab countries such as Saudi Arabia and Egypt, particularly in light of the Iranian nuclear threat and the realignment taking place within the Gulf States. Following the revolution in Egypt in February 2011, the so-called Arab Spring, and the upheavals throughout the Middle East, the Israelis are concerned about the possibility that radical Islamist elements will take over some countries, such as Egypt and Saudi Arabia, either through elections or in violent revolutions. What occurred in Iran in 1979, Israel has pointed out, could one day happen in other Middle Eastern countries.

The Americans counter that if the United States doesn't sell the equipment to these countries, Russia likely will. Further, by selling the planes to the Arab countries, the United States reserves for itself a certain degree of control over their use, since the countries will be dependent on the United States for spare parts and maintenance. The Israelis, however, point to the sale of F-4 fighter jets to Iran in the 1970s. Despite sanctions imposed on Iran and an embargo that has been in place since shortly after the 1979 revolution, the Iranian Air Force somehow continues to obtain spare parts.

While Israel is concerned about the Saudis' receiving additional F-15s, possibly even more worrying is that the proposed $60 billion deal includes joint direct attack munitions (JDAMs), basically freefall satellite-guided smart bombs that can be fired from a standoff position of dozens of miles. The problem with a JDAM, as one senior IAF officer explained, is that unlike other weapons systems, a pilot does not need to "drive" it to its target. "Our pilots are better trained than Saudi pilots," the officer said. "But even an untrained pilot can drop a JDAM and accurately hit a target dozens of kilometers away." Israel can take comfort in the fact that the Saudis are not getting the most advanced JDAMs currently in use in the United States and Israel, such as the Laser JDAM, which adds a laser seeker to the bomb's nose and gives it the ability to engage both moving and static targets.

Major General Nehushtan had fought hard in his previous job as head of the IDF's Planning Division to prevent the George W. Bush administration's sale of JDAMs to Saudi Arabia. In June 2007 he flew with Amos Gilad, head of the diplomatic-military bureau at the Ministry of Defense, for talks with top Pentagon officials about the proposed sale and to voice the Israelis' concerns. Under his watch as IAF commander, however, the Saudis not only ordered JDAMs but were also arming themselves with more than eighty additional F-15s.

Although the impact of the Saudi deal on Israel remains to be seen, two points are increasingly clear: the balance of power in the region is shifting, and Israel's qualitative military edge is no longer as obvious as it once was.

Israel's deterrence does not rely solely on its offensive capabilities, such as fighter jets that can fly to and attack Iran. It also has good defensive measures, such as the Arrow missile defense system, which is said to be capable of intercepting all of the current long-range and ballistic missiles in Iranian and Syrian hands. Until 2009, Israel was the only country in the world with an operational system capable of intercepting incoming enemy missiles. By the end of 2010 it fielded the Iron Dome system, a missile interceptor developed specially to intercept short-range rockets, such as the Kassams and Katyushas that Hamas and Hezbollah have wielded against Israel's northern and southern borders since the early 2000s. By the end of 2011, the Iron Dome had a 75 percent kill rate, intercepting thirty-three rockets throughout the year. Sometime in 2013 Israel plans to deploy the David's Sling, the third and middle layer of the overall missile defense concept that is capable of intercepting the medium-range rockets known to be in Hezbollah's large arsenal.

Israel's first taste of missile attacks came during the Yom Kippur War in 1973, when Egypt fired a few Scuds into Israel. During the Gulf War, Saddam Hussein launched a monumental missile attack in 1991 and fired thirty-nine Scuds into Israel. The assault paralyzed the country and forced millions of people to don gas masks and enter sealed rooms, fearing the missiles were loaded with chemical and biological weapons. At the time, Israel was in complete disarray over this new threat. One of the few people who understood that Hussein's barrage was only the first of a different kind of strike was former IAF chief Maj. Gen. David Ivry (Ret.), who at the time served as director general of Israel's Ministry of Defense.

Ivry knew a fact or two about the Iraqis. On June 7, 1981, as commander of the IAF, he oversaw Operation Opera, in which eight IAF F-16 fighter jets bombed the Osirak nuclear reactor in Iraq. Ivry was responsible for convincing Prime Minister Begin that his pilots were capable of carrying out the strike, and they did without encountering any real resistance. (One of the pilots, Ilan Ramon, later became Israel's first astronaut, but he and six other crew members died in the space shuttle *Columbia* tragedy in 2003.) In a briefing at military headquarters in Tel Aviv after another Scud attack in 1991, Ivry told the IDF's general staff: "What we are currently seeing with forty-something Scuds is nothing compared to what we will see in the future."[23]

In 2006, during the Second Lebanon War, Ivry's prophecy came true when Hezbollah fired more than four thousand rockets into northern Israel, displacing about a million Israelis. On Israel's other front in the south, in 2008 alone Palestinian terror groups operating in the Gaza Strip fired three thousand rockets. "Ivry was right . . . ," said Israeli defense minister and former prime minister Ehud Barak in November 2009. "Hezbollah today already has forty thousand rockets and Hamas is also building up a significant arsenal."[24]

Israel's assessment is that during a future conflict, the country will come under a rain of rockets of different sizes and ranges. "The entire Israeli home front could be part of any future war," Barak's deputy Matan Vilnai said in April 2009.[25] "Everyone needs to know that there is a chance that in the next war a missile will land in their backyard."

The missile threat to Israel encompasses a variety of weapons. On the one hand, the country faces small, short-range, and primitive rockets such as the Kassam, which Hamas produces in the Gaza Strip. On the other end of the spectrum, the long-range, Iranian-made Shahab and Ashura ballistic missiles can easily reach Israel and are capable of carrying nuclear warheads. In between are the medium-range rockets that make up most of Hezbollah's and Syria's arsenal.

What makes the challenge even greater is that Israel's enemies, recognizing the potential damage their missiles can cause, are continuously upgrading their capabilities. Hamas, for example, has increased the range of its Kassam from ten miles in 2005 to thirteen miles in 2006 and twenty-five miles in 2008. The next year Hamas test fired a missile that has a range of close to forty miles and puts Tel Aviv, Israel's main metropolitan city, within its range.

Hamas obtains its missiles from two sources—Iran and local manufacturers in Gaza. The short-range Kassams are developed and manufactured in the Gaza Strip. The long-range missiles are smuggled into Gaza through the network of tunnels the terror group operates along the Egyptian border in a small, nine-mile strip of land called the Philadelphi Route.

During Operation Cast Lead in the Gaza Strip in the winter of 2008–2009, rockets with Chinese markings pounded Israeli cities. These rockets make several stops before reaching Gaza. In many cases Iran or Hezbollah purchase and then transfer them to the Sinai Peninsula, where they are smuggled via tunnels into Gaza. In some instances, the weaponry is believed to come through Yemen and Eritrea, where it is transferred to Sudan, then northward to Egypt, and into Gaza.

Iran provides Hamas with two types of missiles—Grad-model Katyushas, an old Soviet-era rocket with a range of about twenty-five miles, and the Fajr-5, an Iranian copy of a Chinese artillery rocket that has a range of close to fifty miles. Both types of the Iranian-made missile are too big to fit into a tunnel in one piece. Thus, they are dismantled into components, usually four or five, and smuggled into the Gaza Strip. There, Hamas engineers reassemble them.

Hezbollah has a mix of different types of missiles: mostly short-range rockets from the Katyusha family: the 122mm Katyusha with a range of about thirty miles; the 220mm Syrian-made rocket with a range of around forty-five miles; and the Syrian-made 302mm rocket, boasting a range of more than sixty miles. Before the 2006 war, Hezbollah had a significant arsenal of Iranian-made Zelzals and Fajrs, but as noted previously, the IAF destroyed close to 90 percent of them the first night of the battle.[26]

Hezbollah has since significantly boosted its rocket capability and arsenal today. In addition, Hezbollah's missiles are believed to have a range of close to two hundred miles and can reach Israel's most sensitive military installation, its nuclear reactor in Dimona. These missiles are believed to be upgraded models of the Zelzal-2, an Iranian-made missile that can carry more than a thousand pounds of explosives. "Hezbollah has three times the ability it had before the Second Lebanon War and now has forty-two thousand missiles in its possession, as opposed to the fourteen thousand it had before the war," Defense Minister Barak told the Knesset in November 2008.[27] "It has missiles that can reach the towns of Ashkelon, Beersheba, and Dimona."

Israel also works under the operational assumption that Syria, at a moment's notice, could smuggle some of its long-range Scud missiles into Lebanon. "A truck carrying a launcher and a missile can leave Damascus and arrive in the Bekaa Valley Hezbollah stronghold in just a few hours," according to a senior officer in the IDF's Northern Command, which is responsible for Lebanon and Syria.[28] In May 2010 this fear appeared to have materialized when reports surfaced that Hezbollah had received a small number of Scud missiles from Syria. Prime Minister Netanyahu later told Italian prime minister Silvio Berlusconi that the missiles were being stored in a Syrian base immediately north of Damascus on behalf of Hezbollah. In May 2011, Israeli intelligence warned the government that Hezbollah was moving its stored strategic assets from Syria into Lebanon out of fear that the equipment would be jeopardized if President Bashar Assad's regime were toppled.

While the Scuds are of great concern, in 2012 the IDF was more worried about another missile called the M-600 that had made its way from Syrian to Hezbollah hands. Hezbollah received hundreds of these advanced, Syrian-made surface-to-surface missiles, which are clones of an Iranian missile called the Fateh-110. The M-600 has a range of 250 kilometers, carries a 500-kilogram conventional warhead, and is equipped with a sophisticated navigation system, giving Hezbollah a measure of accuracy it did not have previously.[29] The IDF believes that Hezbollah is likely storing the missiles in homes in central and northern Lebanon, just as it did with the Iranian-made Zelzal and Fajr missiles that the IAF destroyed during the Second Lebanon War. The "homes," in many cases, feature retractable roofs and built-in missile launchers.

The largest surface-to-surface missile arsenal in the Middle East is in Syria. Following the 1973 Yom Kippur War President Hafez al-Assad understood that he could not overcome the IDF's air or ground forces. Instead, Assad instructed the Syrian military to invest its money in missiles and create a strategic deterrent against Israel. Syria's first supplier was the Soviet Union. In the 1990s, North Korea and China took the Soviets' place, and today Syria is estimated to have an arsenal consisting of tens of thousands of short-, medium-, and long-range rockets.

In 2005 Syria test fired three missiles in an "airburst" mode, and the warheads likely used cluster munitions that can carry chemical or biological weapons. One of the missiles was an older Scud-B, with a range of about 200 miles, but two were the North Korean–manufactured and improved Rodong or, as they are known in Syria, Scud-D missiles with a range of up to 450 miles. Syria also has an extensive chemical and biological weapons program.[30]

As recently as 2006 Syria had perhaps 330 missiles capable of hitting Tel Aviv; Hezbollah, fewer than two dozen; Iran, about 50; and Hamas in Gaza, none. By 2009 Syria's arsenal of missiles capable of reaching the area had soared to 1,300, Hezbollah's to 800, and Iran's to 300. Even Hamas in Gaza had a handful. By 2010 the numbers jumped again: Syria had an estimated 2,300; Hezbollah, 1,200; Iran, 400; and Hamas in Gaza, dozens.[31]

In testimony before the U.S. Senate Committee on Armed Services in 2009, Lt. Gen. Michael D. Maples, director of the Defense Intelligence Agency, laid out the threat Israel faces from Syria. Maples said that Syria's chemical warfare program is "well established with a stockpile of nerve agents, which it can deliver by aircraft or ballistic missiles."[32] Maples confirmed that during the years preceding his testimony, Syria had continued seeking chemical warfare–related technology and expertise from foreign sources and had set up the facilities and expertise needed domestically to produce, store, and deliver chemical agents.

Israel's greatest challenge, however, comes from Iran, whose combination of long-range ballistic missiles with a nuclear capability poses a threat of an existential nature. On April 22, 2008, the IRGC held its annual military parade in downtown Tehran. As in previous parades, the IRGC marched its guns, artillery cannons, and tanks down the capital's main avenue. In the sky above, some 220 planes flew over the city, including U.S.-made F-5, F-4, and F-14 fighter jets. Except for a modern tank that the IRGC makes in few numbers and a handful of Russian-made MiG-29s, the shah's regime had purchased all of the displayed hardware and military platforms in the 1960s and 1970s. So where is all of Iran's money going today? The simple answer is into the development of nuclear technology as well as long-range ballistic missiles.

Iran began equipping itself with ballistic missiles during the Iran-Iraq War in the 1980s.[33] It first received a shipment of Russian-manufactured Scud-B missiles from Libya and later turned to North Korea, which became its main supplier. In 1988 during the so-called War of the Cities, Iranian forces fired seventy-seven missiles into Iraq.

When the war ended later that year, the Iranians found themselves with only a limited number of Scud-B and Scud-C missiles. Ten years later, however, they already had their first operational Shahab-3 missile, which they originally purchased from North Korea together with a built-in production line. Today Iran is believed to have several hundred Shahabs and dozens of corresponding launchers. The missile has a range of about a thousand miles and can carry a warhead weighing between 500 kilograms and a ton.[34]

Iran made especially impressive technological leaps in ballistic missile development in 2009 with the launch in February of its first homemade satellite, the Omid, and in May of the new Sajil missile, which has a range of more than twelve hundred miles and can easily reach parts of Eastern Europe. Now the Iranians have their own production line of Shahabs and Sajils for which they are building underground silos. In addition, Israeli assessments indicate that the Iranians are capable of independently manufacturing their own version of the BM-25 missile, which they received from North Korea and has a range of close to two thousand miles. According to the same evaluation, the launch of the Omid demonstrated that Iranian scientists have made breakthroughs in guidance technology, which likely has been applied to its ballistic missiles also.[35]

Uzi Rubin, who oversaw Israel's Arrow missile development and served as the head of the Homa missile defense program within the Ministry of Defense, points to three main breakthroughs in Iran's missile program. First, it now uses solid fuel propellant. Second, it has taken unguided rockets like the Zelzal—which are also in Hezbollah's hands—and turned them into guided rockets. Finally, it has built a two-stage satellite launcher, rather than the usual three-stage rockets for space-lift vehicles.

Iran's success in upgrading its missile's propulsion systems from liquid to solid fuel is quite significant, Rubin notes. The main difference is that a missile that operates on liquid fuel needs to be fueled close to launch, making it easier for surveillance satellites or hovering aircraft to discover them. Solid-fuel missiles have a significantly longer shelf life and can be stored in underground silos for an extended period, allowing the Iranians to lift their covers and launch them whenever they choose.[36]

"The Iranians have the technology right now to produce an intermediate-range ballistic missile that can threaten Europe," Rubin says. "Whether they do it or not involves the question of intention, but they are capable of doing it." According to Rubin, these developments indicate a possible reversal in roles between Iran and North Korea. While Tehran bought technology from Pyongyang in the 1990s, today the flow of technology is believed to go the other way.

"This trend of using solid fuel is an improvement, and [is a] central part of their missile program," said Col. Guy Aviram, who works for the Homa program that designed the Arrow missile defense system.[37] "Together with the range and the intentions of the Iranian regime, we get a package of technology and intentions that puts us, as the country most threatened by Iran, in a place that every day that passes is not like the day before."

In December 2009 Iran test fired what is said to be an upgraded version of the Sajil. With a range of more than fifteen hundred miles, its reach could hit six European Union (EU) countries: Poland, Slovakia, Romania, Hungary, Bulgaria, and Greece. Rubin says that with such ranges, Iran can easily hide its missiles and launchers near the city of Tabriz in northwest Iran, an area of about thirty thousand square miles filled with mountains, valleys, and canyons. "You can hide thousands of ballistic missiles there with a very high probability of survival," he says. "So the capability to make a survivable missile that can threaten Europe now exists in Iran."

Israel's hope is that in the event of a future war, its missile defense systems will provide a shield. While they will not succeed in intercepting all incoming missiles, they might knock out a majority and provide relief to the home front. The systems also are equipped with highly advanced radars that can accurately predict where the missiles will land. Thus, if a rocket or missile is heading for an open field, the system will not need to intercept it.

In addition to saving lives, a multilayered missile defense system similar to the one Israel is developing will give the government more diplomatic maneuverability. Until Israel deployed the Iron Dome system along the border with Gaza, the primitive Kassam rocket was a weapon of strategic significance against Israel. Its incessant use in attacks against Israeli towns on numerous occasions pressured the Israeli government into launching an operation inside the densely populated Gaza Strip. If the rockets are intercepted, the pressure on the government to take immediate offensive action decreases.

Israel's interest in missile defense began in the mid-1980s when, together with the United States, it began to develop the Arrow missile defense system. Since then, the U.S. government has invested close to $3 billion in the Arrow, which the IAI outside of Tel Aviv and the Boeing Company in Huntsville, Alabama, manufactures. In 2009 Congress approved additional funding for the development of the Arrow 3, a newer and larger version of the current system with a greater range and the capability of intercepting missiles at higher altitudes.

The U.S. government's cooperation peaked prior to the 1991 Gulf War, when George H. W. Bush's administration sent Patriot missile batteries to help defend Israel against Saddam Hussein's Scud missile attacks. In October 2008 George W. Bush's administration gave Israel a farewell gift in the form of the X-Band radar, one of a handful of such advanced radars in the world. Manned by American troops at a base in the Negev Desert in southern Israel, the radar is capable of detecting targets thousands of miles away and of providing five to seven minutes' warning before a missile from Iran strikes. By contrast, the residents of the southern town of Sderot, Israel, have ten seconds' warning when Palestinian terrorists fire a Kassam rocket from the Gaza Strip.

In some tests, the Arrow successfully intercepted an Israeli missile called Blue Sparrow, which was modified to mimic an Iranian Shahab-3 ballistic missile that carried a split warhead and had advanced radar-evading capabilities. In 2010 the Shahabs in Iran's arsenal did not possess such capabilities, but in a 2009 test the "enemy missile" incorporated the type of threat the IDF believes Israel will face one day from its enemy to the east. "The Arrow technology is always improving, and we cannot forget that the enemy is also advancing and improving its capabilities," says Brig. Gen. Daniel Milo, in 2009 commander of the IAF's Air Defense Division, which is responsible for operating the Arrow.[38]

The close Israeli-U.S. relationship on missile defense reached new heights in October 2009 with Juniper Cobra, its largest-ever joint missile defense exercise. For three weeks thousands of American soldiers—flown to Israel from bases in Europe, the Middle East, and the United States—and Israeli soldiers simulated various threat scenarios to test Israeli defenses.[39] The exercise, held every two years in Israel, has three main components: field training, which focuses on improving cooperation between Israeli and U.S. forces; computer simulation, which examines the interoperability between Israeli and U.S. systems; and, in some years, live fire exercises, which test Israeli and U.S. radars. What made the 2009 exercise unique was that the United States brought all of its own missile defense systems—ships with the Aegis ballistic missile defense system and the Terminal High-Altitude Area Defense (THAAD) system—to Israel for the first time. It set up the necessary infrastructure required to operate the American systems in Israel, in case the United States decides to deploy them in the event of a war with Iran.

One of the IDF's worst nightmares is a simultaneous Iranian and Syrian missile barrage, possibly carrying nuclear or nonconventional warheads and all heading toward Israel, with only minutes to be intercepted. Responsible for civil defense, the IDF's Home Front Command is prepared to deal with potential missile fallout; however, the country is banking on the Arrow to prevent that mission from being necessary. It hopes the missile will provide the thin line that separates the Jewish State's existence from obliteration.

Superior military technology, though considered a necessity in Israel, is only one side of the coin. Since the 2006 war Israel also has invested in training and rehabilitating its reserve corps. In December 2006, while the country was still nursing its wounds from the war and while public criticism of the government and the IDF's top brass was mounting, the changes that would carry the IDF into the next decade were already visible in the field.

In the winter of 2007 Erez Zuckerman, the young colonel who had established the Egoz antiguerrilla unit and during the 2006 war had served as a division commander, stood at the entrance to a training base near the town of Elyakim in the Upper Galilee and observed the rows of trucks carrying the tanks under his command. Once a promising young commander, Zuckerman had failed during the war. His division's official assignment was to be a back-up force in case the Syrians attacked the Golan Heights. But Zuckerman couldn't sit on the sidelines while the IDF fought a war in Lebanon. Several days into the war, Zuckerman asked his commander for permission to enter Lebanon with his men. "I was either going to get a medal for my actions or a demotion," he would later say, right before resigning from the IDF. "Had I succeeded, everybody would have praised me."[40]

But he didn't succeed. After the war ended and Zuckerman conducted a survey of his division, he learned of harsh personal criticism against him. The officers, all reservists, had little regard for military hierarchy, and as in other reserve units in the IDF, the dialogue with their commander was open. The soldiers spoke about years of insufficient training, low levels of professionalism and expertise, errors in decision making, and mainly the deficient qualifications of the division commander. This criticism was foreign to Zuckerman, but it was not baseless.

Zuckerman was not entirely to blame, though. His situation was a symptom of the overall problem. While he was a proven leader and brave commando, he had never undergone tank training, never commanded a tank, and never learned how to mobilize a division. Still, when the war erupted, he was expected to know how to lead his armored division into Lebanon.

Iran, in the first half of 2006, was not on the list of threats for most reserve soldiers. Only the IAF pilots trained knowing that they could one day be asked to fly the distance and bomb the Islamic Republic's nuclear facilities. The IDF top brass did not realize until after the war with Hezbollah that while the next conflict might not be directly against Iran, it would counter Iran's influence in the region and particularly within Israel's immediate vicinity.

Before the war, all of the IDF commanders had their unit's training protocols dictated from above. Two armored brigades in one IDF division, for example, were not allotted any training time. The only exercises the division held focused on the use of standoff power such as artillery and reconnaissance missions. During the rest of their reserve service, the reservists were sent to the West Bank to man checkpoints and patrol highways.

Zuckerman did not shy away from responsibility, and as with the commander of the IDF's Northern Command Maj. Gen. Udi Adam and Brig. Gen. Gal Hirsch, he too decided to resign. "When I took it upon myself to take the division into this war despite knowing that it wasn't ready, I also understood that I would be responsible if it failed," he said in the winter of 2007. "I cannot excuse myself for deviating from the norms by which I have lived my entire life."

Despite the resignations, the changes in the IDF continued at an unprecedented pace. The IDF took regular active units out of the field and sent them to train. Instead of only two months of training a year, the IDF instituted an unbreakable four-four equation, with four months spent protecting Israel's borders and four months in training. Reservists who used to spend their annual service requirement manning watchtowers and checkpoints found themselves wearing their full combat gear instead, running up sand dunes in the Negev and hiking through thick forestry brush in the Galilee. The motivation was simple. The IDF had suffered a heavy blow to its image during the 2006 war and needed to change. As Ehud Barak, the defense minister in 2007, has famously said throughout his extensive military and political career, "There is no pity or respect for the *weak* in the *Middle East*."[41]

To appreciate how dramatic the IDF's change was, one must revisit the State of Israel in the 1950s and 1960s. Prime Minister Ben-Gurion was the first to formulate the idea that the reserve corps was a vital necessity for the newborn country. "We are few and they are many, and naturally the many endeavor to dominate the few," he had acknowledged in a monumental security speech in 1949.[42] As a result, the leadership decided to build an army that would be disproportionate in size to the country's population. But to accomplish this goal, the nascent state had to devote its economy to its security needs or, in other words, forgo economic development for the sake of defense.

The solution was to maintain both a compulsory army, whose soldiers would not receive a salary, and a limited, career-based army of those people who wanted to continue their service. The IDF would be based on a strong reserve corps consisting of all the discharged soldiers, and the National Insurance Institute would pay them a benefit from the taxes that they themselves had paid. Israel's security doctrine viewed the reservists as "strategic human inventory" that could be mobilized quickly and determine the outcome of a war. As Ben-Gurion himself said, "Our security relies first and foremost on our reserve forces."

During the early decades, the reserve soldiers enjoyed the support and understanding of Israeli society. Employers had to come to terms with their employees' prolonged absences, and universities forgave students' absences. A positive folklore developed around the Israeli reservist, who was seen as being full of good humor, encouragement, and self-deprecation. Until the mid-1980s the reserve army was the IDF's primary asset; it was a widespread phenomenon and a source of strength and pride for the State of Israel.

By the summer of 2006, however, the reservists had barely a week of training a year and increasingly were viewed as an excess force or a peripheral power that was no longer the center of the Israeli fighting machine. Recognizing the distant threat in Iran, the IDF presumed that technological superiority and high-level professional expertise, and not the reserve forces, would be required to remain competitive. Nevertheless, when contemplating its strategy to counter the limited Palestinian terror threat, the IDF and political echelons banked on the compulsory army. This new understanding of this army's mission was translated economically. As the government began to neglect the reserve corps, the country limited its financial investment as well.

The change was apparent in late December 2008, when Israel launched Operation Cast Lead against Hamas and other Palestinian terror groups in the Gaza Strip after their incessant Kassam rocket attacks of the preceding eight years. Throughout 2008, Israel's chief of the General Staff Lt. Gen. Gabi Ashkenazi privately had spoken countless times with the members of the security cabinet and various ministers. The trauma from the Second Lebanon War accompanied the ministers' every step and every statement the chief of staff made. "An operation in Gaza requires calling up the reserves," Ashkenazi warned. "If we want to capture the Gaza Strip it will come at a price—you are the ones who will have to make that decision, not me," he repeated.[43]

As the Israelis discovered in Lebanon, the catalyst behind the increased tension in Gaza was Iran and its Revolutionary Guards. Aman reports referred to large arms shipments sent from Tehran to Gaza that were destabilizing the balance of power between Israel and Hamas.

On Saturday morning, December 27, 2008, the call-up orders were ready to be sent out to the reservists. The government had reached its decision and given the green light to launch the operation. The first stage included a week of aerial attacks on hundreds of Hamas targets.

Among the IAF personnel taking part in the operation were many reservists. In this regard the IAF had not changed. Reservists who want to retain their wings are required to fly at least one day a week, and those who do not participate in the training flights are removed from the list of qualified pilots. The Iranian threat, as mentioned, had preserved the IAF's budget even during the years of cutbacks to the ground forces.

During the three-week operation, many commanders who had fought against Hezbollah two years earlier remarked that the new Israeli military was more confident and better prepared. The change was clear from the beginning of the operation, when the first reserve division was drafted and sent into the northern Gaza Strip. The reservists' mission was first to replace compulsory units that had captured the territory and were being sent to rest and then to capture the southern part of the Gaza Strip, including the city of Rafah. According to Israeli intelligence agencies, Rafah is the end point of hundreds of smuggling tunnels and possibly even the location where Israeli soldier Gilad Shalit had been held since his kidnapping in 2006.

Operation Cast Lead ultimately ended before the units had a chance to head to the strip's southern tip. Nonetheless, the IDF and its reservists had restored their image as an effective and powerful fighting machine.

In the heart of Israel, a fifteen-minute drive from Ben-Gurion International Airport, is the Tzrifin military base. Before 1948 the base served the British army, and the old architecture is still recognizable today. In 2007 in one of the low-level buildings on the base, a group of cadets from the IDF's company commanders course had gathered. The first class of cadets to enter the course following the Second Lebanon War, the participants were young men in their twenties and some older reservists. Many of them already had headed companies and battalions in complex missions in the territories and in Lebanon, but they had never undergone any formal training.

The cadets—all officers—were about to set out on the IDF's traditional and compulsory trip to Poland. Since the 1990s, the IDF has sent many of its combat officers to visit the concentration camps in Poland, a journey aimed at demonstrating to the officers the importance of the State of Israel. The officers were of different ethnicities: Arabs, Druze, Christians, settlers, and religious and secular Jews.

At the podium stood Maj. Gen. Benny Gantz, who at the time was the head of the IDF's Ground Forces Command and later would be appointed military attaché in Washington and then, in February 2011, the IDF chief of the General Staff. "We have learned and internalized from our mistakes," he said. "We have learned that in order to be a commander one must undergo organized training. This cannot be neglected."

Previously, the IDF had been occupied with routine security and patrol activities in the territories, reducing the need for reserve soldiers. The tremendous burden of the al-Aqsa Intifada and the threat of suicide terror had caused the senior IDF commanders to ignore the command schools and military academies. To become an IDF officer one had to graduate from the Bahd 1 Officers' Training School located in the Negev, but after Bahd 1 an officer might not undergo formal training before assuming higher positions.

As a rule, in the 2000s the IDF gave precedence to those who had undergone organized training and schooling, but with the army being under tremendous strain, this option was not always possible. Instead, the IDF hastily had to appoint platoon commanders as company commanders, company commanders to battalion commanders, and battalion commanders to brigade commanders. Courses for each position existed in Tzrifin, but not all of the commanders could devote the necessary time to studying.

The first course after the war was intended to address this problem. Commanders who had already accumulated a great deal of field experience came in order to acquire theoretical knowledge and to understand what they had been doing until then and how to improve. Now the IDF required commanders to attend a two- to three-month course. The scenario they trained for was quite simple—an all-out war against Hezbollah, Syria, and Hamas. Interoperability became the focus, as cooperation between the different branches of the army and how to synchronize the army with the air force and navy was emphasized.

The training addressed issues that occurred during the war in 2006. For example, pilots carried updated maps, but the ground forces' maps were not current. Every time the ground forces needed a helicopter to carry away wounded soldiers or drop off provisions, the maps from both branches quickly became superfluous. Meanwhile, communication problems plagued other ground troops, as combat engineers had trouble communicating with tank commanders, who in turn had difficulty speaking with the infantry units. During one complex operation of two elite units, the commanders, young reservist officers, had trouble finding "the rear phone" in the tank accompanying them. This device is meant to provide direct communication between infantry forces outside the tank and the commander inside the tank. Even after searching for several minutes, the soldiers and commanders could not find it. Such was the price of not touching a tank since Israel's withdrawal from Lebanon in May 2000.

By mid-2007, the IDF had built an organized training regimen for all its forces. The results were evident during Operation Cast Lead in Gaza in January 2009. A stranger entering the front command of the 401st Brigade of the Armored Corps, which captured the central Gaza Strip, would have been surprised to encounter officers with blue officers' ranks (signaling they were from the navy and air force) on their shoulders. The brigade commander, a soldier from the Armored Corps, sat in a large protected and sealed shelter, and at tables set up in rows on the side were different work groups consisting of armored officers, IAF pilots, and navy representatives.

On one side, sitting next to a small table lined with radio devices, were representatives of the Shin Bet dressed in civilian clothing. Every few minutes one of them would pick up an encrypted telephone connecting them directly to staff headquarters in northern Tel Aviv. Brigade commanders had direct command over combat helicopter squadrons, infantry battalions, armored battalions, a combat engineer battalion, and special teams from the navy's elite commando unit, the Shayetet. Everyone knew one another and how to communicate. Every morning the representatives of the ground forces handed out folders with lessons learned from the previous day's fighting. While several friendly fire incidents had occurred—almost ten soldiers and officers were killed because of coordination problems—the IDF pronounced the operation a success.

Two divisions effectively operated in a small urban area of 140 square miles. The full coordination and hard training had paid off, but the Israeli chief of the General Staff General Ashkenazi's approach also deserves credit. The IDF had been preparing for a conventional war against a big and strong army, but when faced with a small war—despite all of the predictions, despite the doomsday prophecies, and despite the Israeli trauma suffered in Lebanon—the IDF was able to end the war on its own initiative and with limited casualties. The IDF knew who the real enemy was and kept in mind that the operation in Gaza, as with the war in Lebanon three years earlier, was part of the same war that it was already fighting against Iran. While the IDF did not fight directly against Iranian soldiers, it fought against Tehran's proxies—Hamas and Hezbollah.

When the IDF began pulling out of Gaza, the military had recently completed construction in northern Israel of its first mock "nature reserve," as described in chapter 1. The IDF sought to mimic the Hezbollah bunker systems and rocket launch pads that the guerrilla group had built throughout the thick forests of southern Lebanon. Similar to the Vietcong in South Vietnam, Hezbollah also had created an infrastructure of fortified underground bunkers, weapons storehouses, and tunnels where they hid both terrorists and rockets smuggled from Iran to be fired into Israel.

Hezbollah's camouflage was perfect. Israeli soldiers who stepped next to tunnel openings were unable to tell that they were standing near artificial ground. The only tools that could identify these underground networks were either precise intelligence received from well-placed sources in the enemy's command structure or from specially trained bomb-sniffing dogs. In the IDF the soldiers called the bunkers nature reserves because of their pastoral facade.

But how could a large strong army with tanks, planes, and advanced technology counter primitive tunnels and men fighting with methods that were common during Roman times? During the Second Lebanon War the IDF had tried all possible countermeasures. It purchased specially designed bunker-buster bombs. It used flammable materials such as napalm that were supposed to burn vegetation and expose the tunnel systems, but they did not work on the trees in southern Lebanon. It even sent in heavy engineering equipment to shake up and chase the people outside. In the end, though, nothing really worked. Hezbollah fighters remained inside their forest positions long after the war.

When the fighting ended, the IDF accumulated information that the Syrian Arab Army, which had stayed on the sidelines throughout the war, had begun digging trenches along its border with Israel. As opposed to the Soviet method of building round fortified compounds, which Israel called Syrian pitas, the Syrians adopted Hezbollah's tactic and began digging deep tunnels. Now the IDF's challenge had increased twofold.

To learn how to counter the new threat, the IDF emphasized two different operational requirements—to conquer territory with mobilized forces consisting of combat engineers, tanks, and infantry and at the same time to acquaint itself with tunnel and guerrilla fighting. This effort was the embodiment of collage warfare.

In addition, the IDF also began rethinking the way it employed its Special Forces, such as the Shayetet, the Sayeret Matkal (General Staff Reconnaissance Unit), and the IAF's Shaldag (Kingfisher) Unit, which reportedly conducts target designation behind enemy lines for IAF fighter jets. As opposed to the U.S. Army, which incorporates all of its Special Forces under one command, in the IDF each branch possesses its own elite unit. This arrangement engenders healthy competition between the units and a high level of motivation, but it also creates disparities in professional knowledge and leads to limited cooperation and reciprocal learning. During the Second Lebanon War, the IDF made an effort to publicize the heroic operations that the different units executed. Sayeret Matkal, which operates under Aman, and Shaldag took control of a medical compound in the Bekaa Valley in northern Lebanon.[44] The operation took Hezbollah completely by surprise, but the intelligence upon which the operation was launched—that the kidnapped Israeli soldiers Eldad Regev and Ehud Goldwasser were in the compound—was wrong. Shayetet carried out an operation near the coastal city of Tyre that was deemed a success after the unit captured a Hezbollah command center and killed a senior Hezbollah operative.

The units documented all of their operations with thermal cameras, and festive press conferences were held the same day to present the results to the Israeli public. However, the great celebrations overshadowed the fact that the units that had received the IDF's greatest investments had failed to prove their worth and had achieved weak results. An army study on the subject led the IDF in 2012 to establish a new Special Forces command. Creating the joint command would enable the IDF's top brass to focus on its primary objectives of capturing territory and employing firepower while the single joint command deployed its elite units in areas considered to be more complex, such as the nature reserves or more remote areas where individual skills are required.[45]

The IDF's basic assumption was that in a "missiles and planes" war in which the long arm of the IDF is active, such as in a war with Iran, the only ground forces that would be deployed so far away would be the special units. Their participation in a daring strategic operation, however, had already taken place in mid-2007, less than one year after the war in Lebanon had ended. The target this time was Syria.

3

OPERATION ORCHARD

The governments of Israel and Syria have never confirmed the following sequence of events. Photographic evidence and unofficial reports from American sources privy to the operation, however, reveal one of the most complex and fascinating missions the Bor, the IDF's underground command center in downtown Tel Aviv, has ever overseen—the destruction of Syria's only nuclear reactor. This chapter tells the story of Operation Orchard through the eyes of the Israeli intelligence operatives, the IAF pilots, and, most of all, the politicians who were involved and made the decision to bomb the Syrian reactor, making Israel the only country in the world (as this book went to press) to have destroyed successfully not one but two nuclear reactors from the air.[1]

Despite the months invested in collecting intelligence about the Syrian site, its true nature, and how to attack it, in retrospect the most difficult aspect of this whole process was Prime Minister Ehud Olmert's decision to go through with the attack. The story of those who were biting their nails in the prime minister's office in Jerusalem on September 6, 2007, foreshadows their successors' actions into 2012 when considering what to do about Iran's race toward nuclear power. But this story starts shortly after the Second Lebanon War.

While Prime Minister Olmert and Defense Minister Amir Peretz were fighting for their political survival in the war's aftermath, foreign reports indicated the Israeli defense establishment had received the evidence it was waiting for. The heads of the Syrian project had no idea that Mossad agents had obtained "solid intelligence" that the small facility under construction along the Euphrates River in northeastern Syria was in fact a nuclear reactor. The Mossad took the evidence that agents from one its operational units had obtained directly to the prime minister's office.

As in the Mossad's other operations, it had all begun when Unit 8200, the IDF's SIGINT unit, incidentally intercepted a phone conversation and an electronic reservation a senior Syrian official in Damascus had made while in a London hotel.[2] Israeli and U.S. agencies had tapped the Syrian official's communication lines since 2002. He had cultivated contacts over the years with North Korea, and his numerous trips to Pyongyang had attracted the attention of the CIA and Mossad. At that stage, the existence of a Syrian nuclear program was based simply on speculation. The U.S. National Security Agency (NSA)—the equivalent of Unit 8200—had intercepted an increasing number of phone calls between Pyongyang and a place in northeastern Syria called al-Kibar.

While antennas at Unit 8200's base north of Tel Aviv received the Syrian official's reservation, a group of young agents sitting not far away at Mossad headquarters discussed the Second Lebanon War. Similar to the rest of the Israeli defense establishment, the Mossad was not immune to public criticism after the war. For two years, Mossad agents had carried out dozens of secret missions and had risked their lives to collect information about Iran and its proxies scattered across the Middle East. They had paid particular attention to the smuggling routes Iran used for its nuclear project and scrutinized the smallest clues related to the Iranian Revolutionary Guard Corps' activities in Lebanon, Syria, and elsewhere. Some of this information enabled the IAF to destroy Hezbollah's long-range missile arsenal on the first night of the Second Lebanon War in 2006. Nevertheless, the intelligence achievements and successful covert operations could not prevent the agents at Mossad headquarters from castigating themselves.

The young men and women in the espionage agency were part of the Mossad's Caesarea Branch, known for its covert operations overseas.[3] Despite the months that had passed, they were still frustrated for having been "frozen" during the war. All of the men had served in combat units; almost all of them had undergone arduous training. But during the war, the Mossad did not let them enlist with the reserves. "You are too valuable," explained the head of the department, himself a graduate of an elite IDF unit. "Besides, think about if you were needed for an immediate operation here."[4] The war was still on everyone's mind, and the decision makers were preoccupied with public relations aimed at saving Prime Minister Olmert's image and with approving operational plans for the army. They pushed the Mossad aside.

The call that came through on the red secure phone startled everyone in the room. On the line was the head of the department, who updated them about the Syrian official's trip to London. The agents were familiar with the protocol in these situations and immediately set preparations to put a new operation into motion.

Two days later, after studying the Syrian official's facial features and the layout of the prestigious London hotel where he was supposed to be staying, the agents split up and boarded various planes to different destinations. They would rendezvous at the European capital and wait for their target at the airport and the hotel. During their last briefing before leaving on the mission, their instructions had strongly emphasized gaining access to the official's laptop or, to be more exact, the information it contained. Two days after arriving at the hotel, the intelligence operatives had reportedly succeeded in installing a Trojan horse on the computer and gleaning all of its contents.[5]

The hard drive contained construction plans, letters, and hundreds of photos that showed the al-Kibar complex at various stages of its development. In photos from 2002 the construction site resembled a tree house on stilts, complete with suspicious-looking pipes leading to a pumping station at the Euphrates. Later photos showed concrete piers and roofs, which apparently were meant to make the building look inconspicuous from above, or as if a shoebox had been placed over the structure to conceal it. The pictures of the facility's interior, however, left no room for doubt. The Syrians had built a nuclear reactor.

Despite the signs and speculations during the two years preceding the Mossad's operation, the agents still found this evidence shocking. No one in Israel's intelligence establishment had imagined that Syrian president Bashar al-Assad, who had succeeded his father seven years earlier, had decided to break all known taboos and defy all intelligence assessments to develop a nuclear bomb. Most startling was the advanced stage at which Syria's program was discovered. The intelligence community also was taken aback by the discovery that Iran was involved and had provided funding and support so that Syria could build a reactor right across the border from Israel and at a time when the future of Iran's own nuclear program was so unclear. Officials in the CIA, the Mossad, and the IDF's Aman scoured old files, searching for clues that they might have overlooked and categorized as insignificant but could now help piece together the Syrian nuclear puzzle. It was possibly the biggest intelligence discovery since the beginning of the decade.

Western intelligence agencies reportedly uncovered the first evidence of a connection between Syria, Iran, and North Korea at Hafez al-Assad's funeral in

June 2000.[6] An entourage accompanying the funeral procession had included top Iranian and North Korean officials. Pictures from the funeral had aroused the suspicions of the Mossad's nonconventional weapons investigators. Any link found between North Korea and Iran was always a point of concern, so the Mossad, then under the command of Efraim Halevy, had classified the information that the investigators had collected as top priority. But the meeting of these heads of state at the funeral appeared to be a one-time incident. Nothing seemed more preposterous at the time than the North Koreans and the Syrians cooperating on the development of such nonconventional means as nuclear weapons.

Israeli intelligence agencies, as with those of the United States and other Western powers, missed the clues when they made their assessment of Syria's pursuit of nuclear weapons. The younger Assad had inherited from his father a country that was in the throes of a deep economic crisis and whose army was equipped with outdated Soviet-era weaponry, some rusty and some without spare parts. The eye doctor from London had little time to prepare for his task as successor. His father's team of advisers did not know him well enough, and, fearing a revolution, they accompanied his every step.

As a result, the Israelis felt that Assad had far more urgent missions than to forge diplomatic ties and treaties with such a remote country as North Korea. Engaging in a nuclear project when his country was collapsing was the last thing the Israelis expected Assad to do. Their basic assumption had been that even if Syria in fact established relations with North Korea—in this case, the nuclear peddler—and Iran, they would fizzle out on their own. In 2000, this assessment had seemed logical.

Second, there was the financial issue and the enormous cost of investing in a nuclear project, despite Iran's financial backing. The Israelis concluded that the Iranians would prefer to strengthen their hold over Hezbollah and other terrorist organizations before building such a prestigious project for another country. Meanwhile, the United States already had the admittedly unpredictable North Koreans under tight scrutiny for their own illicit nuclear program.

While the North Koreans' visits to Damascus interested the Israelis, the latter conjectured that the purpose of these visits was to upgrade Syria's aging military equipment. Cooperation between the countries was also not all that new. In the past Pyongyang had helped Damascus develop medium-range Scud ballistic missiles and chemical weapons such as sarin and mustard gas. For North Korea the relationship was all about the money. Pyongyang did not have a problem exporting nuclear technology to a country like Syria, which aggravated the West and was willing to pay top dollar.

The third and most significant piece of information that shaped Israel's assessment was the fact that the late Hafez al-Assad had never pursued nuclear power, even though he had the opportunity to purchase the technology from Abdul Qadeer Khan, more notoriously known as A. Q. Khan or the father of the Pakistani atom bomb. Assad had ruled Syria with a mighty hand for thirty years (1971–2000) and understood very well that his starting a nuclear project would be unacceptable as far as Israel was concerned. Though he had developed weapons in order to deter Israel from attacking, he had never tried to obtain the judgment day weapon. The Yom Kippur War in 1973 and its outcome—Israel succeeded in holding the Golan Heights and the Sinai Peninsula (which it had captured six year earlier)—had prompted major changes in Syrian military strategy. After the war, Assad finally understood that Syria was incapable of defeating Israel militarily and that he would have to pursue alternative methods for creating a balance of power.

As a result, Syria secretly began developing chemical weapons and even attempted, albeit unsuccessfully, to manufacture biological weapons.[7] But the Syrians' ambitions had stopped there. While Israel knew that Syria had limited chemical weaponry, Assad also knew that he could not use it. But as far as he was concerned, having them was enough to restore Syria's pride, which had been damaged during the 1973 war.

When Bashar took over in 2000, the prevailing assessment in the Israeli intelligence community was that he was not a trailblazer, that he was as conservative as his father was in his military ambitions, and that he would not try to develop new capabilities before he first succeeded in stabilizing his new regime. In hindsight, everyone was wrong. They overlooked one factor—the deep level of Iran's involvement and influence over the young Syrian leader.

In 2002 American intelligence received information about a series of meetings between Syrian, Iranian, and North Korean representatives. The intelligence, which had reached Israel as well, illustrated President Bush's perception of the "axis of evil." But other than the news that the meetings had taken place, no one had the details of what the officials had discussed. It was logical that Iran would cooperate with Syria, its main channel for smuggling weapons to Hezbollah in Lebanon. It also made sense that Iran would cooperate with North Korea, a pivotal contributor of technology and know-how for its own budding nuclear project. But the meetings of all three states' representatives together raised more questions.

In 2005 Mohsen Fakhrizadeh-Mahabadi, Iran's top nuclear scientist, reportedly paid a visit to Damascus. Less than a year later, Iranian president Mahmoud Ahmadinejad visited Damascus as well. Warning lights went on in intelligence offices around the world. Various Western intelligence agencies began following, tracking, and infiltrating the lives of senior Iranian, North Korean, and Syrian officials wherever they might be. The Mossad, which in the meantime had undergone major changes in management and character, viewed the contacts among these countries as a high priority and second only to the Iranian nuclear project.

Meir Dagan, the former IDF general who had been appointed to head the Mossad in 2002, ordered his agency to begin scouring for information on what was happening in Syria. Dagan, a field man, immediately infused a new sense of daring in those under his command. During the years he spent as head of the organization, his motto was "Obtain information, take risks, and succeed in the mission."[8]

In 2006, the sketches and documents that the Mossad agents reportedly succeeded in obtaining from the senior Syrian official's laptop clearly showed that the reactor project was concealed under a front, that is, a farm used to conduct agricultural experiments. Few in the Syrian government and defense establishment, however, were privy to the true nature of the mysterious al-Kibar complex.

The complex was located near the Turkish border and about 130 kilometers from Iraq, which since 2003 had been under the control of U.S. and Coalition forces. Dir al-Zur, the desert region in northeast Syria where al-Kibar is located, was declared a closed military zone even for most of Syria's senior commanders. Syria had invested too much money in the project for incidental or intentional information leaks regarding its planning and execution. The vision of the younger Assad and the IRGC, which had financed the project, was that by the time Israel and the West found out about the project, it would be too late for an attack.

Each of the involved parties had a different guiding interest in the project. The North Koreans wanted to make hundreds of millions of dollars and prove how powerful they were in the international scene. In line with their reputation as shrewd economists, the Iranians wanted to spread their nuclear investment to additional locations in order to deter an Israeli attack and, at the same time, establish a reserve facility in case their deterrence did not succeed. According to assessments made after the reactor was bombed, Iran had spent close to $2 billion on the entire project by bringing the North Korean technology to Syria and purchasing additional components for operating the reactor. Iran loaned some of the money to Syria, though Assad could never repay the debt. During Ahmadinejad's visit to Syria in 2006, he guaranteed the money.[9]

But the Syrians themselves had the greatest interest in the project, given that it was in their country. Assad built the reactor in spite of Operation Opera, the Israeli operation in 1981 that destroyed a nuclear reactor in Iraq. Assad's decision must have been made hastily and without prior serious in-depth discussions regarding Israeli intelligence capabilities and the Israeli response once it learned of the reactor. In the eyes of Syria's supreme ruler though, creating additional deterrence against Israel was a way to strengthen his standing in the Arab world, to position himself as a world leader, and maybe even to force Israel to return the entire Golan Heights. For him, nuclear weapons were not only about military might but also about taking Syria from the backbenches of the region to the forefront of the world.[10]

A nuclear Syria would have represented a great failure for the West, but it was not to be. Bits and pieces of information began to leak. The most conclusive evidence came from Brig. Gen. Ali-Reza Asgari, a former senior commander in the IRGC and deputy defense minister who mysteriously disappeared during a trip to Turkey in 2007. A target of various intelligence agencies since the 1980s, when he was involved in founding Hezbollah in Lebanon, Asgari defected to the West in early 2007 and took some of Iran's most closely guarded secrets with him.[11] Already during the first days of his interrogation by the CIA, Asgari revealed that the Revolutionary Guards had started a secret nuclear project in Syria. Since he had not been involved in the details of the transaction, all Asgari could talk about was the Iranian funding and confirm the existence of the nuclear program. For the United States and Israel, which had participated in parts of the interrogation, this information was enough.

At the time of Asgari's defection, Israel was still in the middle of the post–Second Lebanon War probes of the failures and flaws that led to the war and its unsatisfactory outcome. Even as the public was busy demanding that Prime Minister Olmert resign, he had initiated top-secret talks in the spring of 2007 with President Bush, according to senior U.S. government officials.[12] Olmert briefed Bush on the Syrian reactor and asked him to take action. Bush declined. According to U.S. officials who were intimately involved in the talks, Olmert presented

Bush with hard-core, unequivocal data and intelligence, but the president had no intention of initiating another attack on a Muslim Arab country. In his mind, getting America out of Iraq in one piece was more important than any new danger developing in his purported axis of evil. One top Bush administration official said in an interview that Israel tried to pressure the Americans to deal with the problem, but the White House was unwilling to accept the challenge.

Olmert had tried to build on the discussions between the United States and Israel regarding the Syrian reactor that had begun several months earlier. In April 2007, Mossad chief Dagan in Tel Aviv phoned the White House switchboard.[13] He told Stephen J. Hadley, Bush's national security adviser, "We need to meet urgently. The Syrian story is heating up." Hadley, who was intimately familiar with certain details of the Iranian nuclear project, set up a meeting.

On the first Wednesday of May, Dagan slipped inconspicuously into a side entrance of the White House and walked directly into Hadley's office with a large portfolio in hand. Countries have a silent agreement never to inquire about the source of sensitive information, but from the start Dagan revealed his agents' successful mission to gather the secret intelligence about Syria. And then he began showing Hadley pictures, one after the other. In the first one two men, one Asian and one of dark complexion, were hugging. Hadley looked at Dagan quizzically when the latter placed two papers on the desk. At the top of each page was a picture of one of the two men from the first picture and under it ran a summary of the Mossad's file on him. The first man was Chon Chibu, a North Korean scientist who managed the fuel production at the Yongbyon reactor. Hadley asked his secretary to retrieve his CIA file immediately. The second man in the picture was Ibrahim Othman, director of Syria's Atomic Energy Commission. In the photo's background was some sort of industrial facility. While the connection between the two men was clear, Hadley had yet to see the pictures of the facility.

Dagan presented the pictures of the facility in chronological order. In the first ones the basic infrastructure was visible. In the next series of pictures appeared a structure Hadley was familiar with from his experience with other nuclear programs. Finally, Dagan showed him the pictures of an innocent-looking factory being constructed over the reactor.

At this stage, some of Hadley's men had entered the office. One carried pictures of the nuclear reactor Chon Chibu had built thirty years earlier in North Korea. The structures were identical. Hadley looked at Dagan. There was no longer any doubt that Syria was building a nuclear reactor.

Minutes later Dagan was in an armored White House vehicle and on his way to Langley, Virginia, to meet CIA director Michael Hayden. Dagan elicited the same reactions. Hadley, who in the meantime had informed President Bush of the discovery, was already assembling the material he had from the CIA. Bush's orders were clear: they were to study all of the Mossad's evidence and maintain complete secrecy.

Now, it was up to Hadley and Secretary of State Condoleezza Rice to find a solution. They brought the Pentagon into the inner circle and drew up plans for a lightning strike, which was similar to the one Israel eventually would carry out.

Upon his return to Israel, Dagan went straight to the prime minister's office in Jerusalem and briefed him about the meetings. Concerned that time was slipping away, Olmert contacted Bush directly in an effort to impress upon the U.S. president that the Israelis' assessment was that the pictures showed a nuclear reactor on the verge of becoming operational. Washington, however, was a little skeptical and wanted to study the material further.

In their discussions, Olmert told Bush that as far as Israel was concerned the reactor "needed to disappear." Bush did not dismiss this option, but the professional ranks in his office explained to the Israelis that before doing so three basic questions needed to be answered:

1. What is the real purpose of the facility in the pictures?
2. In what stage is the nuclear program?
3. What can be done to stop Syria from going nuclear?

These questions brought about a period of collaboration that continued up until the week of the attack itself. "The relationship between Israel and the United States peaked then," the former top Bush administration official said. "There was unprecedented sharing of intelligence and the dialogue reached an unbelievable level of intimacy."

In the meantime, to answer these questions, the Mossad and Aman ramped up their intelligence-gathering efforts. They thoroughly interrogated people suspected of having knowledge of the Syrian program, and every piece of information justified a new round of investigation. People from the Israeli defense establishment began working according to a timeline, trying to discover the so-called point of no return for the nuclear program, or when it would be too late to attack. According to former defense minister Amir Peretz, if the reactor were allowed to go online, they would have to reconsider whether to take military action. Therefore, in his mind, the attack had to occur before that happened.

Olmert and Peretz invited a small number of military specialists and scientists to discuss the potential consequences of both bombing the reactor and ignoring the project. One of the participants was Maj. Gen. David Ivry, who in 1981 was the IAF commander during Operation Opera's attack on the Iraqi reactor. The arguments for and against a similar strike, as well as about the operational issues, were the same ones they had addressed almost three decades earlier.

Among the meeting's participants were those who claimed that Bashar al-Assad had built the reactor only in order to impress other Arab countries. They claimed that he had no intention of taking the reactor to the stage where it would present an existential threat to Israel. The overwhelming majority thought otherwise. In their opinion, Israel's implicit or quiet acceptance of a nuclear reactor in a Muslim-majority country in the region (as had happened in the Iranians' case, when it first began exploring nuclear power) would start a nuclear arms race among other Arab countries, even the moderate ones.

Olmert was determined to attack, mainly to rebuild the deterrence threat that had been crushed during the Second Lebanon War and maybe to prove to himself and to the Israeli people what he was really made of.[14] According to a senior U.S. government official, the meetings between Bush and Olmert ended with a mutual understanding: the reactor posed an "existential threat" to Israel, a threat that therefore justified a military attack.

Agents gathered more intelligence about the intensifying relations between North Korea and Syria. Ships with foreign flags docked at the Tartus port in Syria; some of the ships' logs said that they had originated in North Korea. As opposed to Syria's maritime capabilities, Israel could fully monitor what happened in the waters in the region. Any freighter or passenger ship that strayed from its route in the direction of Syria was detected by the Israeli military and reported immediately.

In September 2006, for example, spy satellites identified the freighter *Gregorio* with suspicious-looking pipes on its deck. The ship docked in Cyprus on its way to the Tartus port in Syria. The stream of incoming ships kept increasing. In early September 2007 the freighter *Al-Hamed*, which had sailed from Pyongyang, arrived at the Syrian port of Tartus with a cargo of uranium materials.[15]

After weeks of discussions and debates in the administration, Bush contacted Olmert and shared his plan for dealing with the reactor. According to the senior U.S. government official, Bush told the Israeli prime minister that in his opinion the ideal solution was first to approach the International Atomic Energy Agency (IAEA), headed by the Egyptian Mohamed Mustafa ElBaradei. In the event that the IAEA did not help, they could take the evidence to the UN Security Council and ask for sanctions against Syria. If that option failed, then and only then would the United States contemplate a military option.

Olmert, whom his fellow Israelis perceived as a political dove without any backbone, came out of these meetings looking as if he knew how to hold his own. He completely dismissed the American plan. Israel had had a bad experience with ElBaradei, who systematically had chosen to overlook Iran's mounting nuclear violations. In the IAEA's opinion, Iran was simply a law-abiding country whose goals and tactics were all part of a legitimate political game. Moreover, in Israel's view, sanctions were not a reliable tool. In 2007, when Bush spoke about *future* sanctions against Syria, the Israelis already knew that within a short period of time the Syrian reactor would become active.

"Allow me to remind you," Olmert told the president (according to a senior official in the Bush administration), "that at the beginning of these talks, when I presented the intelligence material to you, I said all along that the reactor needs to go away. If we reveal the data to the UN, the Syrians will build a proverbial kindergarten on top of it and prevent a strike forever." According to the same source, at this point Olmert realized that the United States was not going to attack the Syrian reactor. Had he looked closer, though, Olmert would have seen the evidence much sooner.

Three years earlier, during the Sudanese massacre in Darfur, human rights groups had pressured the American administration to take military action to prevent the genocide there. Bush had heard the calls and searched for a viable solution. For him it presented a classical scenario of the forces of good fighting the forces of evil to prevent the murder of the weak and oppressed. The military command suggested attacking the Sudanese Air Force to relay a clear message: no more genocide. Convinced, the president was about to green-light the operation. But then his closest advisers convinced him to back down, claiming that with U.S. troops already in Iraq and Afghanistan, an attack against another Muslim-majority country would only increase hatred toward America and increase public sentiment against him. They persuaded him it was more important to solve his current problems. The attack against Sudan never took place. "Had the Israeli prime minister understood this dilemma," the American official said, "he never would have expected Bush to order an air strike against the Syrian reactor."

On June 19, 2007, a few months before the Israeli strike, Olmert arrived in Washington for a meeting with President Bush. While newspaper headlines claimed the leaders spoke about the Palestinian peace process, they spent the majority of their meeting discussing the nuclear reactor under construction in Syria.

"We plan to strike the reactor," Olmert reportedly told the president. Bush tried to restrain him, suggesting alternative modes of action. From the American administration's standpoint, a war between Israel and Syria would seriously damage the state-building process in Iraq and would even risk the stability of the Coalition in Afghanistan. But Israel's prime minister politely explained that he was not there to ask the administration for permission; rather, he wanted to update him on Israel's intentions. "Israel was not looking for approval from the American government," the top administration official explained. "Israel made it clear that there were no traffic lights and no requests for green lights or red lights."

In his memoir *Decision Points*, published in November 2010, Bush himself supported this description. "Prime Minister Olmert hadn't asked for a green light, and I hadn't given one. He had done what he believed was necessary to protect Israel," Bush wrote in his book.[16]

The Israelis' decision to inform the American administration of its plans derived from a few considerations. First, the Israeli government under Ehud Olmert enjoyed warm relations with the Bush administration. In the meetings held in Israel prior to the attack, participants had raised the question of how it would affect Israel's relationship with the United States. Some of the participants, like Ivry, remembered the aftermath of Operation Opera. When Menachem Begin sent the IAF jets to strike Saddam Hussein's nuclear reactor, Israel used American military equipment without prior coordination with the United States, and the U.S. administration felt it had hurt the chances for peace in the Middle East. Two weeks after the 1981 attack the UN assembly approved a resolution denouncing Israel, with support from the United States, which usually prevented anti-Israel votes.[17] The Reagan administration even decided to freeze deliveries of F-16 fighter jets to Israel temporarily. A decade later, however, when the American army was fighting in Iraq, the administration recognized the importance of the Israeli operation.

The Olmert administration of 2007 showed it had learned its history lesson. Despite the Americans' opposition, Olmert's advisers still argued in favor of sharing the operation's full itinerary with the Bush administration. This decision proved to be correct. According to a senior official in the Bush administration,

"From the beginning, both leaders said that Syria could not have a reactor. Bush agreed and was not disturbed with Israel's actions, nor did it affect his relationship with Olmert." That same source also referred to the Israelis' expectations that Bush would not leave office before stopping Iran's nuclear program. "I think that an Israeli who knew of Bush's decision not to bomb Sudan and Syria would have been hard-pressed to think that he was going to bomb Iran, which was a far more dangerous operation," he said.

But in the Syrian case, the relations between Israel and the United States were not the only consideration in keeping the Americans informed. The Syrian nuclear reactor was close to the border with Turkey, a NATO member, and 130 kilometers from American-controlled Iraqi airspace. Carrying out the attack without U.S. tracking devices identifying Israel's movements would have been extremely difficult. As opposed to the 1981 strike, an attack inside Syria without proper reporting to the American forces in the area could have caused friendly forces to open fire against each other; indeed, American air control might have interpreted the jets flying at high speed as a Syrian or Iranian attempt to attack Turkish or Iraqi targets. To avoid this scenario, someone in the American command had to know what to expect.

By the middle of 2007 the Olmert administration already clearly saw that a military strike on the Syrian reactor was its only viable option. The next stage involved transferring the operational order to the army. The administration had briefed few in the Israeli security establishment on the discovery. Only a handful of Mossad agents and top officers from Aman had the necessary security clearance to review the material taken from the senior Syrian official's laptop. The defense minister and prime minister limited the size of the inner circle of decision makers. They decided to leave top officials in the dark and brief them only after the pilots reported that the target had been successfully hit.

The operational preparations began inside the spacious office of the IAF's chief commander in the command building in Tel Aviv. Maj. Gen. Eliezer Shkedy, an F-16 fighter pilot, understood that he was tasked with one of the most important operations ever assigned to the IAF. The instructions he had received were clear: maintain complete compartmentalization until a final decision is reached. As a result, when the pilots began training, they did not know what their target was.[18]

"In order to understand how any air strike is executed, you must understand the chain of command," explained a senior IAF commander in early 2010. "From the moment it is decided that the air force will carry out a strike, the IAF commander calls the head of the operations department into his office. From there the order is handed down to the fleet commander, and from him to the operations officers and pilots. All along, this process takes place with the participation of the executing force, intelligence analysts, and an operations research team, whose job is to quantify the chances for success."

As was the case in 1981, the IAF also conducted a similar procedure before the attack against Syria, but the necessary compartmentalization made the entire process different. The IAF commander, the head of the operations department, and the head of the intelligence team knew the target, but how were they supposed to prepare pilots for a target that no one was supposed to know existed?

The IAF solved this problem by building matching replicas of the target in Israel's expansive desert areas. When the IAF wants to train for high-altitude bombings, it does so in live fire training fields in the yellow and sun-scorched land of the Judean and Negev Deserts. The date of the attack was set for September, and its summer weather guaranteed clear skies with few clouds. The pilots thus repeatedly practiced destroying a target reinforced with concrete, but what the target was and where it was located, the pilots would only discover on the day of the actual operation.

The air force was simply one component in the decision-making process. From a military perspective, Syria did not have significant antiaircraft capabilities that could prevent the IAF aircraft from penetrating its airspace and carrying out the strike. Without belittling the Syrians, Israel's advantage in the air against Syria was quite obvious. The Israelis' advantage, however, was not as clear cut on the ground. As plans for the airstrike moved forward, concerns grew in the IDF over the potential retaliation and the possibility that a large-scale war could break out in northern Israel with Syria, an enemy Israel hadn't fought against since 1973. No one knew how Assad would respond. The IDF, which only months earlier had fought a painful war against Hezbollah, needed to prepare for a potential war after the strike against the nuclear reactor.

The question also was how to sell the increased military training to the country and the world, which likely would suspect a move was afoot if Israeli troops returned to train in the Golan Heights. Thus the defense establishment began using a new English word, "miscalculation"—a reference to a potential misunderstanding between military commanders stationed along the border that can evolve, owing to high tensions, into an all-out war between the two countries.

In Israel, though, random civilian observers had difficulty believing that the Syrians would attack that quickly. The disparity between the two countries' strengths was too obvious. Since the Syrians could see Israel preparing for war along the border, they also knew what kind of obstacles awaited them should they decide to enter on foot: mine fields, tank trenches, harsh ground conditions, and heavy artillery fire. From their standpoint such a foray, given Israel's firepower advantage, would almost definitely fail.

However, the IDF explained that the Syrians had taken a new approach called opportunist strategy. Lacking the military capability to defeat and capture territory, the Syrians developed a new military theory, according to which they did not have to recapture the Golan Heights to achieve a blow against Israel. Instead, to send a message of strength to the entire world, they only had to capture a borderline town or even raise a Syrian flag over the Israeli side of Mount Hermon.

"We know that Israel is superior over us in some military fields. But we have decided to stand fast," Assad was quoted as saying in an interview in 2001 with the Lebanese newspaper *As-Safir*. "We will stand fast and repulse the [Israeli] aggression even if we estimate that the enemy will destroy many of our installations."[19]

After the 2006 war, Israeli sources claimed that the Syrians had applied each and every one of the lessons from the way Hezbollah fought, and that they were building a guerrilla army with the goal of achieving a psychological victory and not a military one. No one in Israel was surprised then when IDF chief of the General Staff Lt. Gen. Gabi Ashkenazi reinstituted training in the Golan Heights. Everybody in Israel agreed in the aftermath of the Second Lebanon War that Israel needed to be prepared for every contingency, including the Syrian challenge.

The Israeli media was full of stories about the Syrians' new Hezbollah-style antitank units and how they had transformed the border with the Golan Heights into a bustling construction site. From the Israeli side the Syrians' engineering tools, reinforcements, and renovations were easily visible. It seemed that Syria was investing in constructing underground defense systems similar to Hezbollah's infamous nature reserves, which had made the previous war so difficult for the Israeli soldiers. The nature reserves were intended to replace the previously mentioned Syrian pitas—small, pita-shaped positions atop little hills—along the defense lines. Apparently the Syrians had adopted underground warfare as a combat doctrine suitable for its regular army forces as well.

But particularly concerning for Israel was Syria's increased missile production. The facts were simple and stark. As recently as 2007, Syria had perhaps 330 missiles capable of hitting Tel Aviv. By 2009, Syria's arsenal of missiles capable of reaching the Gush Dan metropolitan area had soared to 1,300; the following year it had had jumped again to an estimated 2,300 missiles. So when the Syrians began maneuvering their military forces and increasing their training, the IDF responded accordingly.

In 2007 at Tel Aviv University's Institute for National Security Studies, a prominent Israeli think tank, an officer who was on sabbatical from Aman claimed that Bashar al-Assad lacked backbone and had not participated in the 2006 war because he was deterred by Israel's power. Since then, however, Assad had surrounded himself with radical advisers, primarily his brother-in-law, Assef Shawkat, the notorious Syrian intelligence chief who in 2009 was promoted to deputy chief of staff. All of the moderates who had served Assad's father had disappeared from the scene. For example, Farouk al-Sharaa had been removed from the Ministry of Foreign Affairs, and Abdul Halim Khaddam, the former vice president, was forced to resign and was exiled to Europe. Under such conditions it was no wonder Assad was thinking about the option of war.

Few in the Israeli security establishment, meanwhile, knew that the growing tension between Israel and Syria was not simply based on speculation and rumors about a brewing conflict. The Israeli attack on Syria's most carefully guarded secret—a project in which the Iranians had invested $2 billion—could have so many repercussions that a belligerent Syrian response might be the best-case scenario.

Before the Israelis could carry out the strike against the reactor, they needed more solid evidence that the facility Syria was building was in fact using nuclear materials. In August 2007 a pair of Yas'ur (Sikorsky CH-53 Sea Stallion) helicopters took off from a base in Israel and flew northward at a low altitude.[20] Through their night vision goggles, the pilots could clearly see the many small canyons branching out of a river in a nearby mountain. Behind the Yas'urs and at a higher altitude, attack helicopters and a rescue chopper with a team from the unit circled while an airborne command plane flew over all units. "Two minutes to landing," the flight technician called out to the camouflaged fighters assembled in one of the Yas'urs.

Sayeret Matkal is the IDF's most elite reconnaissance unit and is world renowned for missions that have taken its operators far behind enemy lines. This time their mission was to gather soil samples from the al-Kibar facility's ground and to conduct surveillance. The battle procedure was shorter than what the soldiers were used to, as they began training in the beginning of June and engaged in a month and a half of strenuous exercises. No one went home. The IDF's Information Security Department made the operators sign special confidentiality forms, as they did before every sensitive mission. The preparations for the operation were nonstop. Every few days senior officers showed up to take part in the training or to watch with their own eyes as the soldiers ran through the model one more time.

As far as the two participating teams were concerned, this assignment was a once-in-a-lifetime opportunity. Statistics show that every Sayeret Matkal soldier trains for three to four special operations during his military service. Fifty percent are cancelled at the last second. The reasons vary. Sometimes it's the unpredictable weather conditions; other times enemy forces change their positions. Once in a while the Israeli prime minister calls off the mission after deciding that the risks outweigh the benefits. This time the preparations—constructing a model in comparable terrain, training, learning the navigational axes and outlines of the target, and boarding the helicopters—demonstrated it was fast and safe.

The atmosphere at the final briefing was festive. In the two front rows of the unit's state-of-the-art conference room in the center of the country were seated the chief of Aman, Maj. Gen. Amos Yadlin, and General Ashkenazi, the IDF chief. A few questions about hypothetical scenarios and reactions were asked, and then everyone present wished the soldiers good luck.

The soldiers went through their equipment one more time. As always happened before a mission, a conversation began about how much weight to carry and whether it was more important to load up on firepower or scouting and camouflage materials. They finally boarded the waiting helicopters, knowing that as soon as they hit the ground at their target they would be on their own. If they encountered trouble, the chances of being rescued were extremely slim.

After a short flight, the helicopter's back ramp opened, and the Sayeret Matkal operators all stood ready. With their equipment loaded into large bags slung over their shoulders, they checked their thermal night vision goggles. "Start moving," signaled the commander. They marched forward, with the advance scout team leading the way. Every half hour the commander ordered a planned stop. A long straw that extended from each soldier's equipment bag ended next to his mouth, and they drank as ordered.

The scouts moved at a distance of about a hundred meters in front of the main force. Before entering a new area, the commander of the navigating force would press twice on the two-way radio, an agreed-upon sign that it was safe to proceed.

At an observation point, the soldiers concentrated on security positions. An assignment team under one of the team leaders' command went out to an area that had been identified and located during the planning stages. The team left its heavy bags in the concentrated area and packed all of the assignment gear into small military packs.

The team leader and a squad commander began filling plastic boxes that Aman had supplied. One of the soldiers in the squad began collecting small rocks and another picked wild plants growing in the area. The entire assignment took a few minutes. When they were done, another soldier walked around with a device that resembled a small broom and ensured that they hadn't left any tracks. On the way back to the meeting point, the force commander radioed the command plane flying high overhead, and within seconds the command post deep underneath military headquarters in Tel Aviv heard his report. One part of the mission was accomplished successfully, but it was still too early to relax.

The days the two teams spent on the ground in Syria with long-range scouting gear and camouflaged positions caused two generals, a defense minister, and a prime minister insomnia. But after the soldiers returned to Israel with their samples and the lab results came in, they were able to declare the mission a complete success. Israel now possessed incontrovertible and tangible evidence of Syria's nuclear intentions. If Olmert needed one more push to green-light the mission, Sayeret Matkal gave him one.

The first days of September 2007 saw heightened tensions along the Israeli-Syrian border. Given the harsh exchanges of words between the leaders of both countries, the reinstitution of training in the Golan Heights, and the large exercise drill a year after the Second Lebanon War, it was clear why the military was on such high alert.

Due to the increase in tension, the IAF followed the guidelines it created after the 2006 war broke out when it moved some of its fleets' air drills to southern Israel. While this location meant extra flight time and wasted fuel, at least they were farther away from enemy missiles. Flights that needed to stay in the north required parking the planes in protected shelters. For the soldiers and commanders, the exercise during the summer of 2007 was a simulation of the previous war. The IDF's Northern Command engaged in a practical expression of Ashkenazi's credo that an army should be either preparing for war or fighting one.

For these reasons, the exercises were a natural part of the changes being made throughout the entire IDF, including the air force. At the Ramat David Air

Force Base in northern Israel, fighter pilots conducted bombing drills. They figured that something important had prompted the arduous training exercises, but their squadron commander kept his lips sealed.

In the meantime, at Mossad headquarters in Tel Aviv, a group of people reportedly studied a batch of new surveillance pictures. The *al-Hamed* ship from North Korea that the Israelis had been following for many weeks finally had docked in Tartus. While under way, the crew had managed to change flags and courses, but Tartus had been the ship's destination the whole time. A few weeks earlier, with assistance from the Americans, Mossad agents had successfully identified uranium being loaded onto the ship during its stop in Pyongyang. Time was running out. Israel feared the reactor was on its way to becoming operational.

On September 5, 2007, an operational order arrived in the squadron's conference room. The participants had to sign an additional confidentiality form. Only then were they informed of the target by their commanders. They all looked at each other in complete shock. Only once in a generation is an Israeli pilot able to participate in such a critical operation, one that will be studied for years in flight schools around the world. They understood the success or failure of their mission clearly influenced the future of the State of Israel.

The takeoff command came at 22:45. Ten F-15I fighter jets took off and waited for instructions to proceed north. Command ordered three of the planes to abort. They shot straight up into the air and turned around. These provisional jets would wait in the air until the mission was completed in case something went wrong. The young pilots, though pained that they could not take part in the strike itself, were still pleased to be part of the operation.

The command to proceed came through for the seven remaining planes, which began accelerating. Their target was close to the border. Seconds after entering Syrian airspace, the formation leader dropped his first bomb on a Syrian radar station. Less than twenty minutes later, the planes flew over the final target. The front four jets dropped AGM-65 bombs, each one weighing approximately half a ton. The formation commander reported that the target had been destroyed.

Then the pilots detected antiaircraft rockets. "They're firing," barked the commander over the radio.

The jets were already on their way back to Israel when, in order to pick up speed, the pilots dropped their detachable fuel tanks, which landed over the border in Turkey. On the landing strip the technical teams were waiting for them. Someone opened a bottle of champagne, and someone else pulled out a camera that would later be sent to the squadron headquarters. The pilots were warned that the moment they left the squadron room, they never would be able to discuss what they had just done. Already that night a primary inquiry was conducted by the IAF.

Some in the political establishment celebrated as well. Ministers who were close to Olmert called to congratulate him. Officials in the defense establishment and generals who had not been privy to the operation were briefed and updated about what had just occurred. All were genuinely impressed with the courage shown by the prime minister, who up until then had been the most criticized person in Israel. But the operation's real stars, however, were the men and women of the IDF's Information Security Department for creating one of the largest decoy operations in Israel's history.

In such bombing operations, the next step belongs to the diplomats from the Ministry of Foreign Affairs, which at the time was under the direction of Tzipporah "Tzipi" Livni. As foreign minister, Livni had aspirations of one day replacing Olmert as prime minister. She knew about the plans to carry out the mission but had not been involved in the technical meetings.

During the operation, pre-addressed envelopes in the ministry's war room were ready to be sent out in diplomatic pouches. Inside the envelopes were material and evidence meant to explain Israel's mission and the true nature of the target. Attached to the diplomatic documents was the foreign minister's letter summarizing the events. Livni, who as a student had served in the Mossad and had even undergone an operational course, had personally supervised the preparation of the briefs. Other Ministry of Foreign Affairs workers had minimal exposure to the materials.

When the operation ended and the planes returned home, Livni called the war room and ordered the officials there to send out the bags. The next day at noon, the Israeli ambassadors to Germany, Britain, and France delivered the materials to those countries' leaders.

The ministry's explanation was comprehensive. Israel revealed everything. Everyone, with no exceptions, remained quiet—even well afterward—and astonished by the operation. One diplomatic bag was addressed to Turkish prime minister Recep Tayyip Erdogan. The Turkish media had publicized the fact that a detachable Israeli fuel tank was found on the ground in eastern Turkey. It was the first piece of evidence linking Israel to the strike. (Later on, one of the IDF's most senior officers claimed in a closed conversation that just as infantry soldiers know how to burn off the Hebrew writing inscribed on their boots, erasing any link between them and Israel, it was about time the Israeli Air Force learned to remove Hebrew writing from parts that could fly off a plane.)

The bag that reached Erdogan did not surprise him. As soon as the planes had landed in Israel, the Israeli prime minister had placed his first call to the Turkish prime minister. "We attacked the Syrian reactor," Olmert told him. "Please send the Syrians the message that we are interested in peace and not war, but we will not tolerate a reality with a nuclear Syria. If they adopt an ambiguous position with respect to the media, we will as well."

The Turkish premier, during whose term Israeli-Turkish relations had reached an unprecedented nadir, was silent. A month later, though, Erdogan dispatched several top aides to Damascus to confront the Syrians with the Israelis' claims.[21]

A few hours after the strike, while Israeli officials were both celebrating their victory and anxiously waiting for a Syrian response, the official Syrian news agency reported that Israeli planes had infiltrated the country's airspace but were quickly chased back. Aman's Syria Desk immediately tried to interpret the meaning of the message. Did the Syrians want to drop the whole thing? Or had the Syrian military not completely understood the significance of the defeat? Few knew about the reactor and its purposes. Assad was left to deal with the shattered pieces of the nuclear dream almost all by himself.

On September 11, North Korea issued a public condemnation of the Israeli strike.[22] This announcement was not coordinated with the Syrian government. Seemingly, there was not supposed to be any stable, ongoing relationship between Syria and North Korea and certainly not relations that would prompt the dictatorial regime in Pyongyang to stray from its normal policy of expressing an opinion on events in the Middle East. The North Koreans' announcement turned the media's speculations on the attack into established information. The Americans, meanwhile, remained completely silent. President Bush avoided questions on the matter at press conferences.

The quiet that prevailed on the northern border increased the tensions. The cloud of ambiguity that hovered over the operation also succeeded in confusing Western intelligence agencies, which had been informed when the Israeli Ministry of Foreign Affairs sent the evidence of the Syrian nuclear reactor to their respective governments. In the Golan Heights, the forces were on the highest state of alert. The IDF imposed curfews on soldiers who left their bases, and the IAF kept fighter jets, loaded with fuel and bombs, ready for takeoff at any given moment.

On September 22, it seemed for a brief moment that the Syrians had decided to respond. One of the IDF's air control units reported the disappearance of a Syrian airplane from the radar screen. Within minutes, two fighter jets took off from the Ramat David base. The chief of staff and defense minister were put on line in case an interception would be needed.

There was commotion in the Northern Command's operation room, but a few minutes later the air control unit reported that in its estimation the plane had either landed or crashed. Why did the Syrians send up an old plane with an untrained pilot toward the border? Aman's top analysts tried their best to answer this question. One idea was that it was a test to check Israel's state of alert.

The army's original assessment remained unchallenged: the Syrians did not have the military capability to start a war. If anything, they would seek a psychological victory in the style of a Hezbollah-like attack. In order to demonstrate Syria's power to the Arab world or, more likely, Bashar al-Assad's power for the Syrian people, Syria only needed to put on a good show.

Five days later, on September 27, this scenario seemed to be inevitable. A group of Syrian helicopters moved in the direction of Israel and began circling next to the border. The IAF once again sent up fighter jets from Ramat David Air Force Base. Then air control units saw the helicopters turn around.

With no other reports available, the Arab world tried to offer some explanations of its own. Al Jazeera reported that American warplanes had attacked the Syrian nuclear reactor using small nuclear bombs.[23] The IAF, the organization claimed, had covered the American planes from the rear. Similar reports, some fantastical, were aired on other Arab and Western media outlets. Syria, however, was absolutely silent.

On October 10 Western spy satellites identified a huge explosion in the area where the reactor had been bombed. An examination of earlier satellite footage taken on October 6 showed the Syrians had been working hard to conceal the debris with enormous canvas sheets. The explosion had flattened the remaining debris. By October 24, workers had plowed over the land and removed any evidence that Syria ever had a nuclear reactor.[24]

But the rest of the world did not buy this story. Three weeks after the controlled explosion ElBaradei's IAEA approached Syria, requesting to examine the destroyed reactor. Syria declined. The IAEA officials decided to condemn the Israelis' strike on the facility, claiming that Israel did not have sufficient evidence to pass on to the IAEA.

The White House finally broke its silence in April 2008 and announced that not only was the structure that the Israelis attacked indeed a nuclear reactor but also that it had been erected in collaboration with North Korea in order to produce plutonium. Four days later, President Bush openly stated that by exposing the cooperation between Syria and North Korea, he was sending a clear message to Damascus, Pyongyang, and even Tehran.

CIA director Michael Hayden, who was first made aware of the reactor during Mossad chief Meir Dagan's visit in early 2007, briefed Congress and declared that the Syrian reactor could have manufactured two nuclear bombs a year. Despite the revelations, Israel, Iran, and Syria all remained silent.

In December 2009 Japanese diplomat Yukiya Amano replaced Mohamed El-Baradei as head of the IAEA. During ElBaradei's twelve-year term, Iran had succeeded in finishing its reactors and was on the verge of manufacturing a nuclear bomb. The IAEA had not interfered as Syria built a reactor but had condemned its destruction.

On February 19, 2010, for the first time in years, it was possible once again to see why the agency was so important. Amano ignored the politics and Syrian pressure and decided to publish a report that established the bombed al-Kibar site was likely a nuclear reactor. It also included that inspectors had found traces of processed uranium in the vicinity of the structure that Israel had destroyed. In response, the Syrian ambassador to the agency, Bassam al-Sabbagh, claimed that Israel was responsible for the uranium found in Syrian territory. According to him, IAF planes had scattered uranium in Syrian territory after bombing the facility near al-Kibar.

Amano also changed the agency's approach toward Iran. Under ElBaradei, the agency had turned a blind eye to Iran's nuclear program, giving the Iranians a big head start without requiring them to pay a price for their continued violations. This situation changed almost immediately under Amano's watch.

In Israel, which had proven twice that it is capable of destroying an enemy's nuclear reactor, intelligence operations officers continued to ponder the possibility of a third strike, this time against Iran. They understood, though, that exerting a political backbone, such as Olmert had demonstrated, would not always be enough. After the successful bombing in Syria, one major question remained unresolved: how could Israel repeat its success in Iran?

4

THE SHADOW WAR

As on most summer days in Tel Aviv, the air was still. Guards stationed around the Kirya Tower—the IDF's headquarters located off Kaplan Boulevard—wiped the sweat from their brows.

Suddenly a suspicious figure popped into their sights.

Wearing a long coat in the hot summer weather and pulling a small suitcase, the man immediately grabbed the guards' attention. Swinging their M16 assault rifles into position and fearing a suicide bomb attack, the guards headed toward the man while transmitting instructions back to the control room through their handheld communication devices.

"Atzor (stop)!" the guards yelled out in Hebrew as they cocked their weapons.

The man, visibly sweating and mumbling something inaudible under his breath, kept moving. Suddenly he looked straight at the guards and yelled out, "Allahu Akbar (God is great)!" It was only then that the guards noticed in his sweaty palm a small trigger connected by a black wire to the suitcase.

At first nothing happened. Then a big flash engulfed everything.

This scenario, while fictional, stands at the heart of the Israeli defense establishment's concerns when contemplating the danger of a nuclear Iran. All of Israel's intelligence agencies constantly analyze and debate the feasibility of a lone terrorist carrying a small nuclear bomb or even a "dirty" bomb into Israel. Thus when Israel warns about the Iranian nuclear threat, it is not simply talking about a Shahab or Sajil long-range ballistic missile fitted with a nuclear warhead and fired into downtown Tel Aviv. To Israel, no less concerning is the dirty bomb and the possibility that Iran will provide a nuclear weapon to one of its many terrorist proxies placed strategically throughout the Middle East.

"The primary danger is that a nuclear weapon will reach a terrorist group which will not hesitate to use it immediately. They will send it in a container with a GPS to a leading port in the US, Europe, or Israel," Israeli defense minister Ehud Barak said in 2008.[1]

This chapter chronicles the story of the secret war Israel and the West are waging against Iran and its proxies. While mostly fought in the corridors of the United Nations or on the battlefields of Lebanon and the Gaza Strip, the battle against Iran and its proxies takes place also in the dark shadows of Europe, the cities of Tehran and Damascus, and elsewhere around the world. This struggle is called the shadow war.

Spearheaded by Israel's Mossad and the CIA, this shadow war against Iran is partially responsible for Iran's failure to cross the technological threshold of its nuclear program until mid-2009. It reportedly includes key assassinations, the sabotaging of equipment destined for Iran's nuclear program, and the defection of key members of Iran's nuclear program. Most of these events can be attributed to either of the two intelligence agencies.

The most significant blow to the Iranian-led axis thus far was the assassination of arch terrorist Imad Mughniyeh on February 12, 2008. Until he was killed, Imad Mughniyeh had served as Iran's primary terror emissary, was one of the most-wanted terrorists in the world, and until the attacks on the United States on September 11, 2001, was considered responsible for killing more Americans than any other terrorist since World War II. In his short life of forty-five years, Mughniyeh personified what can be described as a nexus of terrorism encompassing the Middle East and possibly the entire world, serving as a link between Hezbollah, Iran, Syria, al Qaeda, Hamas, and Islamic Jihad.

He was on the most-wanted list of the U.S. Federal Bureau of Investigation (FBI) with a $5 million reward on his head for his involvement in the 1983 bombings of the U.S. Embassy (in April) and the Marine barracks (in October) in Beirut that together killed more than 360 people as well as the 1985 hijacking of a TWA airliner.

While Argentina, France, and a host of other countries also wanted his head for various crimes, Israel hunted him for his direct involvement in two bombings in Buenos Aires: the 1994 bombing of the Argentine Israelite Mutual Association (AMIA) center that killed eighty-five people and the 1992 bombing of the Israeli

Embassy that killed twenty-nine people. IDF intelligence also believes that Mughniyeh masterminded the July 12, 2006, abduction of IDF reservists Eldad Regev and Ehud Goldwasser, the cross-border attack that sparked what later became known as the Second Lebanon War.

On February 12, 2008, after decades of evading capture, he met his demise in a meticulously planned assassination. The bomb was planted in the headrest of a car that exploded as he walked past it on his way into the Iranian Cultural Center in Damascus. He was to be the center's guest of honor at an event marking the twenty-ninth anniversary of the Islamic Revolution of 1979.

As Mughniyeh's infamous career demonstrated, the world of terror is quite small and even intimate. Iran is the known financial backer of Hezbollah, whose military forces he commanded. Syria is the primary supplier of weaponry to Hezbollah, and he was killed, fittingly, in Damascus. Israeli intelligence services also claim to know Mughniyeh and Osama bin Laden met at least once in the early 1990s in Sudan, where the two discussed possibly collaborating on a terror attack that never took place.

Looking back on Mughniyeh's life one better understands how far both Hezbollah and Iran have come from their early days as a small-time terrorist group and patron, respectively. At the same time, his story demonstrates the threat of what the Western world will face if Iran is allowed to continue supporting terrorism and to develop a nuclear bomb that further bolsters and empowers its proxies across the globe.

Mughniyeh was born in 1963 in the southern Lebanese village of Tayr Dibba. His father was a poor farmer and vegetable salesman. At the age of sixteen, Mughniyeh joined Fatah, climbed the ranks fairly quickly, and eventually became a member of its elite military unit, Force 17. One of Mughniyeh's first missions was to protect Khalil al-Wazir, or Abu Jihad, the cofounder of Fatah.

One of the first Israeli intelligence officers to hear the name "Mughniyeh" was Brig. Gen. Shimon Shapira (Ret.), who in the late 1990s served as Binyamin Netanyahu's military secretary during his first term as Israel's prime minister. "It was unusual for the Palestinians to give such a senior position to a Shiite like Mughniyeh," said Shapira, who wrote his doctorate on Hezbollah and its rise to prominence as one of the most sophisticated terrorist groups in the world. "This was a clear indication of Mughniyeh's skill, talent and looming greatness."[2]

Mughniyeh left Fatah in 1982, after Israel invaded Lebanon and deported Yasser Arafat. Mughniyeh did not remain unemployed for long. Within several months, Ali Akbar Mohtashemi, Iran's ambassador to Lebanon at the time, who had spent several years in the country and had become intimately familiar with Fatah, offered him a job. Mughniyeh became the bodyguard for Sheikh Mohammad Hussein Fadlallah, the Lebanese Shia community's spiritual leader.

After Mughniyeh's first year as a bodyguard, Hezbollah began to gain strength, bombing the American Embassy and Marine barracks in Beirut in 1983. "Following those attacks, he came up on our radar," said Uri Lubrani, the venerable former Israeli envoy to Iran before the revolution in 1979.[3] After the revolution, Lubrani became the coordinator of Israeli government activities in Lebanon in the 1980s.

The 1983 attacks in Beirut led Lubrani back to Tel Aviv, where he met with Yitzhak Rabin, then Israel's defense minister. Lubrani told Rabin that he believed Iran was behind the bombings and was becoming a major threat to Israel. Rabin concurred. He gave Lubrani $200,000 in cash to recruit sources, to buy information, and to verify or refute his suspicions. "I was sure that Iran was behind the attacks because Ayatollah Khomeini had already said that he wanted to export the revolution," Lubrani recalled. "The Shiite population in Lebanon was a persecuted minority, and I knew that it would be an easy target to infiltrate and convince to get on Iran's side."

In 1994, Israel had decided that Mughniyeh needed to be stopped once and for all. In the south side of Beirut, outside his brother Fuad's store, agents set off a 50-kilogram car bomb. The blast killed Fuad and three others.[4] (Mughniyeh's other brother, Jihad, had been killed nine years earlier during an attempt on the life of Hezbollah spiritual leader Sheikh Fadlallah, whom he was guarding.) Lebanon attributed the attack on Fuad to the Mossad. According to later news reports, agents had hoped Mughniyeh would attend his brother's funeral, scheduled for several days later, and kill him too. Sensing a trap, Mughniyeh never showed.

Another attempt to capture the terrorist was planned in 1995 after Washington received a tip that Mughniyeh was on a plane from Beirut to the Persian Gulf. The Americans, who had implicated Mughniyeh in the 1983 Beirut bombings, asked Saudi Arabia to intercept the plane. Fearing revenge from radical Islamists, the Saudis refrained.

"Israel and other countries have watched him for years," former Mossad chief Danny Yatom said. "He was very slippery. He never gave interviews and there were only a few pictures of him. . . . He had special capabilities—a satanic and creative mind—and he never left tracks behind him. He was the mastermind of every major Hezbollah attack."[5]

Mughniyeh's involvement in attacks against Israeli soldiers in Lebanon was not a secret; eighteen soldiers were killed in 1987 and another twenty lost their lives the following year. At the end of 1988 internal power struggles forced Mughniyeh to flee Lebanon for Iran. In 1989, the year he was in exile, the numbers of IDF soldiers attacked dropped—two killed in 1989 and another seven in 1990. By the mid-1990s, when he returned to Lebanon, the numbers again started to climb.[6]

In 2000, following Israel's withdrawal from Lebanon, Mughniyeh traveled to Iran, where he met with the Iranian Revolutionary Guard Corps' top brass. He suggested that Iran not limit itself to supporting Hezbollah, as it had been doing; rather, Iran should turn Lebanon into a forward base for the Islamic Republic against Israel.

While Iran previously had supplied Hezbollah with weaponry, after 2000 the shipments arrived weekly. "This is when Iran decides to turn Hezbollah into their front against Israel and into a real strategic asset and begins deploying thousands of missiles in Lebanon. Mughniyeh is responsible for all of this," Shapira said.

Mughniyeh's assassination in 2008 was significant for a number of reasons. His death was first a major setback for Hezbollah operations as he not only was the commander of its military forces but also served as the group's liaison with the Iranians, the Syrians, Hamas, and Islamic Jihad. At the time of his death, Israeli intelligence assessments indicated that Mughniyeh was planning an attack against Israel under the orders of Syrian president Bashar al-Assad to avenge Israel's bombing of Syria's nuclear reactor five months earlier.

The assassins' success in infiltrating Hezbollah's top echelons undoubtedly bolstered Israeli deterrence, as it was the first high-profile assassination following the 2006 Second Lebanon War, which had stained the IDF's image. Mughniyeh's assassination also sent a clear message to every Hezbollah, Hamas, and Islamic Jihad terrorist around the world: Israel could take them out too.

More important, while his assassination disrupted the Iranian-Hezbollah-Syrian triangle that Mughniyeh exclusively had coordinated and directed, it was also a blow to Hezbollah Unit 1800, which Mughniyeh had set up in the late 1980s. It was responsible for the terror group's overseas operations and provided assistance to Palestinian terrorists in the West Bank and the Gaza Strip.[7] Under Mughniyeh, Hezbollah had an extensive terrorist infrastructure overseas. Its attack on the Israeli Embassy in Argentina in 1992, only two months after Israel assassinated Hezbollah leader Abbas al-Musawi, and the bombing of the Jewish community center in Buenos Aires clearly demonstrated those capabilities. And according to Col. Eitan Azani (Ret.), former head of Aman's Lebanese Desk, Hezbollah now maintains an active presence and terror infrastructure in more than fifty countries around the world.[8]

In September 2006, a month after the Second Lebanon War, the U.S. Congressional Committee on International Relations held a hearing entitled "Hezbollah's Global Reach" to discuss the potential fallout from the monthlong Israeli-Lebanese conflict and the possibility of attacks against American and Western targets. The transcript of the hearing provides a frightening and detailed description of Hezbollah's long-arm capabilities, which none other than Mughniyeh established and directed.[9]

One of the witnesses at the hearing was Frank C. Urbancic, Jr., then the principal deputy assistant secretary in the Office of the Coordinator for Counterterrorism in the U.S. State Department. In his testimony, Urbancic mentioned Hezbollah strongholds in South America—particularly in the tri-border area connecting Brazil, Argentina, and Paraguay—where Hezbollah supporters are actively involved in drug smuggling, arms trafficking, money laundering, fraud, and intellectual property piracy. Hezbollah, Urbancic told the committee, also maintains a strong presence in West and Central Africa within Shiite Muslim communities whose members have significant control over the import of basic commodities and the diamond trade. "Hezbollah has assets around the world and it can mobilize them on a moment's notice," he said. "I am quite sure of that."

Another witness John G. Kavanagh, then the chief of the FBI's International Terrorism Operations Section, told the committee of fears that Hezbollah operatives were also infiltrating the United States via the border with Mexico. In 2006, he said, the FBI concluded an investigation in Detroit in which it had obtained 107 federal indictments leading to the arrest of fifty-eight Hezbollah operatives and the seizure of $5 million in property. "What we are seeing is a lot of supporters and sympathizers who are funneling a lot of money back to Lebanon for the cause, for the suicide bombers and the terrorist operations that are occurring in the Middle East," Kavanagh said.[10] This infrastructure, he added, was responsible for supplying Hezbollah with millions of dollars annually.

Urbancic said the United States was particularly concerned about growing ties between Hezbollah and the Venezuelan government of Hugo Chávez. "There is a large Hezbollah nexus to Venezuela . . . it is something that we are conscious of, that we are watching, and that we are very concerned about, and given the proclivities of the Chavez government, it is not a reassuring situation at all," the State Department official said.[11] All of this work, the testimony indicated, was attributed to Imad Mughniyeh, a single man who personified an "axis of terrorism." Evidence that a suitable replacement for Mughniyeh had not been found, General Shapira said in early 2010, was reflected in the group's repeated failure to avenge his assassination. Several known plots had been thwarted, including a plan to bomb the Israeli Embassy in Baku, Azerbaijan, and a plan to shoot down an Israeli airliner over Turkey with shoulder-fired surface-to-air missiles.

Mughniyeh's assassination also left a major vacuum in Hezbollah, which by 2012 it still had not managed to fill completely. Because of the numerous roles that Mughniyeh held in the organization, no other single person could do all of those jobs at once. As a result, many people, including Iranian military officers, were appointed to some of his previous positions.[12]

Israel had made the decision to assassinate Mughniyeh before the 2006 war, but the plan became urgent immediately after the cease-fire went into effect on August 14. The Mossad was tasked with the assassination and immediately recruited as accomplices Palestinian militants based in Lebanon who were ideologically opposed to Hezbollah.[13] After receiving a tip that Mughniyeh was planning to attend the Islamic Revolution's twenty-ninth anniversary celebrations at the Iranian Cultural Center in Damascus, Mossad director Meir Dagan convened top IDF and intelligence officials for a meeting in early February 2008 to discuss a plan.

Tasked with the actual mission was the Mossad's Kidon Unit, an elite group of expert assassins who operate under the Caesarea Branch of the espionage organization. Not much is known about this mysterious unit, details of which are some of the most closely guarded secrets in the Israeli intelligence community. The members of Kidon (Spear) are taught to be stealthy and lethal, to move in the shadows.

Kidon is reportedly responsible for all overseas assassinations and recruits former soldiers from the elite IDF Special Forces units. The commander of Kidon chose three of his top men to carry out the assassination. According to one account, the three flew into Damascus on European passports, which Jews living abroad loaned to them.

Using local Lebanese conspirators, the three Kidon operatives obtained explosives, loaded them into a rental car, and parked it in front of the Iranian Cultural Center, which is located in the Syrian capital's upscale neighborhood of

Kafar Soussa.[14] As they waited that February night in Damascus, the skies were clear and a cool breeze ran through the tight alleys. Then Mughniyeh's silver Mitsubishi Pajero SUV entered the street.

Mughniyeh left the car and begin walking toward the party. Persian music could be heard coming from the building. As he passed the rental car, the entire street shook. Mughniyeh's body parts were later found scattered across the street. Another report claimed that the Israeli agents had planted a bomb inside the headrest of Mughniyeh's jeep while he was inside the cultural center. When he got back in his car, one of the agents pressed the button and the vehicle went up in flames.

Two years later, Kidon reportedly struck again. The location was Dubai. The target was Mahmoud al-Mabhouh, a top Hamas operative, whose body was discovered in January 2010 on the second floor of the luxury Al Bustan Rotana Hotel.

Next to his bed police found medications. Reportedly his assassins had planted them there to cover their tracks and make his death look natural. For some time it worked, but ten days after his body was discovered, an analysis of forensic evidence that had been reviewed in France arrived at Hamas headquarters in Damascus. The terror group announced that Mabhouh had been murdered.

The Dubai police conducted an investigation and published pictures of twenty-six people who allegedly entered Dubai on forged British, French, Irish, German, and Australian passports. They traced some of the identities to Jewish citizens of these countries who had immigrated to Israel. Dubai's sophisticated closed-circuit television (CCTV) system had recorded the alleged spies wearing wigs and frequently switching clothing and hotel rooms. Others had disguised themselves as tennis players.

While Israel neither denied its involvement nor claimed responsibility for the assassination, the passport fiasco left little doubt about the role the Mossad had played in killing Mabhouh. Even before Dubai released pictures of the passports that the alleged assassins had used, the smiles on the faces of several Israeli government ministers as they entered the cabinet room the Sunday after Mabhouh's assassination made Israel's involvement quite clear.

"All the [Israeli] security services make, thank God, great efforts to safeguard the security of the State of Israel," Israeli minister of internal affairs Eli Yishai told reporters at the entrance to the cabinet room.

Science and Technology Minister Daniel Hershkowitz added that Dagan was one of the best Mossad directors in Israeli history. "My impression is that that the

Mossad knows how to get the job done and it is a known thing that anyone who lifts a hand against a Jew is putting his life on the line," Hershkowitz said.

Mabhouh made his way onto Israel's most-wanted list in February 1989. In one of the terror group's first kidnapping attacks, a Hamas terrorist cell of which Mabhouh was a member kidnapped and murdered IDF soldiers Ilan Sa'adon and Avi Sasportas. Knowing that Israel was hunting for the murderers, Mabhouh fled Gaza and went to Egypt with his wife and children. He eventually made his way to Syria, where he settled into the Damascus-based political bureau of Hamas, headed by Khaled Mashal. Mabhouh's rise to prominence came in 2004 when he succeeded as head of the Hamas-Iran axis Izz a-din Subhi Shaykh al-Khalil, who was killed in a Damascus car bomb attack that was also attributed to the Mossad. Mabhouh became responsible for coordinating weapons shipments from Iran to the Gaza Strip.

During his time overseas, Mabhouh established strong ties in Sudan that Hamas used to smuggle weaponry from Iran and into the Gaza Strip. One of the more well-known smuggling routes is from Eritrea, up into Sudan, through the Sinai Peninsula, and then under one of the hundreds of tunnels along the Philadelphi Route. Mabhouh was behind the weapons convoy, for example, that Israel bombed during Operation Cast Lead as it was making its way to Gaza through the Sudanese desert. Israel believed this convoy carried long-range missiles that could reach Tel Aviv. Hamas eventually did obtain the missiles, likely thanks in part to Mabhouh, and in late 2009 test fired one estimated to have a 60-kilometer range.

From a policy perspective also, it made sense that Israel would have wanted Mabhouh as well as Mughniyeh dead. "The response to Munich [Olympics massacre of 1972] was the last time Israel killed people for what they did in the past," said Ram Igra, a former senior Mossad operative who was in charge of the agency's Missing in Action Desk in the late 1990s. "From Munich and on, the policy was to eliminate people for what they could do in the future, not only for what they did in the past."[15]

Mabhouh had been a target of many foreign intelligence agencies for a number of years. Several days before his assassination, he called his brother and said he believed Arab-looking spies had him under surveillance.

The intelligence on Mabhouh's planned trip to Dubai arrived in Israel in late 2009, and Kidon was immediately put into action, rehearsing the assassination in Tel Aviv hotels.[16] On January 19, Mabhouh boarded Emirates flight EK912 in Damascus to Dubai, where he was expected to lay the logistical groundwork for a large Iranian arms shipment to the Gaza Strip.

A Mossad informant had followed Mabhouh to the airport and knew that he was on the plane even though the forty-nine-year-old Palestinian had used an assumed name. The informant sent a message, reportedly via a pre-paid Austrian mobile phone, to reconnaissance teams that were already on the ground in Dubai and waiting for their target.

The teams followed Mabhouh from the moment he stepped off the plane in Dubai. CCTV footage shows two of the hit team's members, wearing tennis clothes, sharing an elevator with him up to the second floor. One of the men is seen looking down the hallway as Mabhouh enters room 230. Less than an hour later, the team books room 237, directly across the hall.

Mabhouh then left the hotel, giving the team time to set up inside room 237. He returned later that evening, likely after meeting a contact. Twenty minutes later, CCTV footage shows four men wearing baseball caps entering an elevator on the second floor. Less than two hours later the team members were at the airport, boarding flights for Hong Kong, South Africa, and Europe. Mabhouh's body was only found the next afternoon, giving the team plenty of time to escape Dubai.

The CCTV videos provide a unique insight into the way the Mossad operates. Using passports that belong to Jews who immigrated to Israel helps create identities for its agents and enables them to travel freely throughout the Arab world, which is off-limits to Israeli passport holders.

The man behind the Mughniyeh and Mabhouh assassinations, former Mossad director Meir Dagan, is believed to be one of the most dangerous people in the world today, even if he doesn't look the part. A short, stout man in his sixties who walks with a cane, Dagan was appointed director of the Mossad in 2002. (Tamir Pardo replaced him in January 2011.) Until then, the agency had appeared to be paralyzed under the tenure of his predecessor Ephraim Halevy, who, according to one former Mossad operative, preferred to talk with Arab diplomats at cocktail parties in Europe rather than undertake dangerous and risky operations in the Middle East.

This paralysis had taken hold of the Mossad following its failure to assassinate Hamas's Mashal in 1997 in Amman. Two Mossad agents were caught in the botched operation. In exchange for their release, Israel was forced to provide an antidote to save Mashal's life and to release hundreds of Palestinian prisoners. "Under Halevy, the motto was 'Don't get in trouble,'" explained the security source.

On one occasion in the early 2000s, Mossad trainees attended a lecture about how to behave if the police captured them during an operation overseas. The example used was from 1998 when a team of Mossad agents was caught trying to tap a suspected Hezbollah operative's phones in Switzerland. One cadet asked the instructor why they shouldn't resist arrest, fight back, and try to escape. The instructor answered that it was not the way the Mossad operated.

That attitude completely changed under Dagan, who brought a new sense of boldness and courage to the agency. When Dagan received his appointment, Prime Minister Ariel Sharon gave him one task—to stop Iran's pursuit of a nuclear weapon.

Born in 1945 in the Soviet Union, Dagan tried out for the IDF's most elite Special Forces unit called Sayeret Matkal. After failing to pass the grueling selection process, Dagan enlisted in the Armored Corps and slowly climbed the ranks, proving to be a daring soldier as well as a smart tactician. As a young officer in basic training, Dagan reportedly flung knives at trees and telephone poles like a circus entertainer. Renowned for his bravery, he earned a medal of valor for grabbing a grenade from an enemy fighter's hands.

In 1970, Sharon, then head of the IDF's Southern Command, chose Dagan to command a unit of elite Special Forces called Sayeret Rimon. The unit's soldiers disguised themselves as Palestinians and raided the Gaza Strip to assassinate Palestine Liberation Organization fighters.

As Dagan fought against Palestinian terrorists in the Gaza Strip, the Mossad was waging the same fight on the streets of Europe. The Israeli espionage organization was in its prime, assisting the CIA in uncovering Soviet spies around the world and helping America fight the Cold War. After the massacre of Israeli athletes at the Munich Olympics in 1972, the Mossad was tasked with avenging their deaths and carried out a string of complex assassinations of PLO commanders across the globe.

In light of the Mossad's decline under former chiefs Yatom and Halevy, Sharon needed a leader who could restore the organization's earlier glory. Dagan was the right man at the right time. He took the deteriorating organization by the reins and embarked on daring operations around the world.

The way Dagan decorated his office set the tone for his tenure. On one wall of his modest Tel Aviv office was a black-and-white picture of an old bearded

Jewish man wearing a tallith, or Jewish prayer shawl, as he kneels in front of two Nazi soldiers, one with a stick in his hand, the other carrying a rifle slung over his shoulder. As Israeli prime minister Netanyahu recalled during a farewell cabinet meeting held in Dagan's honor in early January 2011, Dagan would tell visitors to his office, "Look at this picture. This man, kneeling down before the Nazis, was my grandfather just before he was murdered. I look at this picture every day and promise that the Holocaust will never happen again."[17]

Dagan's work reportedly paid off. Iranian scientists began to disappear; equipment sent to Iran for its nuclear program arrived broken, likely sabotaged. Warehouses in Europe where equipment for Iran's nuclear program was stored before being shipped mysteriously went up in flames. In 2005, a number of mysterious plane crashes plagued Iran, killing dozens of IRGC officers, including several senior officers. All of the above were attributed to the Mossad by Iran.

During one of his last cabinet meetings before leaving office in 2009, Prime Minister Olmert said: "I believe the processes the government of Israel has enacted under my leadership in various areas, those that can be told and those that cannot, will yet receive their proper place in the history of the State of Israel."[18] Thus, it came as no surprise when Olmert decided twice to extend Dagan's term, making him the longest-serving Mossad chief in Israeli history.

On the one hand, the Mossad's successes did generate some criticism. By 2010, three of Dagan's deputies had resigned out of frustration with the government's decision to extend Dagan's term repeatedly, halting their chances to advance. On the other hand, with the agency's success also came money. According to one former senior intelligence operative, by 2007, the Mossad's annual budget had jumped by close to half a billion dollars, which Dagan used to help battle Iran and its terror proxies. Israel's intelligence work on Iran and some of its discoveries led several top European intelligence agencies—primarily in Germany, France, and Great Britain—to side with Israeli assessments over the White House's claim in its 2007 National Intelligence Estimate (NIE) that downplayed Iran's nuclear progress. Meanwhile, relations with the CIA also peaked with Dagan at the helm, owing to the Mossad's once again providing critical intelligence and proving itself to be a major player. "There is unprecedented cooperation today between the agencies," one top Israeli security official said in mid-2010, giving Israel's work on various top secret missions as an example.

During his tenure, Dagan was careful not to speak publicly about his assessments regarding Iran's nuclear progress, with one exception. In 2009 he had stirred controversy in an appearance at the Knesset when he said that Iran would not obtain the bomb until 2014, pushing back Israel's earlier assessments by a number of years. At the time, officials explained that Dagan was referring to the stage when Iran would have the ability to fire a missile tipped with a nuclear warhead into Israel. Iran could very well develop a testable nuclear device before then, they said.

After his resignation on January 6, 2011, Dagan broke tradition and convened his first-ever press conference. Iran, he said, had encountered major technological complications and as a result would not be able to develop a nuclear weapon successfully until sometime around 2015. "Even if the world sits and doesn't do anything it will still take the Iranians several years," Dagan said. He felt this delay meant there might be some time before Israel would be required to take unilateral military action to stop the Iranians' nuclear program.

Dagan's replacement was announced on November 29, 2010, the same day two bombs went off in downtown Tehran, killing top nuclear scientist Majid Shahriari. Despite his bodyguard's presence in the car, two assassins on a motorcycle drove up along Shahriari's small Peugeot sedan and attached a magnetized bomb to the car. The explosive device killed him. Several minutes later a different motorcycle approached another car in Tehran carrying scientist Fereydoun Abbasi-Davani, a specialist in nuclear isotopes and known for his involvement in Iran's nuclear program.[19] Abbasi-Davani survived by jumping out of the car after spotting the assassin. Three months later, he became head of the Atomic Energy Organization of Iran. Not much was known about Shahriari's role in Iran's nuclear program, but some reports claimed he was working on designing new nuclear reactors.[20] Shahriari was one of four Iranian nuclear scientists killed in similar assassinations between 2010 and 2012.

There is no such thing as a coincidence in Iran. Within a matter of hours the Islamic regime officially blamed the Mossad and its resigning director Meir Dagan for the assassination.

Assassinations overseas are rare and extremely complicated. As a matter of principle, intelligence organizations such as the Mossad do not approve overseas assassinations unless they are deemed the only course of action available and are believed vital for national security. In Israel's case, both the Mossad and Aman maintain lists of terrorists and enemies of the state who are deemed legitimate targets. While Aman's list focuses mainly on Israel's direct military enemies and

Hamas and Islamic Jihad terrorists based in the Gaza Strip who can be targeted from the air, the Mossad's list includes terrorists and enemy operatives who cannot be reached in standard IAF missile strikes. The prime minister usually sanctions the lists, and in many cases he will meet with the agents assigned to an overseas assassination mission before giving the green light. Israeli prime ministers have traditionally done the same before sensitive military operations as well.

For example, ahead of the assassination of PLO military chief Khalil al-Wazir, also known as Abu Jihad, in Tunis in 1988, Aman and the Mossad reportedly watched his every move for several months. They reportedly followed the same tactics ahead of the Mughniyeh and Mabhouh assassinations.

"Targets are followed for years," said a senior former Israeli intelligence officer who participated in past covert missions.[21] "We learn every detail, where the target sleeps, what he eats, who he spends his time with and what his day looks like. Only then do we start planning operations."

Another senior Israeli intelligence official explained the importance of assassinations. "When someone like Mughniyeh, [Syria's liaison to Hezbollah and North Korea, Gen. Mohammed] Suleiman or Mabhouh is assassinated, it sends three clear messages: that the respective terror groups or countries are penetrable, that the leaders of the groups can also be assassinated, and that they should be careful."

Contrary to the way assassinations are depicted in books and movies, they are extremely complicated to carry out and many times are canceled at the last second. In many cases, a secretive committee of the heads of the three main intelligence agencies—the Mossad, the Shin Bet Security Agency, and Aman—debate the planned operations. One of the key changes that led to Israel's successes in its shadow war was the increased in cooperation between the different intelligence agencies, a direct result of the Iranian threat. The close work yielded great dividends. Further, IDF generals and their Mossad counterparts cultivated relationships, and each side learned how the other worked and how they could better utilize one another.

Dagan, for instance, developed good working relationships with top officers in the IDF, particularly Chief of the General Staff Lt. Gen. Gabi Ashkenazi and the IAF commander Maj. Gen. Eliezer Shkedy. They closely worked on a series of complicated missions, many still classified. In the government, Dagan also found an ally with a love for covert operations in Defense Minister Ehud Barak, who is said to have a soft spot for assassinations. In 1973, as a team leader in Sayeret Matkal's Operation Spring of Youth, he once disguised himself as a woman, infiltrated a PLO hideout in Beirut, and killed three top operatives.

In 1992, as the IDF's chief of staff, Barak convinced the government to approve the assassination of Sheikh Hassan Nasrallah's predecessor at the helm of Hezbollah, Abbas al-Musawi.[22] Later that year, he oversaw the training for a planned (but aborted) assassination of Saddam Hussein in retaliation for firing Scud missiles into Israel during the 1991 Gulf War.[23]

Following Mughniyeh's assassination in February 2008, cooperation between the Mossad, Aman, and the Shin Bet made another dramatic leap. While the different heads of Israel's intelligence agencies do meet monthly—as per the recommendations of the Agranat Commission, which investigated the intelligence failures that preceded the Yom Kippur War in 1973—the assassination of Mughniyeh brought them even closer together. Anticipating Hezbollah's acts of revenge led them to establish a number of interagency teams that met daily, over a period of several weeks, to assess the threat.

Unique in Mughniyeh's case, the teams not only shared intelligence with one another—as they have done many times in the past—but also analyzed and assessed the threat level. One of the teams consisted of analysts who gathered and analyzed raw intelligence data and then assessed the threat to Israelis in specific countries. One of Israel's main concerns was that Hezbollah would strike at a target overseas, such as an embassy, a consulate, or an Israeli airliner.

Israel is a world leader in aviation and embassy security, however, a status obtained from hard-earned experience after a number of successful terror attacks and hijackings in the 1970s. On a military base in the center of the country, the Shin Bet has built a facility where it trains security guards who are later stationed on El Al airplanes or in embassies and consulates around the world. While it appears to be a completely ordinary building, inside is a long room that is built to replicate the interior of a passenger airliner, with rows of seats and a cockpit door in front. There the security guards train, with live fire, to thwart hijacking attempts. Down the road, in another building, the agency has built a replica of the inside of an Israeli embassy abroad. Security guards who are deployed in missions around the world are trained here how to operate in the event of an infiltration.

Following Mughniyeh's assassination, Israel took immediate further precautions. El Al flights from India, for example, were no longer allowed to take off during the day since shoulder-fired surface-to-air missiles are harder to lock on a target at night. In addition, helicopters escorted civilian flights in Europe and Southeast Asia upon takeoff and landing. Large security contingents also accompanied Israeli government ministers who traveled abroad on private vacations.

Intelligence work is split into three main divisions: intelligence obtained from human agents (HUMINT), intelligence gathered from electronic eavesdropping and signals (SIGINT), and intelligence collected from visual surveillance equipment, such as satellites, and unmanned aerial vehicles such as the Israeli-made Heron drone, capable of flying undetected to Iran (VISINT). All three are important and each has its advantages and disadvantages.

Human agents can go places that listening devices and satellites cannot access and vice versa. In addition, electronic signals can always be intercepted, decoded, and traced back to their source.

Following the 2006 war in Lebanon, Aman's budget increased significantly and continued to grow with every successive year. Israel launched new satellites into space that could track Iranian developments and developed new UAVs that are capable of flying reconnaissance missions far from Israel and undetected.

In addition to the Mossad's fieldwork, Unit 8200 is a military intelligence group that is similar to the U.S. National Security Agency in that it is responsible for signals intelligence and code encryption. Officers and soldiers who serve in the unit, the largest in the IDF, develop most of its technology in-house. Their main task is simply to listen to the enemy, read its newspapers, watch its television shows, and eavesdrop on its most sensitive conversations.

The unit has two basic tracks—the technological track and another for the intelligence gatherers, who are mostly young eighteen-year-olds fluent in Arabic and Persian. Finding such soldiers with these language skills is not easy, considering that the IDF's new recruits in 2012 were not born in Arab countries as some of their parents were thirty years earlier. Thus, few soldiers are fluent in Arabic or Farsi. As a result, in 2005 Aman opened a special language school for nonnative Arabic and Farsi speakers. By 2010, Aman had more than tripled the number of Persian speakers in its ranks. The school, one of a kind in the world, teaches soldiers one of the two languages in record time—only twenty weeks—after which they are stationed in Unit 8200 and begin collecting and deciphering intelligence on Israel's neighbors and enemies.

One of the few known examples of Unit 8200's work was provided during the 1967 Six Day War. The unit had intercepted a phone call Egyptian president Gamal Abdel Nasser made to Jordan's King Hussein during which he claimed that the Egyptian Air Force—which the Israeli Air Force already had mostly destroyed in a preemptive strike—was actually bombing Israeli airfields. Nasser also urged Hussein to declare that American and British fighter jets were behind the attacks on their airfields. Fearing that Nasser was trying to draw the Soviets into the war by accusing the United States and Great Britain of being involved, Israeli defense minister Moshe Dayan decided to broadcast the intercepted phone call on public radio. The move worked. It embarrassed Nasser and Hussein and, more important, stopped the Russians from coming to Egypt's assistance and joining the war.[24]

Unit 8200 is also responsible for Israel's cyber warfare capabilities, said to be some of the most advanced in the world. The effect cyber warfare can have in a low-level skirmish was demonstrated during Israel's Operation Cast Lead in early 2009. Alongside the fighting in Gaza, Hamas sympathizers from across the Arab world launched hundreds of cyber attacks against Israeli websites. Israel's retaliation was swift. It culminated in the breaching of Hamas's al-Aqsa TV network and airing an audio message in Arabic addressed to regular Gazans, saying: "Hamas leaders are hiding and they left you on the front line." The following day, Israel again broke into the network with a more elaborate message that showed an animated clip of Hamas leaders being gunned down with a warning that "time is running out."[25]

While shrouded in secrecy, Israel's cyber warfare technology is believed to be as advanced as that of the United States, China, and Russia—that is, capable of knocking out an enemy's war grid or shutting down its economy. The man who helped Israel develop this new weapon is Maj. Gen. Amos Yadlin, the head of Aman between 2005 and 2010. A former air force pilot, Yadlin knows firsthand what flying the distance to deal a devastating blow to an enemy is like. In June 1981, Yadlin was one of the eight F-16 pilots who flew to Iraq and destroyed Saddam Hussein's French-built Osirak reactor. "Fighting in the cyber dimension is as significant as the introduction of fighting in the aerial dimension in the early 20th century," Yadlin said in a policy speech at a Tel Aviv think tank. "Preserving the lead in this field is especially important, given the dizzying pace of change. . . . Like unmanned aircraft, it's a use of force that can strike without regard for distance or duration, and without endangering fighters' lives."[26]

The three largest known cyber attacks provide insight into what this capability can do for Israel. In 2005, in what is called the Titan Rain attack, Chinese hackers are believed to have penetrated hundreds of U.S. networks in the Defense Department and other government agencies. In 2007 Estonia came under a massive cyber attack from Russia, which was also believed to have been behind similar cyber attacks against Georgia in the war of 2008.

Israel has also invested heavily in the cyber field in recent years. After the United States decided in 2009 to establish the Cyber Command, Israel began considering its own move. At one point it even deliberated the possibility of setting up an entirely new command within the General Staff, but after a short study, the General Staff decided to divide the responsibility between Aman and the C4I (Command, Control, Communications, Computers, and Intelligence) Directorate. The Aman Unit 8200, being already responsible for signal intelligence, eavesdropping on the enemy, and code decryption, was entrusted with offensive cyber capabilities. Defense was left with the C4I Directorate.

To ensure that the two branches continued to cooperate and work together, the IDF in mid-2009 assigned an Aman lieutenant colonel to Matzov, the unit in the C4I Directorate that is responsible for protecting IDF networks. Matzov is also responsible for writing the codes that encrypt the IDF, Shin Bet, and Mossad networks as well as the mainframes in national corporations, such as the Israel Electrical Corporation, Mekorot, the national water company, and Bezeq, a telecommunications group.

The Aman officer's job is to receive the information from Aman on enemy capabilities and coordinate with the C4I Directorate to make any necessary changes to IDF computer defenses. In addition, C4I has established a special team of computer experts that tries to breach IDF firewalls and encryptions, acting as if it were the enemy.

On the offensive level, a possible taste of Israel's capability was revealed in the summer of 2010. Reports circulated that a piece of malware, or a worm known as Stuxnet, had severely infected Iranian computer systems at its main enrichment facility at Natanz and its reactor at Bushehr. The first to detect the worm was a computer security company in Belarus. News spread quickly about the malware as Iran blocked its computers to the outside world to prevent leaking the exact extent of the damage.

In November 2010, the International Atomic Energy Agency openly confirmed that Iran had encountered major technological difficulties and had suspended work at its nuclear-field production facilities, likely a result of the Stuxnet virus. A few days later, Iranian president Ahmadinejad admitted that malicious software had damaged the nation's centrifuge facilities. He downplayed the extent of the damage, but some analysts have claimed it was far worse than Iran made it out to be and that Iran faced a dwindling number of working centrifuges at Natanz.

Ralph Langner, a German information technology expert, was the first independent expert to assert that the malware had been weaponized to attack Iran's centrifuges. In his analysis, he said that the worm had succeeded in setting back Iran's nuclear program by two years.[27] "It will take two years for Iran to get back on track," Langner explained. "This was nearly as effective as a military strike but even better since there are no fatalities and no full-blown war. From a military perspective this was a huge success."

When Langner learned of the infection, he immediately got his hands on the code and began studying it. His mouth practically dropped open as he stared at the fifteen thousand lines of code, something only a country or two could have been capable of writing.

To succeed, simply inserting the worm into the Iranian systems would not have been enough; rather, the attacker had to have the exact layout of the Iranian computers down to the wire in order for it to effectively damage every single computer and control system. Intelligence agencies would have needed to obtain these specifications. In addition, the complexity of the worm led experts to conclude that at least five or six writers were working on the code simultaneously with quality control teams and project management teams supervising the work. Likely the crew grew to several dozen people over a period of many years. One foreign analyst claimed that the code was of the quality of military applications similar to the type of software found in cruise missiles.

For the West, it is extremely difficult to measure the extent of the damage Stuxnet caused Iran. In September 2010, the cyber security firm Symantec determined that more than thirty thousand computer systems had been infected in Iran. A few days later, however, Iran put up a firewall to stop information on its computer systems from reaching the outside world. It has yet to be removed.

But Symantec was able to determine that Stuxnet was designed to target systems that have a frequency converter, or a device that controls the speed of a motor, such as a centrifuge that spins around using a motor to enrich uranium. The Stuxnet code modifies programmable logic controllers in the frequency converter drives used to control the motors. It changes the frequencies of the converter, first to higher than 1,400 Hz and then down to 2 Hz—speeding it up and then nearly halting it—before setting it at a little more than 1,000 Hz.

Essentially Stuxnet causes the engines in Iran's IR-1 centrifuges to increase and decrease their speed. Iran usually runs its motors at 1,007 cycles per second to prevent damage, while Stuxnet seemed to increase the motor speed to 1,064 cycles per second. The increase is small but enough, according to experts, to damage the enrichment process.

"If you start changing the speed, there are vibrations and they become so severe that it can break the motor," said David Albright, a Washington-based expert on nuclear proliferation who studied Stuxnet. "If it is true that it is attacking the IR-1, then it is changing the speed to attack the motor."[28]

During his investigation, Albright discovered that in early 2010, Iran had mysteriously decommissioned a thousand centrifuges, or a tenth of the total number at the Natanz facility. That only a thousand were damaged could mean that Stuxnet—if it caused the breakage—was meant to be subtle and work slowly, causing small amounts of harm without leading the Iranians to suspect that something foreign, such as malware, had infiltrated their computer computers.

But how did it infiltrate the Iranian computers?

Simple, Langner explains: "You don't have to get the infected drive into Natanz, but all you need to do is make sure that someone who has access to the facility has his or her computer infected and then connects to the server."

While it sounds simpler than it actually is, such techniques have worked in the past. In 2008, an American soldier walked into a bathroom on a military base in the Middle East and found a few memory sticks scattered on the floor. The sticks had been deliberately infected with a computer worm, and the foreign intelligence agency behind the operation was counting on a soldier's human nature to pick up a stick and attach it to his computer to see what is on it. When it happened, the result was nearly devastating, delivering a worm into the computer system of the U.S. military's Central Command that took fourteen months to eradicate.[29] The Stuxnet malware could have been introduced in a similar fashion, by infecting the computer of a Russian engineer or technician who supports the Iranian facilities or of an employee at Kalaye Electric Company, the Iranian company that is suspected of serving as Iran's primary centrifuge developer and manufacturer.

Widespread speculation has named Israel's Aman Unit 8200, known for its advanced SIGINT capabilities, as the possible creator of the software as well as the United States. Langner said that in his opinion at least two countries—possibly Israel and the United States—were behind Stuxnet.

In January 2011 the *New York Times* reported that Israel had tested the Stuxnet virus on Iranian centrifuges constructed inside its nuclear reactor in Dimona.

The account maintained that the United States and Israel, with help from the Germans and the British, had developed Stuxnet.[30]

Israel has traditionally declined to comment on its suspected involvement in the Stuxnet virus, but senior IDF officers had confirmed in late 2010 that Iran had encountered significant technological difficulties with its centrifuges at the Natanz enrichment facility.

Meanwhile, in December 2010, Eric Byres, a Canadian computer security expert, ran a daily review of traffic to his Tofino Industrial Security Solution website, an obscure specialized site for companies seeking information technology security solutions. What he discovered was groundbreaking: while his site usually averaged one or two Iranian visitors a year, it had received close to a thousand visits from Iran in the span of a few weeks.

"Iran was never on the map for us, and all of a sudden we are now getting massive numbers of people going to our website and people who we can identify as being from Iran," he said. "We are talking about hundreds. It could be people who are curious about what is going on, but we are such a specialized site that it would only make sense that these are people who are involved in control systems."[31]

This information led Byres to a simple conclusion: six months after it first attacked Iran, Stuxnet was still running wild through Iranian computer systems. By 2012, Iran claimed that the virus had been neutralized.

But more important, in Israel and Iran it was understood that Stuxnet—regardless of who was behind it—was likely only the beginning of the world's new art of warfare. Cyber warfare is quieter, being fought in the shadows and on adversaries' computers, but it is as deadly as a missile or rocket.

As head of Aman, General Yadlin was one of the key players in formulating Israeli policy vis-à-vis Iran. In the United States, he once said, his job would be split among five different generals: one in charge of the NSA's SIGINT, another in charge of the Cyber Command; a third to command the military intelligence unit's Special Forces, similar to the renowned Sayeret Matkal or the U.S. Special Operations Command; a fourth to serve as the chief intelligence adviser, or the J2 Joint Staff Intelligence officer for the Joint Chiefs of Staff; and a fifth to serve as the director of national intelligence, advising the president's cabinet.

When Yadlin assumed his post in 2005, while Iran was one of Aman's primary targets, the organization was more focused on research and analysis and less on creating target banks for the event that Israel would one day decide to attack the Islamic Republic's nuclear facilities. One of the first decisions Yadlin made was to establish small teams of officers from various intelligence units and direct them to sift through all of the intelligence collected on different targets and work with the Operations Directorate to plan potential missions.

Intelligence is not used merely on a tactical level. It can also influence political processes, especially when Israel shares it with partners around the world. In 2004, for example, Prime Minister Ariel Sharon sent the head of Aman at the time, Maj. Gen. Aharon Farkash, to Rome, Paris, and London to brief world leaders about Iran's nuclear military plans. While some of the European officials were adamantly skeptical that Iran was developing a bomb, after Farkash briefed them on Iran's advanced missile program and its extended ranges and the growing size of their warheads, they walked away convinced that the mullahs were after the bomb. The question that remained was how to stop them.

The results of his visit, Farkash later confessed, were not encouraging. "The Europeans said they did not understand why Israel was trying to scare them with a nuclear military threat since they had lived with such a threat during the Cold War," he later said.[32]

Assassinations have not been Israel's only instrument in its battle against Iran's nuclear program and support of terrorism. Western intelligence agencies have also focused their efforts on the financial hierarchy in Iran. They have used high-tech tools to hack into Iranian computers and bank accounts and to cause money that was intended for procurement or nuclear technology to disappear.

There have also been countless reports of sabotage. One well-known example occurred in 2007 when power supplies used to regulate voltage and current at the Natanz enrichment plant blew up, destroying dozens of centrifuges. In other cases, the U.S. and European governments recruited companies around the world to sell the Iranians faulty components manufactured with undetectable flaws. This sabotage, focused on the supply chain that the Iranians were relying on for their nuclear program, was instrumental in delaying Iran's nuclear progress. Nonetheless, by 2010, despite some continued technological complications, the Iranians had succeeded in mastering the technology needed to make a bomb.

"It is now just a political decision to go to the breakout stage, to enrich uranium to higher levels, and begin developing the bomb," Amos Yadlin said in November 2011.[33]

While Israel by 2010 was investing tremendous resources in collecting intelligence on Iran, the Iranians were fighting back. In the mid-2000s, the Iranians or Hezbollah would announce the discovery and capture of another Israeli spy ring every few months. While they fabricated some reports to unify public opinion behind the regime, others were likely genuine.

Insight into this battle of wits was provided in 2008 when the Iranian Ministry of Intelligence and Security captured Ali Ashtari, a forty-five-year-old businessman from Tehran, and accused him of working for the Mossad. Ashtari confessed to meeting Mossad agents in Thailand, Turkey, and Switzerland, where he received $50,000 and was asked to bug communication devices that he had sold to the Iranian military and members of the nuclear program. Ashtari also apparently revealed that he had tried to recruit figures involved in Iran's nuclear project on behalf of the Mossad.

Another spy ring was discovered in May 2009, this time in Lebanon, where the Mossad reportedly used it to infiltrate Hezbollah. In this case, the Lebanese discovered the ring members' equipment, including a red Igloo cooler with an advanced electronic mapping system hidden inside, encryption devices, a can of Mobil motor oil hiding mini tapes, forged identification papers, and a car battery charger that police said was used to store and transmit data.

Reportedly a Lebanese man named Marwan Fakih, the owner of a car dealership and garage in the southern Lebanese town of Nabatiyeh, led one cell. According to the Lebanese Internal Security Force, Fakih installed tracking devices and eavesdropping equipment inside cars that belonged to Hezbollah operatives when he serviced them. If the allegations against Fakih are true and he was working for Israel, then the devices he installed in the cars could have enabled Israeli intelligence to locate and identify secret and otherwise unknown Hezbollah installations.

Iran, meanwhile, also tried to recruit Israelis as spies for its regime. In April 2007, the Israeli Shin Bet security agency revealed that it had uncovered an Iranian scheme to approach Israelis at the embassy in Turkey when they requested visas to visit Iran. The Shin Bet said that Iran's intelligence gathering focused on three main points: Israel's decision-making echelon, its military and defense establishments, and the strengths and weaknesses of Israeli society.

Because Iran does not allow anyone into the country whose passport bears an Israeli entrance stamp, Israelis who want to travel to Iran must pass through the Iranian Consulate in Turkey, where they are issued special documents that allow them into to Iran or, alternatively, to take out an Iranian passport. From the interrogation of ten suspected spies, it emerged that Iranian intelligence officers disguised as diplomats worked at the Iranian Consulate in Turkey. They took Israeli visitors into a separate room and questioned them for hours about their military background, their families, political issues in Israel, and possible connections to defense officials.[34]

When the Israelis arrived in Iran, they were taken again for questioning and, in many cases, had their travel documents confiscated. In some cases, these Israelis were stuck in Iran for several months. Their next contacts offered to help them trace their documents and leave Iran. Once the contacts returned the documents, they usually asked the Israelis to begin gathering information to pass on to their handlers. In some cases, they requested research papers and photos of classified military installations in exchange for up to thousands of dollars.

To combat the penetration of its nuclear program, in 2005 Iran established the Oghab-2, a counterintelligence bureau whose mission is to prevent information regarding Iran's nuclear program from leaking out of the country. The regime also tasked the bureau with monitoring top Iranian scientists on their trips overseas to conferences and with ensuring that equipment procured for the nuclear program had not been sabotaged.

Putting the most pressure on the Iranians by 2012 appeared to be the systematic defection or assassination of Iranian scientists affiliated with the republic's nuclear program. In 2007 the International Monetary Fund (IMF) released a report that claimed that Iran had the highest rate of "brain drain" among the ninety countries it had measured. According to the report, more than 150,000 Iranians leave the Islamic Republic annually, and an estimated 25 percent of Iranians with postsecondary education live abroad.[35]

Not in the IMF's report was a top secret program called Brain Drain that the CIA's Counterproliferation Division started in 2005 and ran for years, attracting some of Iran's best graduates. Much of the recent intelligence obtained about Iran's nuclear progress has come from Iranian scientists who defected to the West. Between 2005 and 2008, for example, four Iranian scientists fled to the United States and provided critical information about Iran's nuclear program, including revelations about Iran's secret uranium enrichment facility that was being built in a mountain near the holy city of Qom and was off-limits to UN inspectors.[36]

The U.S. government relocated the scientists throughout the United States. Many of them became rich, pocketing millions of dollars for their acts of betrayal. Some opened businesses, others returned to academia. Some even kept their original names. The work done on convincing scientists to defect, as well as the identities of the scientists, are some of the most closely guarded secrets in the corridors of CIA headquarters in Langley, Virginia; of other Western intelligence agencies; and of Mossad headquarters near Tel Aviv.

For Israel, the reported focus on nuclear scientists was not new. In the late 1970s, Israel reportedly assassinated a number of Iraqi scientists who were involved in the Osirak program. Then, too, faulty equipment also made its way to Iraq, allegedly after Israel sabotaged it.

In the CIA, the folders on the scientists and the operations that led to their defection are given top secret code names that only a few people know. The notes are printed out on typewriters and stuck in folders covered with the letters RH (restricted handling), which means that only a select group of senior American officials can read its contents. Then an armed courier takes the folders directly to the offices of those individuals, usually including the head of the CIA, the director of operations, the national security adviser, the secretary of defense, and many times the president himself. Once each official reads the enclosed document, he or she signs his or her name on the respective folders and hands them back to the armed couriers who brought them.

One defector scientist the United States welcomed is Masud Naraghi. Currently living in upstate New York, where he runs a company that manufactures high-end industrial lasers, Naraghi came to the United States in 1958 to earn his PhD in nuclear physics from Case Western Reserve University. Mohammad Rezā Shāh Pahlavi later brought him back to Iran to launch the country's nuclear program.[37]

In the mid 1980s Naraghi met with German and Swiss businessmen who represented Pakistani nuclear scientist A. Q. Khan, who, the media has demonstrated, was running a black-market ring for the worldwide distribution, sale, and proliferation of nuclear technology. In 1987 Naraghi's work culminated in the procurement of blueprints for the P-1 centrifuge—based on an aluminum rotor— as well as a list of companies from which they could buy the necessary parts. By 1992, however, after he lost his post as head of the Iranian nuclear project, Naraghi walked into the U.S. Embassy in Bern, Switzerland. Several days later he was already undergoing intensive debriefings on American soil.

The importance of the Pakistani blueprints cannot be overstated. While it took Iran more than a decade to get the centrifuges working on an industrial level,

A. Q. Khan's materials gave Tehran the boost it needed to arrive at the nuclear threshold in 2010. His proliferation ring did the same for Libya, which in December 2003—likely feeling the pressure following the invasion of Iraq—revealed that it too had purchased nuclear components from A. Q. Khan.[38]

Regarded as a national hero, Khan has left no room for debate about what his and Iran's intentions were in collaborating on nuclear technology. In a 2009 TV interview, the Pakistani scientist said that if Iran succeeds in "acquiring nuclear technology, we will be a strong bloc in the region to counter international pressure. Iran's nuclear capability will neutralize Israel's power."[39]

Meanwhile, one of the more recent defections included one of Naraghi's assistants, who also had studied at a prestigious U.S. college. According to U.S. officials, another scientist who defected in 2006 was one of the designers of the P-3 and P-4 centrifuges that were installed at the Natanz enrichment plant and that began testing in 2008.

In 2008 the CIA turned another nuclear engineer who revealed details about the Qom facility, which Israel suspects was being built to enrich uranium to the high military-grade levels needed for a bomb. Another scientist who also defected had worked on the mysterious Project 111, which is the code name for Iran's military nuclear program. Still, little is known about the project's director, a scientist named Mohsen Fakhrizadeh-Mahabadi, but he is believed to be the brains behind Iran's efforts to manufacture a nuclear warhead.

"One scientist points to another and then another like a family tree," explained one former U.S. intelligence officer who was familiar with the defection work being done in the CIA. "It was like one big happy family."[40]

The Qom facility actually first appeared on America's satellites and NSA intercepts in 2006, about a year after Mahmoud Ahmadinejad was elected president of Iran. He had ordered a resumption of uranium enrichment after work had been suspended following the U.S. invasion of Iraq in 2003. Qom is the ideal location for a secretive site and represents everything the West has to be scared of when planning strategy against Iran. One of the holiest cities in Shia Islam, Qom is home to some of the greatest Shia scholars and texts as well as the resting place of Fātimah bint Mūsā' al-Kādhim, daughter of the seventh imam. It is also the city where Ayatollah Khomeini planned the Islamic Revolution before he was exiled to France in 1965. Thus, Qom is the ideal place to hide a facility to manufacture the highly enriched fissionable material needed for the Shia regime's bomb.

While careful, the Iranians' attempts to hide the plant did not succeed, but the CIA only discovered the true nature of the facility in late 2008. It learned the facility was supposed to contain some three thousand centrifuges to enrich uranium to military levels and was slated to become operational by 2012.[41] At the same time, Israel and the United States also learned that Iran was attempting to build a next-generation centrifuge, called the P-4, which is capable of spinning faster and enriching uranium in record time.

America updated its allies in Israel and some European capitals but decided to keep quiet about the new facility for a number of reasons, first and foremost that it hoped to prevent another embarrassing intelligence mishap, such as the erroneous reports of Saddam Hussein's weapons of mass destruction (WMD) that led to the invasion of Iraq.[42] As important was the fear that if Iran learned that the world had discovered Qom, then it would build another facility in an even more secret location that the world might not uncover.

"Sometimes it is better to let them continue thinking that we don't know about it so this way they won't feel the need to build something new that we won't know about," an Israeli intelligence official said in an interview with one of the authors.

Fears that Iran has built additional facilities have been the focus of Israeli, American, and European intelligence work for the past two decades. The construction at Qom represented the materialization of that fear. Some speculate it is likely only the beginning of Iran's construction program.

A centrifuge plant requires uranium hexafluoride (UF6), which is derived from refined uranium ore and produced at a conversion plant. Iran, therefore, would probably not risk diverting the UF6 from the known conversion plant in Esfahan, which the International Atomic Energy Agency has under supervision. As a result, Iran more likely planned to build or was already working on an accompanying clandestine conversion facility.[43]

"They likely do have additional facilities that we still don't know about," said former ambassador Uri Lubrani in October 2009 after the Qom revelation.[44] "This is based on past experience and taking into consideration that the Iranians are experts at deceiving the world."

Brig. Gen. Mike Herzog, a top aide at the time to Israeli defense minister Ehud Barak, had expressed this fear during an appearance before a Washington audience.[45] Referring to a "bomb in the cellar" and the possibility that Iran has a fully clandestine production line and enrichment program in unknown facilities, Herzog said, "We suspect that they will want to have some sites unknown to us. But, again, you don't know what you don't know. I can't rule out this possibility."

One scientist involved in exposing Qom was Shahram Amiri, an award-winning atomic physicist who worked at the heavily guarded facility near Qom. He was also reportedly a nuclear physics researcher at Malek-e-Ashtar University, a research institute closely associated with the Iranian military. The CIA apparently had approached Amiri when he accompanied Iran's representative to the IAEA during a trip to Vienna. A few months later, in May 2009, he went on the Muslim pilgrimage, the Haj, to Mecca—home to Kaaba, Islam's holiest site—and disappeared off the face of the earth.[46]

The Iranians took his disappearance hard. Foreign Minister Manouchehr Mottaki, known for his cynical ever-present smile, raised the issue with UN secretary-general Ban Ki-Moon.

"We have found documents that prove US interference of the Iranian pilgrim Shahram Amiri in Saudi Arabia," Mottaki reportedly told the Fars News Agency in October 2009. "We hold Saudi Arabia responsible for Shahram Amiri's situation and consider the US to be involved in his arrest."[47]

Meanwhile, during the summit of the Group of Twenty Finance Ministers and Central Bank Governors, known as the G20, in Pittsburgh in September 2009, American president Barack Obama, French president Nicolas Sarkozy, and British prime minister Gordon Brown hastily called a press conference. Apparently a one-line letter that Iran sent to the IAEA disclosed the existence of the second enrichment plant. While the letter did not include details, it prompted Obama, Brown, and Sarkozy to go public. "What has been revealed today is exceptional, following the enriching plant at Natanz in 2002, it is now the Qom which is revealed," Sarkozy said. In unusually harsh language, he continued, "It was designed and built over the past several years in direct violation of resolutions from the Security Council and from the IAEA."[48] Citing the need for "peace and stability," Sarkozy went on to threaten tough sanctions by December 2009 if what he called "an in-depth change by the Iranian leaders" was not achieved.

Despite the lack of diplomatic follow-up to the intelligence successes, the information that the Western agencies obtained from the defecting scientists was crucial and at the same time fascinating. The men provided the West with an insider's look into Iran's nuclear program and installations. Some of the information was later believed to have been used in an IAEA report in November 2011 that raised some of the most serious concerns ever regarding various experiments Iran was conducting that could only have a military application.

Possibly one of the greatest and most significant modern-day defections from Iran was that of the former deputy defense minister Brig. Gen. Ali-Reza Asgari.

A product of the Islamic Revolution, Asgari was reportedly born in the late 1940s in the town of Shiraz. He joined the IRGC following the 1979 revolution and in the early 1980s was appointed IRGC commander of Lebanon, positioning him in charge of Hezbollah activities as well. His climb to prominence came during the lengthy Iran-Iraq War, which ended in 1988. He eventually became something of a national security adviser for former president Mohammed Khatami and was later appointed deputy defense minister in 1997, a position he held until 2005 when Mahmoud Ahmadinejad was elected president of Iran.

At this point, Asgari is believed to have become disillusioned with the revolution. Removed from power and disenchanted with Ahmadinejad's policies, Asgari was a safe bet for the CIA, which succeeded in turning him.

He reportedly began spying for the CIA in 2005. In early 2007, fearing that his cover was blown, he used a business trip to Damascus to cross secretly into Turkey, where his handlers picked him up and spirited him out of the country. The operation took several months to plan and according to various reports involved Iranian dissidents and a complicated getaway from an Istanbul hotel. Some reports have claimed that the defection was a joint CIA-Mossad operation.[49]

"He is very high-caliber," former Mossad chief Danny Yatom said following reports of his defection. "He held a very, very senior position for many long years in Lebanon. He was in effect commander of the Revolutionary Guards there."[50]

Asgari was taken to a military base and immediately began his debriefing. In most cases, debriefings of Iranian defectors took close to a year, during which the scientists underwent what is called a "data dump" and provided information that went into the minutest details.

Department of Defense scientists who are members of the Red Team—a squad of nuclear scientists whose job is to see scenarios through the eyes of an enemy and could speak the same technological language as the Iranians—head up the debriefings. In some cases, they re-create three-dimensional computerized models of the facilities where the scientists worked based on their testimonies. Later these models can be used to build mock-ups for training the Special Forces and the U.S. Air Force in attacking the facilities.

The information that Asgari supplied began to leak out quickly. Asgari is believed to have provided key incriminating evidence regarding Iran's financing of the Syrian reactor, which Israel destroyed seven months after his defection.[51] He also told his interrogators about a covert Iranian program to enrich uranium by using laser beams held in a special weapons facility in the program's main enrichment facility in Natanz. Also conflicting reports circulated regarding the role he played in formulating the controversial National Intelligence Estimate of December 2007 that claimed Iran had suspended its nuclear weapons program. While some reports say he was the "physical" intelligence that brought about the change in the U.S. intelligence community's assessment, other reports assert that the information he supplied was not applicable to the NIE.[52]

The preparatory work required before approaching a scientist or someone in Asgari's position was extensive and took anywhere from a few months to a few years. Agents never approached the targets in their home countries. Instead, they met them when they went overseas, as they frequently traveled to attend scientific conferences or to meet with suppliers.

A good agent basically has to be a good salesman when approaching a target. "It is all about the pitch and the package that the scientists are offered that is usually too tempting for them to pass up," said a former American intelligence official who is familiar with the CIA's work.[53]

One scientist told a former American intelligence official of a secret meeting he had had with Iranian supreme leader Ayatollah Ali Khamenei. His detailed questions about the production of Natanz's centrifuges left no doubt in the Iranian scientist's mind about the mullah's direct involvement in the nuclear program that he officially heads.

Defectors sometimes differed on the progress of Iran's nuclear program. They were all clear about Iran's true intentions, however: the Islamic Republic was developing the bomb so it could one day attack Israel.

In most cases, work on turning a defector is coordinated between allied agencies such as the CIA and the Mossad. In one instance in 2006, according to a former U.S. official, the Mossad informed the CIA that it was planning to eliminate a particular Iranian scientist whom it had approached and tried to persuade to defect without success. The CIA immediately asked the Mossad to stop since the CIA had already scheduled a meeting with him in several days' time.

"They had failed to recruit the scientist and then told us that they were going to kill him, and we told them to back off," said the U.S. government official who was involved in the coordination with Israel at the time.[54]

The close cooperation entails sharing a great deal of the intelligence that the different agencies obtain. While most agencies do not reveal the source of their information to their allies, they do issue them what are called sanitized reports, which are "cleaned" of information deemed overly sensitive.

They also observe precautions even when dealing with agents from friendly countries. Off the lobby at the entrance of CIA headquarters in Langley, not far from the wall with the stars memorializing fallen agents, is a side room used for VIP visits. Here, CIA directors and top operatives meet with intelligence officials from other countries.

An urban legend that has made its way through the agency is that in the 1970s a Mossad delegation was invited to the building for a meeting. Afterward the agents swept the room for bugs and found one under the table where the Israelis had sat. Since then, the urban legend goes, Mossad representatives meet their American counterparts in safe houses off-site.

Whether the story about the Mossad bug in the CIA headquarters is true or false, Israel was caught off guard when the White House released the National Intelligence Estimate of December 2007. Entitled "Iran—Nuclear Intentions and Capabilities," the lengthy report stated that Iran had ceased its military efforts to manufacture a nuclear bomb in 2003. While uranium enrichment had since been renewed in 2005, the report's authors wrote that they assessed "with moderate confidence Tehran had not restarted its nuclear weapons program as of mid-2007."[55]

The report was nothing less than earth shattering and not only in the Bush administration. In Israel some officials in the Olmert government still hoped that in his last year in office President Bush would embark on one last military adventure in the Middle East—particularly against Iran's nuclear program.

The NIE rendered this prospect impossible. While Israel did not have assurances that Bush would attack Iran, they did not have any indication that he had decided to the contrary. The possibility, the Israelis had assumed, still existed. As one former head of Aman said quite frankly, "I was sure Bush would attack by May 2008."[56]

When the NIE, representing a consensus of all sixteen U.S. intelligence agencies, was released, all of the Israelis' assumptions went down the drain. The NIE's conclusion was even more surprising given that President Bush had said at a White House press conference in October 2007 that Iran needed to be stopped to avoid World War III: "We've got a leader in Iran who has announced that he wants to destroy Israel. So I've told people that, if you're interested in avoiding World War III, it seems like you ought to be interested in preventing them from having the knowledge necessary to make a nuclear weapon."

Taken by surprise, Israel launched a major diplomatic initiative to share its own assessments that Iran was indeed working on a nuclear weapon. Its one ally in the Bush administration was Vice President Dick Cheney, who sent a message to Prime Minister Olmert several weeks after the NIE's publication and claimed that it would not have an impact on the administration's decisions regarding how to handle Iran.[57]

Shortly after the report's release, meanwhile, Aman and Mossad officials met to see if maybe they had misinterpreted their own intelligence. After obtaining what one Israeli official called "hard copy" intelligence that backed up Israel's claim that Iran was pursuing a nuclear bomb, the government dispatched an intelligence delegation to Washington, D.C., with a classified dossier to try to convince the Americans that they were wrong. Less than a week after its publication, Adm. Michael Mullen, the chairman of the U.S. Joint Chiefs of Staff, visited Israel and attended numerous briefings on Iran.

Israel was convinced about the authenticity and veracity of its intelligence. "The evidence that we, in the State of Israel, have is such that I have no doubt that Iran is advancing towards a [nuclear] weapons program," Ilan Mizrahi, the head of Israel's National Security Council and a former deputy head of the Mossad said a week after the report came out.[58]

A week later, IDF Maj. Gen. Benny Gantz, then the newly appointed military attaché to Washington, D.C., said he believed the world did not appreciate the gravity of the Iranian threat. "The world understands [Iran is a problem] since they [countries] are holding talks and imposing sanctions . . . but I am not sure that it understands the severity of the problem and its urgency," Gantz said. While refraining from referring directly to the NIE report, he continued, "Therefore, one miss can put us it in a place with a different course of action and where the Iranians are already nuclear and only then will you want to take action."[59]

Avi Dichter, an Israeli cabinet minister at the time and a former head of the Shin Bet Security Agency, went a step further. "American misconception concerning Iran's nuclear weapons is liable to lead to a regional Yom Kippur [War] where Israel will be among the countries that are threatened," he said in the strongest rebuke of the U.S. report.[60]

Israel had constantly been updating its intelligence assessments on Iran per the flow of intelligence. In 2005, for example, when General Yadlin became head of Aman, the assessment was that the moment the Iranians obtained enough low-enriched uranium (LEU) to work with and extract from it the quantity of high-enriched uranium (HEU) needed for a nuclear bomb, the Iranians would make a run for the bomb. During its reevaluation following the NIE's publication, Aman came up with a new assessment on Iran's nuclear strategy that remained true through 2010. Based on new intelligence obtained and carefully analyzed in Tel Aviv, it indicated that Iran was looking to stockpile several tons of LEU, or enough so that when it decided to do so, it could make not one but several bombs.

"They want to have all of the necessary components so one day, when they perceive that the price they will pay for their violation will be low, they can break out and make the bomb," Yadlin said in November 2011.[61]

What concerned Israel most was that the NIE represented a direct break from all previous American assessments until its publication in December 2007 and demonstrated how politicized the entire intelligence business had become in the United States.

Adm. Michael McConnell (Ret.), the director of national intelligence and the man in charge of the office that produces the NIEs, had said in congressional testimony in February 2007—that is, as the NIE was being written—that Iran was seeking to develop nuclear bombs. "We assess that Tehran seeks to develop nuclear weapons and has shown greater interest in drawing out the negotiations rather than reaching an acceptable diplomatic solution," McConnell had told the Senate's Armed Services Committee.

The question for Israel thus came down to what exactly transpired between February and November—the month the report was finalized—that completely altered McConnell's analysis of the Iranian nuclear threat. According to some accounts, it was the result of a major CIA intelligence coup that included the successful penetration of Iranian computer networks and the obtainment of a so-called treasure trove of reports that detailed Iran's nuclear weapons program. The problem was that the Americans were suspicious of the material and could not determine if the Iranians had renewed the weapons program that had been in place before 2003.

At the same time, while Israel doubted the U.S. assessments, there was doubt in the other direction as well. In one diplomatic cable from March 2005 the U.S. ambassador to Israel at the time, Dan Kurtzer, said that Israeli intelligence assessments were based on "worst-case scenarios and may not match current USG [U.S. government] assessments."[62]

The U.S. government never explained the reason behind its assessment. By November 2011, however, it appeared that the world had accepted Israel's assessment, and the IAEA published a report that claimed Iran had developed and tested all of the necessary components it would require one day to build a nuclear bomb.[63]

Some Israeli officials believed that the NIE from 2007 was completely politicized. One was Finance Minister Yuval Steinitz, who at the time was a high-ranking Israeli parliamentarian, a former chairman of its prestigious Foreign Affairs and Defense Committee, and the serving head of its discreet subcommittee on intelligence. Three weeks before the report's release, Steinitz had led a delegation of Knesset members to Washington, D.C., and met with Vice President Cheney, National Security Adviser Stephen Hadley, and other assorted senators, congressmen, and administration officials. "No one mentioned a word about the new assessment," Steinitz said less than a week after the report came out in reference to meetings he held while in the United States. "If you ask me, it came to them as a complete surprise."[64]

Steinitz says he was convinced that the report was politicized and indicated that the American intelligence services were suffering from what he called the "Pendulum Syndrome." As he explained, the United States, on the one hand, was influenced by the trauma it had suffered after its blatant intelligence failure regarding Iraq's alleged WMD, and it did not want to be caught raising a false alarm again. Israel, on the other hand, was shocked by its failure to learn of Libya's nuclear program before Col. Muammar Gaddafi struck a deal in 2003 with the United States and abandoned it.

As a result of these traumas, both countries interpret the Iranian situation a little differently. Israel takes the more stringent track since "it is better to be safe than sorry," and America takes the more lax approach so as not to find itself in the midst of an unjustifiable war.

"In Iraq they [the Americans] made a mistake by overestimating," Steinitz said. "Now they are making a mistake by underestimating with Iran."

Another Israeli official went so far as to call the CIA the CPIA, or the Central Political Intelligence Agency, for inserting so-called political considerations that would prevent a U.S. attack against Iran into its intelligence assessments.

Whatever the truth is about the origins of the report, Israel became acutely aware that it would likely ultimately be alone in stopping Iran's race toward nuclear power. This remained true even in 2012 when the world was in agreement with Israel about Iran's true intentions and as international sanctions were, for the first time, targeting Iran's energy sector and banking systems and were having an effect.

A mere six months after the NIE came out, Israel flexed its military muscle to the world and demonstrated its will and firepower by sending a fleet of its most advanced fighter jets and support craft to fly nine hundred miles and over Greece—the same distance it would take to reach Iran—in what many viewed as a practice run for an attack. Israel's point appeared obvious: despite the NIE and its sabotage and espionage successes, Israel still retained a viable and realistic military option for stopping the ayatollahs from getting their hands on a nuclear bomb.

5

HAMAS: IRAN'S OTHER ARMY

June 2007 remains the turning point in Iran's love affair with Hamas. A year and a half after Hamas won the general elections that the U.S. government had imposed on the Palestinian Authority, Hamas violently conquered the Gaza Strip, becoming its exclusive ruler. The streets of Gaza emptied as armed Hamas terrorists with an easy finger on the trigger roamed the streets in search of not Israelis but their so-called Fatah brethren.

A local member of Fatah risked his life to tape a group of Hamas men capturing his party's members, taking them to the top of a three-story building, and throwing them alive off the roof. They tied up and shot others. Hamas members overran the hexagonal building in Gaza that had served as the Palestinian Authority's counterintelligence headquarters, which Israeli intelligence had thoroughly bugged.

Palestinian Authority (PA) officials in Ramallah were absolutely stunned as the vision of a united Palestinian state—combining the West Bank with the Gaza Strip—was being shattered right before their eyes. Later on, behind closed doors, PA president Mahmoud Abbas requested assistance from Israel to topple the Hamas government.[1] Word of this request was leaked to the media when immediately after Operation Cast Lead Abbas blamed Israel for a disproportionate military response.

The rest of the world was already discussing the Palestinians' self-destruction and the PA's ongoing internal struggles since Yasser Arafat's death in 2004, but Israel's defense establishment was busy dealing with a far more tangible danger. For the first time since Iran had begun its efforts to export the ideas of the Islamic

Revolution, its investment had paid off and generated real results. Without getting involved itself, Iran had taken over an area packed with activists full of anti-Israel sentiment and motivation. Dr. Yuval Steinitz, chairman of the Knesset's Foreign Affairs and Defense Committee at the time, called Gaza a "forward Iranian base." While Aman toyed with different scenarios with the aim of restoring Fatah's control in Gaza, Hamas and its patron, the Iranian Revolutionary Guard Corps, made it clear that they had no intention of surrendering their new territory.

The Israeli defense establishment was not prepared for Hamas's takeover of Gaza, according to a trove of diplomatic cables published by WikiLeaks. One cable dated June 11, 2007, summed up a meeting between Yuval Diskin, then the head of the Israeli Shin Bet Security Agency (the equivalent of the FBI), and Richard Jones, who was then the U.S. ambassador to Tel Aviv. Diskin said clearly that he did not believe Hamas was capable of taking over Gaza.[2] Another cable quoted the head of Aman at the time, Maj. Gen. Amos Yadlin, as saying that Israel would be happy if Hamas took over Gaza since then it could declare it "hostile territory" and Iran's influence would subsequently diminish.[3] Both Diskin and Yadlin were wrong. Hamas took over the Gaza Strip, and Iran set up another forward base along Israel's southern border.

Until June 2007, Iran had threatened Israel mainly through Hezbollah. The message coming from Tehran was that if Israel attacked Iran's nuclear program it would face a war of unbearable consequences from the north. This threat changed immediately after Hamas took over the Gaza Strip. Israel quickly understood that Iran was sitting not simply to the north but also in its southern backyard. The scope of the risk, intelligence officials concluded, rested in Iran's ability to arm the Hamas forces.

To understand this development one must first acknowledge Hamas's starting point. Approximately 1.7 million people live inside the 360 square kilometers of the Gaza Strip. One third live inside Gaza City itself, in the heart of the tense political climate, but the people are psychologically removed from the fighting and unaccustomed to the sights of Israeli tanks driving through the streets of the northern or southern refugee camps.

In the summer of 2005, Israel decided to withdraw from the Gaza Strip unilaterally, evacuating thousands of Jewish settlers and its military positions. Prime Minister Ariel Sharon's decision was based on a "carrot and stick" policy. Pulling out of Gaza would give the PA a large and open space to control, or the carrot. But if it attacked Israel from there, Israel would have the legitimate reason to respond aggressively with a very big stick.

This basic assumption was proven wrong already in the first week after the withdrawal. Resistance movements, such as Hamas, had no intention of granting Israel even a moment of peace and quiet. Kassam rockets, manufactured domestically in Gaza, began flying into Israeli towns in the western Negev, an already weak socioeconomic region. The Israeli government made threats, but for the most part, it refrained from taking real action.

In 2005 the terrorists inside Gaza created an internal division between the different populated areas. They only shot rockets out of peripheral settlements and made sure not to fire from Gaza City. Their refraining from launching Kassams from inside Gaza City did not mean that the city was void of terrorists. In reality it was full of hiding places where Hamas's upper echelons gathered. From these hideouts they plotted and carried out the border attacks and Kassam firing. While in hiding, they also continued to control the Palestinian security industries, or the factories and assembly lines that produced the Grad and Kassam rockets and would undergo a series of Iranian-supported major upgrades after Hamas took over the Strip two summers later.

With the encouragement of Damascus and Tehran, Hamas alternated between two different policies. The first preserved the calm with Israel. During this time, as in the summer of 2007 when it took over Gaza, its weapons were turned "inward." As soon as Hamas established its sovereignty, the calm with Israel ended and the weapons once again turned against the Israel Defense Forces.

On the eve of Operation Cast Lead in late 2008, the Hamas movement had two armed militias—the Palestinian police force, which Hamas took over from the Fatah government, and the movement's military wing, the Izz ad-Din al-Kassam Brigades. Hamas had planned to unify the two militias and create a mega terror force that it hoped would succeed in preventing the IDF from ever reaching the main Hamas strongholds deep inside the Strip.

The Palestinian police force had close to ten thousand men. They were all armed with light weapons, from old Kalashnikovs to M16 assault rifles stolen over the years from Israel. On November 27, 2008—the first day of Operation Cast Lead—the Israeli Air Force bombed a police graduation ceremony in Gaza City. Hamas later claimed that the IAF had attacked innocent policemen, but the IDF argued that many of the men had dual identities and served in the ranks of the Kassam Brigades. In their forays into Gaza before the operation, mainly after Hamas abducted Israeli soldier Gilad Shalit in June 2006, the Israelis spotted the policemen actively taking up their arms to fight Israeli soldiers.

Even before Hamas's violent takeover of Gaza, the IDF noticed that despite its limited resources, Hamas occasionally succeeded in tapping into the military's radio network and intercepted footage taken from reconnaissance drones. When the number of attempts continued to increase, intelligence officials remembered that Iran had begun its involvement in Lebanon in a similar fashion—that is, by providing intelligence and monetary support to Hezbollah. One of the biggest surprises the IDF encountered during the Second Lebanon War in 2006 was Hezbollah's broad intelligence coverage. For example, the IDF uncovered listening posts along the borders that contained Hebrew-Arabic dictionaries so the listeners could immediately translate and relay to headquarters what they had heard.

With Iranian-supplied technology, Hezbollah successfully intercepted telephone conversations, identified soldiers carrying radiophones, and tapped into secure networks. All this data was translated into precise artillery firing and sometimes direct hits. Guerrilla units have many intelligence advantages, including the ability to mobilize a civilian population and prevent large armies from obtaining vital information. However, alongside these advantages they suffer from limited resources and do not possess the intelligence-gathering systems that proper countries do. In Hezbollah's case, the Iranians' support compensated for its limited resources. Officials in Israel identified a similar process taking place with Hamas.[4]

At the beginning of Operation Cast Lead, Izz ad-Din al-Kassam had almost ten thousand operatives spread out in different areas in Gaza. The activists operated in a clear hierarchical mechanism similar to that of regular armies and were under the operational command of Ahmed Jabari.

Not much is known about Jabari, whose nom de guerre is Abu Mohammed. In a rare appearance he was seen in October 2011 escorting Shalit through the Rafah Crossing on his way back to Israel. In the 1980s and through the 1990s he spent about thirteen years in Israeli prisons. He became closely affiliated with the Hamas leaders who were also in prison at the time, including Mohammed Deif, his predecessor as Hamas's commander in chief.[5] Jabari, who is in his forties, used to be in charge of Hamas's fund-raising mechanisms. In the mid-2000s, after two of his predecessors were either killed or injured, he rose to power and took over the Hamas military wing, later leading the Hamas coup and swift takeover of Gaza in 2007. Afterward he became notorious in Israel and throughout the moderate Arab world.

Jabari then shifted the movement's focus to building the military's strength inside Gaza instead of carrying out attacks in Israel. He revolutionized the organization, changing its focus from serving as an underground terrorist group capable of small-scale, tactical-level attacks to acting as a small army with both offensive and defensive capabilities of larger, strategic proportions. To meet the challenge, Jabari embarked on an ambitious draft to increase Hamas's ranks and constructed a clear chain of command within the organization, establishing professional units with advanced weaponry. He also developed and organized training and exercise regimens.

He knew Hamas needed assistance and anticipated that it would come mainly from Hezbollah and the IRGC. The most significant change occurred right after the Second Lebanon War, when clearly Hezbollah had successfully stood up to the most powerful military in the Middle East and survived. Hamas began to think that it too could deter Israel with Iranian support.

"This is a fusion of ideas and operational capabilities," a senior Israeli intelligence official explained in a private conversation.[6] "The Palestinians are learning from Hezbollah which is learning from the Iranians who are developing additional means against Israel based on the operational experiments carried out by the organizations which fight against Israel."

Operationally, Hamas made significant advances. It began developing specialized professions: sniper units, antitank specialists, combat intelligence, tunnel diggers, infantry, antiaircraft, artillery, and even naval commandos who were supposed to work in cooperation with the coast guard. It then split the Gaza Strip into five sections, with each corresponding to a brigade. Each brigade had battalions, and each battalion had specialized units.

On another level, Hamas fighters continued to upgrade the local Gaza military industry with almost complete reliance on Iran and its continued supply of weaponry. On the eve of Operation Cast lead, Israel agreed to extend a six-month period of calm that was expiring even though it had been marred with hundreds of rocket attacks. The idea was to hasten a deal for the release of abducted soldier Gilad Shalit and to give the inhabitants of southern Israel a few months of quiet. Iran expressed its implicit consent to the process by refraining from ordering Hamas to launch an all-out attack, even as it increased its assistance to Hamas. The IDF's Southern Command later discovered that in only a few months, Hamas had managed to import large amounts of advanced antitank missiles and had made improvements to its domestic-made weapons.

Iran's support for Hamas is diverse and all-encompassing. Ahead of Cast Lead, Iran supplied Hamas with standard 122mm Katyusha rockets, which are more accurate and cause greater destruction than Hamas's homemade rockets. The Katyusha rockets have ranges of between 20 and 40 kilometers, allowing Hamas in 2008 to put a million people in their range. Israeli missile experts analyzed the 122mm rockets with a 40-kilometer range and discovered that they were identical to those Iran had supplied to Hezbollah and were fired into Israel during the Second Lebanon war.[7] By 2012, Hamas was believed to have established rocket production lines and storage centers in the Sinai Peninsula where they would be protected from IAF airstrikes under the assumption that Israel would not easily violate Egyptian sovereignty.

The IDF first noticed the fundamental change in Hamas's rocket capability in the beginning of 2008, or about nine months before Cast Lead, when Hamas fired eighteen long-range rockets into the city of Ashkelon, located south of Tel Aviv along the Mediterranean coast. They were modular 122mm rockets with a range of up to 20 kilometers. The difference between modular rockets and the Grad rockets that Hamas had previously used is that the motor is composed of four 50-centimeter sections. Only a few countries in the Middle East, including Iran and Syria, know how to manufacture modular rockets. Israeli intelligence assessed that Hamas used the modular rockets because they are easier to dismantle and therefore easier to smuggle into the Gaza Strip.

Iran also helped Hamas improve its mortar shell capability and stocked the Palestinian terror group with standard 120mm mortar shells, which are far more accurate and lethal than Hamas's homemade mortar shells. Hamas first used these updated shells in the beginning of 2008. An examination of the remains of a Hamas-fired shell into Israel on February 24, 2008, for example, indicated that it had been manufactured in Iran and was a copy of an Israeli military-industry mortar that the Israeli company Soltam Systems had supplied to the shah of Iran in the 1970s. The shell had an auxiliary motor that increased its range from 6 to 10 kilometers.

In addition to supplying weapons to Hamas, Iran regularly trains hundreds of Hamas terrorist operatives, who take courses for infantry, guerrilla warfare, sabotage, and antitank operations. The instructors belong to the IRGC, and some of the courses are taught in Tehran. Some operatives then return to the Gaza Strip, where they instruct new Hamas recruits, but those who excel remain in Iran for more advanced training, sometimes for up to six months.

One example was Alaa' Jihad Awad Abu Mudeif, a resident of a small village near the Gaza town of Khan Yunis. Before the IDF arrested him on April 15,

2008, Mudeif had been involved in rocket attacks against Israel and was slated to have been dispatched on a suicide bombing attack. During his interrogation he said that in May 2007, he was part of a group of operatives sent to Iran for training. The group left the Gaza Strip through the Rafah crossing into Egypt, and from Cairo the men flew to Damascus and on to Iran. Their passports were not stamped either when they entered Iran or when they left to conceal the fact that they had been there. They were sworn to secrecy and told to say nothing both about what they learned and about their contacts with Iranian intelligence personnel.

Once in Iran, he said, the men were transported to isolated military camps in a mountainous location. There they received extensive military training for about a month in navigation and how to use various weapons, such as light arms, machine guns, hand grenades, and antitank missiles, as well as assembling and detonating improvised explosive devices.

From a planning perspective, Israel, the IDF presumed, would need to eventually take action to counter the growing threat of a stronger Hamas. Defense analysts and former senior officers claimed that an IDF incursion into the Gaza Strip could not take place as quickly as it had after the 2006 abduction of Gilad Shalit. The media reported that the roads and paths leading into Gaza were heavily booby-trapped, and as a result a ground offensive would be extremely difficult and slow. However, the IDF claimed that it did not really matter how many explosives had been sent into Gaza because Hamas simply could not booby-trap all of the paths in a populated civilian area.

Nevertheless, under guidance from its Iranian patrons, Hamas found a creative solution to this problem by laying mines inside deep underground pits. The IDF identified diggings in areas where they were not needed for smuggling tunnels. It took analysts a few months to realize that these areas were "terror tunnels." Hamas would dig a tunnel, cover it, and, when the time came, fill it with explosives. Operatives then could detonate it by remote control. In some cases, they left tunnels with explosives inside them that Hamas field operatives could arm as soon as they identified the direction of the IDF's movement.

Hamas became experts at digging tunnels and pits, a system of warfare that Judean rebels used during the first century CE, Viet Cong fighters during the 1960s, and Hezbollah in its 2006 war against Israel. Hamas began by enhancing the Strip's tunnels in Rafah that it had used to smuggle goods during the 1980s. It continued to make improvements to the tunnels dug for terrorist attacks near the border fence with Israel and to the underground defenses and bunkers similar to the famous Hezbollah "nature reserves" in Lebanon. When Hamas assembled its defense doctrine, with assistance from Iranian instructors, it planned to have parallel tunnel systems for its offensive alignment as well as for booby-trapped defenses to stop an Israeli ground offensive.

The IDF became well acquainted with Hamas's offensive setup in 2008. Some tunnels were intended for sending in terrorists—as was the case in Kerem Shalom, where Gilad Shalit was abducted—and explosives tunnels were supposed to blow up anyone on top of them. What the IDF could not understand was the Hamas's defensive alignment.

The IDF identified mine pits dug on the outskirts of populated areas, on central roads, and in vital passages, but behind them Hamas had dug out an enormous network of tunnels that was supposed to make camouflaged guerrilla attacks possible. The information obtained from HUMINT heightened the IDF's fear of the surprises that Hamas was preparing in the event of an IDF land incursion. In February 2009, after the operation, the IDF published photos from a document that paratroopers had obtained showing an intricate network of tunnels in the northern part of the Strip. Hamas had dug all of the tunnels' entrances in entirely civilian areas. The outline of the tunnels was strikingly similar to North Vietnamese plans that had been sent to Gen. William Westmoreland during the Vietnam War.[8]

The IDF discovered most of the tunnels were on the eastern side, close to the Israeli border. Hamas carefully had planned the locations of their tunnels and sometimes even planted mines in them while still working. Most of the tunnel openings that the IDF uncovered during Operation Cast Lead were cleverly concealed inside closed homes. Hamas had also established a number of underground silos from which it could launch rockets by using a timer. This new capability gained importance after Operation Cast Lead in 2010.

Another component poised to create a shift in the balance of power was Hamas's growing antiaircraft capability. During the Second Lebanon War, Hezbollah succeeded in shooting down an Israeli helicopter transporting troops, a rare success in a battle against the powerful Israeli Air Force. As presented in chapter 2, the threat to Israel's air superiority has grown considerably in recent years, and by 2008, with Iranian assistance, Hamas was believed to have obtained a small but significant number of SA-7 shoulder-fired surface-to-air missiles. Prior to the next operation in Gaza, the IAF had already altered its flight patterns over the Strip under the assumption that Hamas was capable of shooting down helicopters or fighter jets.

In mid-2007, Brig. Gen. Yossi Baidatz, head of Aman's Research Division, walked into one of Israel's premier think tanks for a meeting with its top researchers. A career intelligence officer, the soft-spoken Baidatz knew most of the participants personally, and perhaps that familiarity is why he felt comfortable speaking openly, without reservations. Some of the researchers were former generals and diplomats, and two had commanded Aman. From the myriad of assessments and reports they had written, one would have thought that nothing could have surprised them. But Baidatz did.

After reviewing the threats facing Israel, Baidatz then went on to list the terrorist organizations that menaced their country. Iran, he said, supported each one. "This is how we recognize the globalization of terror," he told the small and intimate group.[9] To explain what he meant, Baidatz told the participants about a secret training base not far from Tehran. He tried to omit certain details so as not to reveal the source of his information. At this base, he said, the Iranian Revolutionary Guards Corps trains several different terrorist organizations simultaneously. The training covers all of the different fields an advanced terrorist must know: explosives, shooting, communications, reconnaissance, and mortar firing. The Revolutionary Guards even conduct classes on psychological warfare.

The base is divided into four quarters, with Hezbollah using one quarter, Hamas another, and Islamic Jihad another. The fourth rotates among the Iranians' other proxies, sometimes Iraqi militias and sometimes Taliban fighters. They follow a set schedule of prayers, meals, and training. At night they meet around a campfire, eating freshly roasted lamb and brainstorming ways to attack Israel and the United States. They also share stories of their personal exploits. A Hezbollah terrorist will take pride in how he took down an Israeli tank; a Hamas fighter will speak about laying a roadside charge. Both already have experience in identifying Israeli forces, and both have insights into what the next war will entail. Some of the Hamas men will remember their time at this camp as a period of indulgence, a hotel for terrorists. It is where the roots of the Hamas plan to escalate its conflict against Israel in the summer of 2008 took hold.

Operation Cast Lead began as a result of the *tahadiya* (truce) signed between Israel and Hamas in June 2008. During this period of calm, both sides were supposed to lay down their weapons. Instead, according to Israeli intelligence, the Revolutionary Guards used the opportunity to operate freely throughout Gaza. Their goal was to prepare the ground for the next conflict with Israel. For the Israelis who live in the south and had experienced daily rocket attacks, the truce was supposed to give them finally some peace and quiet. Unfortunately, most of the Palestinian terror groups in Gaza refused to accept Hamas's uncharacteristic concessions to enter a truce with Israel and continued to fire rockets into Israel's "backyard."

The artificial agreement between Hamas and Israel barely survived. On the second day of the truce Hamas claimed Israel breached the agreement when it fired at a group of men approaching the border fence. Hamas claimed that these men were innocent farmers, but Israel did not take any chances. Rockets and mortars fell from time to time in Israel, and in response, its blockade of Gaza continued.

On July 22, 2008, Shin Bet director Yuval Diskin arrived at the Knesset's Foreign Affairs and Defense Committee. Diskin had come up through the ranks of the Shin Bet as an agent in Nablus, then in Lebanon, and had even spent some time in the Mossad. He was considered an expert on Hamas and is attributed with mastering the art of targeted killings, that is, those assassinations of terrorist chiefs throughout the years of the Second Intifada and mostly in the Gaza Strip.

The purpose of Diskin's meeting was an annual review for the committee members. Just a few weeks earlier, several more rockets had been fired into southern Israel, despite the truce. Diskin looked straight at the committee members and said: "In Gaza there are already rockets that can reach Kiryat Gat and possibly even Ashdod and it does not matter how many times we attack there, we need to have a presence on the ground. We have excellent intelligence, but it does not help us because we cannot use it."[10]

It was the first time a senior Israeli official admitted that Hamas in Gaza, once a small terrorist group, had rockets and missiles that could reach almost half of the State of Israel. It was also the first time a senior Israeli official admitted that Iran was already in Gaza, with its capabilities and weapons.

"Personally," he said, "I opposed the truce in Gaza before the agreement, and I oppose it even now, because it strengthens Hamas and because in exchange for the calm, Israel did not demand an end to the smuggling and the return of Gilad Shalit. Hamas, on the other hand, got what it wanted."

Finally, Diskin presented the data that he had obtained: 222 tons of explosives, 10 million bullets, and dozens of Russian-made antitank missiles had recently been smuggled into Gaza. Diskin made sure not to say a word about the IRGC, which had sent antiaircraft weapons and Iranian instructors to Gaza, but many committee members knew already about the IAF's new safeguards when flying over Gaza.

On November 3, 2008, one of the Shin Bet's intelligence officers received concrete information about a tunnel that Hamas was digging from the al-Bureij refugee camp inside Gaza toward the direction of Israeli communities located right over the border.[11] Workers were seen entering one of the houses in the neighborhood and carrying out piles of sand. Commander of the Southern Command Maj. Gen. Yoav Galant, an officer who came up in the navy commando unit, approved a preemptive mission immediately. He understood very well that the population in Israel would have a difficult time accepting another kidnapped soldier.

One day later, loud explosions were heard in the al-Bureij refugee camp and in nearby Israeli communities. A unit from the IDF's Special Forces had been sent deep into Gaza to destroy the tunnel, which a small group of Hamas men had been guarding. The Hamas operatives fled after the IDF had hit a few of them. The IDF then destroyed the tunnel, removing a threat to Israel but at the same time providing Hamas with the excuse it needed to let loose its rocket teams and officially put an end to the so-called truce.

A few weeks later, Hamas fired more than sixty rockets into Israel, the most ever, in a single day. For the next two weeks the IDF failed to respond, and the Israeli media tried to decipher what Defense Minister Ehud Barak was thinking. The newspapers reported that IDF chief of the General Staff Lt. Gen. Gabi Ashkenazi was opposed to a counter operation, but the Kassams kept flying. It seemed as though Hamas was trying to demonstrate at any cost that the tahadiya had ended. Israel's minister of defense, a Labor Party member who had used the coalition to restore his old post, guaranteed again and again that the rocket firing would be met with a harsh response. But when the IDF did not counterattack, the media began to criticize him harshly. "A country is obligated to provide security for its citizens," argued those on the Right. In reality, however, the IDF had already begun planning an operation months before. The IAF had prepared a "target bank" of dozens of Hamas facilities, some built with Iranian money. Meanwhile, the Home Front Command, which is responsible for protecting and defending the civilian population, completed its inspection of bomb shelters in the south and ensured air sirens were in working order.

The security cabinet held long meetings and discussions, far from the media's attention. Ministers who were close to Prime Minister Ehud Olmert approved the operation; however, when an announcement was released to the press it seemed indecisive. In Israel, voices protesting the government's inaction were growing louder. Barak, a master of deception from his days in the Sayeret Matkal

Unit, opened the land crossings into Gaza, making Hamas think that Israel had no intention of initiating a military operation.

On Saturday morning, December 27, 2008, IAF jets took off from the Ramon and Palmachim Air Bases and headed toward the Gaza Strip. Within a few minutes and in an operation called "Birds of Prey," they crossed into Gaza and fired precise bombs at more than a hundred targets, which had been updated in the flight computers. In the first fleet were fighter jets, and immediately behind them were attack helicopters. In the first two air attacks they killed 155 Hamas men.

Later on, in subsequent attacks, the Israeli Air Force attacked almost seventy additional targets. At the end of that day, the Palestinians reported 270 dead and more than 700 wounded. These numbers would change drastically, however, by the time the United Nations appointed a commission of inquiry at the end of the operation.[12]

Operation Cast Lead continued the next day as the IDF carried out more aerial attacks deep in Gaza. The precisely targeted bombings stunned Hamas, which could not believe the extent to which Israel had succeeded in infiltrating the organization. But no one in the IDF's Operations Directorate rested, not even for a minute. Every known launch site for the Kassam rockets was recorded and almost immediately attacked.

During the early days of the operation, Israel targeted Hamas's arms infrastructure: rocket operators, launch pads, hidden ammunition storehouses, and underground passageways into launching areas. Palestinian sources reported that almost half of their concealed launching capabilities had been destroyed. Iran's enormous investment had been nullified, and the remaining launching equipment was difficult to operate owing to the surrounding destruction. In addition, the IAF struck the smuggling zones in Rafah, that is, the tunnels that passed from Egypt into Gaza. In a short air attack lasting only several minutes, IAF fighter jets destroyed forty tunnels in the area.

The army's next target was the Hamas leadership.[13] During the first round of bombing, the IDF hit Hamas's field commanders, and the "shock and awe" element of the initial aerial bombardment caught Hamas completely by surprise. But within a number of hours, the leaders had disappeared into underground bunkers. The IAF had flown 213 sorties (including 56 helicopter sorties) within two days. Hamas understood that the rules of the game had changed.

Prior to the operation, the inhabitants of the Israeli territory surrounding the Gaza Strip clearly saw that some exercise was about to happen on the ground. The IDF began preparing the agricultural fields around the Gaza Strip as its base for operations. Large encampments were erected, tents shot up as quickly as mushrooms, and massive trucks delivered tanks and heavy engineering equipment.

On December 29, 2008, two days after the air strikes had begun, the ground forces began spreading out in the field and awaiting an order. Sixty-five hundred reserve soldiers were called up. The IDF had learned its lessons of the Second Lebanon War, during which the government and the military had hesitated before calling up reservists or using ground forces, and applied them.

Israeli civilians from the region and from central Israel stood outside the army units' assembly areas, waving flags in support of the IDF. In one of the small towns near the Gaza Strip, the owner of a chain of coffeehouses from Tel Aviv opened a makeshift coffee stand and distributed free coffee and cake to the soldiers. The feeling in the air was that the war against Hamas was a fight for Israel's existence.

As soon as the order came in, the soldiers began marching forward. Artillery was aimed at suspicious spots near the refugee camps in central Gaza Strip. South of Gaza City, tanks from the 401st Armored Brigade passed the remnants of the old Netzarim settlement on their way to the sea. Despite the forecast of large numbers of casualties and the dangers of the ubiquitous charges and mines that Iran had supplied and the terrorists had planted along the roads, not to mention the antitank weapons and the underground traps, the Merkava tanks succeeded in crossing the Strip in less than five hours and effectively divided Gaza in two. The brigade prevented the passage of terrorists or weapons from one place to another.

Col. Yigal Slovik, commander of 401st Brigade, led the forces, knowing that all eyes were on him. The Armored Corps had lost much prestige during the Second Lebanon War when Hezbollah, with Iranian assistance, succeeded in hitting Israel's Merkava tanks, the highlight of Israeli defense industries. It seemed as though they had turned Israel's strong point, its heavy machinery, into a weak spot. Some in the Israeli media had termed the tanks "sitting ducks." But Slovik redeemed the brigade and the Merkava tank during Cast Lead. Despite encountering close to twenty antitank mines planted by Hamas, he succeeded in quickly crossing the entire Gaza Strip without losing a single tank or soldier. "The firepower with which we entered into Gaza, and the direct hits that we scored against the enemy, severely diminished Hamas's capabilities," he said.[14]

On the first day of the ground offensive, the IDF killed some forty terrorists. The rest hid in bunkers. While the IDF commanders had received extensive intelligence briefings on the widespread use of IEDs and booby traps through-out Gaza, they were constantly surprised by the sheer numbers. As the troops moved further into the built-up areas, they saw how Hamas used its explosives. Special units that penetrated deeply into areas evacuated of civilians reported seeing coiled ropes, gas containers, and stretched-out metal wires. The IDF had difficulty distinguishing real explosives from metal scrap. They disarmed those charges that they caught, and they destroyed others in the field. It was the IDF's Combat Engineer Corps' finest hour. Its members prevented many casualties, and at the same time, in labs back in Israel, they worked to identify the source of the materials. It all led back to Iran.

One night, a commando force surrounded a seemingly abandoned structure on the outskirts of Gaza City. Its white walls, beautiful ornaments, and gleaming windows indicated that people of means lived there. The deafening sounds of the nearby tanks made it virtually impossible to listen for people inside the structure. A stray dog startled the soldiers. Someone aimed his gun at it and mumbled that Hamas was even capable of sending suicide dogs.

The force commander stayed close to the structure's low fence and whis-pered to the lead soldier to call the bomb squad. According to intelligence, the building was supposed to be completely empty, without explosives. During the previous night military scouts had seen a person approach the building and exit it with a medium-size package. Intelligence had concluded that one of the residents who had fled earlier had returned to the house after dark to retrieve clothes and supplies for his family. The entire neighborhood had completely emptied out the night the IDF crossed the fence.

Colonel Slovik's armored brigade was visible everywhere. Despite the intel-ligence assessment that the house was clear of explosives, the force commander instructed a pair of bomb sappers to enter the structure and comb it.

Over the radio, the commanders at headquarters pressured the force to en-ter the structure quickly. "Outside the soldiers are exposed to gunfire, inside is safer," said the division's operations officer. Approximately thirty soldiers were thought to have obeyed and entered the building. The unit's bomb-sniffing dog ran ahead of the sappers, jumped wildly from wall to wall, and then stopped in its tracks. He began to bark. The specialists approached the dog and found two gas balloons attached with barbed wire to a detonation device.

"Bomb," one of the soldiers announced over the radio while signaling to the other sappers at his side. Within two minutes all soldiers evacuated the entire structure. The last to leave were the members of the bomb squad, with the neutralized device resting safely in a special pack they had brought along for the mission. In an inquiry conducted later, the bomb sappers explained that the bomb's charge could have caused the entire building to collapse, killing everyone inside. Operation Cast Lead produced many similar stories of disasters avoided and casualties spared.

After the operation in Gaza, the head of Aman Maj. Gen. Amos Yadlin explained that one of the IDF's most significant achievements had been preventing Hamas from obtaining a "victory image"—a kidnapped soldier, a bombed-out tank, or a downed helicopter. Their failure, Yadlin explained, was essentially Israel's success. Hamas had survived the operation but had failed to take it to the next level.

If during the Second Lebanon War the IDF was surprised to discover the quantities of antitank, antiaircraft, and even antiship missiles that Iran had sent to Hezbollah, Operation Cast Lead stunned the IDF with the amount of explosives it found scattered throughout Gaza. For two years, Hamas operatives sat with maps, analyzed every route and every street, dug mine pits, and scattered explosive charges in every spot they thought the IDF would step on one day.

An elite unit's company commander who operated in Gaza during Operation Cast Lead later said that during the fighting it was impossible to be around the forces without seeing soldiers from the Combat Engineering Corps' elite unit Yahalom. Dressed in their ceramic combat vests and protective helmets equipped with night vision goggles, they all had screwdrivers sticking out of their stuffed pockets.

Yahalom's headquarters is located in a base in central Israel. In the IDF they call the combat engineers *shahids* (Arabic for martyrs) since they go in front of the rest of the forces and are unprotected in the face of enemy threats. According to the IDF's fighting doctrine, the engineering forces always are the first to penetrate enemy lines. They are also the first to come under fire, the first to encounter IEDs, and the first to absorb the other side's antitank missiles.

It is a dangerous profession to "lie down on the fence" so that the mobilizing forces can enter enemy territory. "Dangerous, and gray, just like the color of our beret," explained one of the unit's commanders. In a calculated risk assessment prepared before the operation, the combat engineers were expected to suffer the highest number of casualties during the first days of fighting. In the end, the unit lost one soldier, who was killed while trying to locate IEDs that Hamas had planted inside a home in northern Gaza. The "brain" behind these fighters is the National Institute for Ammunition Research, where the IDF analyzes the products of Hamas and Hezbollah terror assembly lines. Army engineers study the charges and the fingerprints of their producers, trace the origin of the explosives, and determine the way they were assembled. Every IED brought in from the field carries a unique seal, engravings of its production line. The investigators know how Hamas works and the characteristics of Islamic Jihad's products and even those of independent IDF manufacturers. But their main occupation is studying the Iranian methods of assembling explosive devices.

A visit to the institute is similar to taking a tour of Israel's various war fronts. On one shelf sit rockets discovered during the 2006 Second Lebanon War. On another shelf are IEDs that were discovered in a Gaza hothouse as well as medicine grenades, or emptied drug bottles refilled with explosive materials. Next to the bottles are syringes that were supposed to be delivered to hospitals in Gaza. The bottoms of the syringes, however, had been cut and filled with gunpowder to serve as fuses in explosive devices.

In the past, Israel imposed restrictions on shipping materials and fertilizers that might serve the Hamas weapons production system, but the medical components were delivered directly before Operation Cast Lead itself and in humanitarian shipments that the IDF had initiated. In 2009, during a visit to Israel, U.S. chairman of the Joint Chiefs of Staff Adm. Michael Mullen brought with him analyses of IEDs that insurgents in Iraq and the Taliban in Afghanistan had used against U.S. and Coalition forces.

A comparative analysis of the IEDs and the firing mechanisms that the IDF discovered in Gaza and Lebanon in 2006 and 2009 revealed that while the IEDs did not originate from the same production plant, they were basically made in the same way. This conclusion confirmed that a larger force—Iran—was teaching most of the terrorist elements in the region how to manufacture improvised explosive devices.[15]

The IDF commanders' desire to expose the crimes Hamas committed and to fight the war without hurting innocent civilians was naive. Despite the IDF's enormous effort, the war could not be sterile, and the world would not refrain from criticizing Israel, no matter how hard Israel tried to avoid such criticism.

For example, 81 percent of the fifty-four hundred bombs that the IAF dropped during the operation were smart bombs. (During the Kosovo War of 1999 only 35 percent of munitions dropped were smart weapons.)[16] Using precision munitions was meant not only to increase the chances of success but also to avoid hitting innocent civilians. While Israel was mostly successful in its targeting accuracy, it still incurred international criticism.

Hamas, however, should bear much of the blame for Israel's inability to avoid civilian casualties. For example, videos taken by IAF drones showed Hamas gunmen using Palestinian children as human shields. Additional footage and intelligence showed how Hamas has established command centers and Kassam launch pads inside and next to more than a hundred mosques and hospitals during Operation Cast Lead, in direct violation of international law. During the operation IDF troops found a classified sketch of the village of Beit Lahiya in northern Gaza that detailed Hamas's extensive deployment of IEDs and snipers inside and adjacent to civilian homes. The sketch, together with several IEDs and Kalashnikov rifles, was discovered in a home that belonged to a Hamas agent.[17] And according to a previously undisclosed interrogation of a Hamas operative, one Hamas cell used a wagon on which children were sitting to transport rockets. In other cases, the operative said, Hamas fighters disguised themselves as women carrying babies to ensure that IDF troops would not target them.

The IDF has videos that back up the intelligence information. One declassified air force video dated January 6, 2009, shows a terrorist shooting at troops from a building's roof. After spotting an Israeli aircraft, the terrorist goes to the building's entrance and calls to nearby civilians to help him escape. A few moments later, a group of children arrive at the entrance to the home, and the terrorist walks out to them. Another video of January 13 shows a senior Hamas terrorist— again spotted by an aircraft—walking alone down a street. After seeing the aircraft, he runs over to an elderly woman walking nearby and continues walking next to her. Later, the IDF discovered that the "elderly woman" was also a Hamas operative in disguise.

One of the main principles of the Law of Armed Conflict is that the parties to a conflict should distinguish, at all times, between the civilian population and the combatants. On the one hand, Hamas clearly did not observe this difference when it fired thousands of weapons into Israeli cities.

Israel, on the other hand, made great efforts to minimize Palestinian civilian casualties—placing a quarter of a million phone calls to homes and cell phones in Gaza before airstrikes and dropping millions of pamphlets warning residents to flee their homes before invading—at the price of losing the element of surprise.

The Israelis even developed a new bomb that an airplane could drop on a rooftop and have the effect of a stun grenade. In other words, without causing any damage or injuries, it scared and chased people off the roofs of buildings they planned to bomb with explosives. The IAF called this new tactic roof knocking since the stun grenade on the roof literally knocked on the home and warned the inhabitants to leave. No other military in the world had developed and employed such means, but adopting this procedure made no difference for Israel on the international diplomatic front.

After the operation ended, the Palestinians claimed that 1,400 people had been killed and that two-thirds were civilians, mostly women and children. The IDF disputed the figures and said that 1,166 people were killed and that two-thirds of them were known terrorists.[18]

During the operation, the IDF had swept through most of northern Gaza, going in some villages door-to-door while searching for terrorists and weapons caches. Some soldiers later admitted that however unrealistic, they carried a hope, if only a glimmer, that behind one of those doors they would find their missing comrade Gilad Shalit, whom Hamas had kidnapped in a cross-border raid near Kerem Shalom on June 25, 2006.

In the end, they did not find him. Instead, Operation Cast Lead, which started with a massive aerial onslaught against Hamas terror targets in Gaza, ended with a complete withdrawal of Israeli forces from the Gaza Strip, except for Shalit, who remained in Hamas captivity.

Finally Hamas returned Shalit to Israel in a prisoner swap in October 2011. Israel received Shalit after releasing 1,027 Palestinian prisoners, including 279 people who were serving life sentences. He might have been returned much earlier had it not been for the Iranians' meddling.

During his five years and four months of captivity, Shalit had become a household name around the world in reference to the Israeli-Palestinian conflict. During his captivity his parents, Aviva and Noam, flew frequently to European capitals and met with world leaders. They hoped to raise awareness of their son's continued captivity and lobbied the leaders to increase pressure on Hamas. In a report that the Shin Bet Security Agency had submitted to Prime Minister Ehud Olmert in 2008, the agency claimed that Hamas in Gaza wanted to see their own men returned in exchange for Shalit but that someone else was blocking the deal. Israeli officials identified Khaled Mashal—the Damascus-based Hamas leader who had been saved from a Mossad assassination attempt in 1997 in Jordan—as preventing an agreement. Many more months elapsed before the Israelis identified the Iranians' involvement in sabotaging the deal as well. The IRGC did everything possible to prevent Hamas from achieving normalization with its neighbors. The Revolutionary Guards did not factor in the price that the Palestinian inhabitants of Gaza paid for the continuing unrest.

The Egyptian-mediated talks that ultimately led to Shalit's release were held in six rounds beginning in July 2011 The final deal was reached with Egypt's mediation. Israel understood Cairo's interest in securing Shalit's release was an attempt by the interim military-run government to show the world its strength although the country appeared to be in disarray and on the verge of governmental collapse following President Hosni Mubarak's downfall. By mediating the Shalit deal, Egypt was able to show that it still is a player with major regional influence. Egypt was also concerned with Hamas and even more so Hamas's founding movement, the Muslim Brotherhood. Egypt expected the Muslim Brotherhood would gain significant political power in the first elections scheduled following Mubarak's resignation. By striking a deal with Hamas, the Egyptian military hoped to gain some political influence over what happens in the Gaza Strip.

In the meantime back in Israel, the role Iran had played in the conflict was becoming clear. Operation Cast Lead showed how Hamas had become increasingly similar to Iran's other proxy, Hezbollah in Lebanon.

Moreover, Shin Bet chief Diskin's greatest fear had materialized: not only had Iran successfully supplied Hamas with long-range missiles, but also Hamas was firing them by the hundreds into Israeli cities dozens of miles from Gaza. Once assumed to be out of Hamas's range, additional cities in southern Israel—Beer Sheba, the capital of the Negev; Kiryat Gat; Ashdod; and Yavne—now found themselves in the line of fire. The Home Front Command had to deal with close to a million people, or a seventh of the entire Israeli population, being under threat from Hamas missiles. But even worse was that suddenly Israel's sensitive security and strategic installations that it had positioned in the southern part of the country were now in Hamas's range, or, in other words, Iran's range. Power stations, army bases, logistical centers, and facilities that Israel had never acknowledged existed, such as the Dimona reactor—all faced a clear and present danger.

Nevertheless, in a final analysis, when it came to intelligence failures, Hamas had made the greater miscalculation. Major General Yadlin was reminded of this situation the day after Operation Cast Lead ended when he entered his office in IDF headquarters in Tel Aviv. There, in the hallway leading to his secure bureau, where Israel's secrets are discussed daily, hang the pictures of Yadlin's fifteen predecessors as the heads of Aman since the State of Israel's establishment in 1948. On the photo-lined wall are well-known former generals, such as the country's sixth president, Chaim Herzog; Defense Minister Ehud Barak; and former chiefs of the General Staff Moshe Ya'alon and Amnon Lipkin-Shahak. But there are also pictures of five intelligence chiefs who were forced out of their positions prematurely. Some had provided inaccurate predictions that led to disasters, such as the Yom Kippur War in 1973. Looking at these photos, Yadlin confessed that he could not help but think about how Hamas, similar to five of his own predecessors, had inaccurately read its adversary—in this case, Israel—in the run-up to the three-week war.[19]

Since its violent coup d'état in the summer of 2007, Hamas had been preparing for a showdown with the IDF. To meet the challenge, Iran stepped in to assist, not only providing weaponry and money but also by creating a comprehensive defensive and offensive plan to fight Israel and strike deep inside its cities. The plan had three main pillars. The first rested on defensive structures and measures in Gaza, including dozens of kilometers of tunnels and bunkers, and thousands of roadside antipersonnel and antitank bombs planted next to booby-trapped homes. The second rested on giving Hamas an improved rocket capability and the third on obtaining a victory image in the form of a burned-out Merkava tank or another abducted soldier.

Despite the tens of millions of Iranian dollars poured into Gaza, Hamas's plan failed. The tunnels and booby traps were unsuccessful in stopping the IDF as it pushed into the Strip on January 3. As noted, the 401st Armored Brigade succeeded in crossing and cutting the entire Strip in half in mere hours. Hamas also did not exact a heavy toll through its rocket attacks. Though its missiles did hit cities within a 40-kilometer range, they went no farther. According to Israeli intelligence, the operation caught Hamas as it was finalizing plans to obtain rockets that could reach Tel Aviv.

During the operation, a convoy of trucks carrying long-range rockets that would have provided Hamas with the ability to hit Tel Aviv was making its way to Gaza through the Sudanese desert. The Israeli Air Force destroyed them. The two men responsible for the convoy were Gen. Qassem Suleimani, commander of the al-Quds Force, and Mahmoud al-Mabhouh, the Hamas operative in charge of smuggling (see chapter 4). Before the operation, Aman had predicted that Hamas planned to fire a hundred to two hundred rockets a day, but after losing most of its underground launchers and missiles in the air strikes, the average number throughout the three weeks of fighting was closer to forty daily.

Hamas would have been willing to overlook all of this bad news had it succeeded in creating a victory image. But it failed to accomplish this goal as well.

According to intelligence assessments, when predicting what Israel would do after the previous cease-fire expired, Hamas made five critical mistakes. First, it assumed, despite its intensifying rocket attacks, that the Israeli government would be paralyzed by general elections in March 2009 and would not launch an operation in Gaza. Its second mistake was to predict any operation would not include a ground offensive. Third, Hamas failed to anticipate that the so-called moderate Arab countries, such as Egypt and Saudi Arabia, would turn a cold shoulder and refuse to offer any support. Hamas's next mistake was miscalculating what the radical axis in the Middle East would do. While Hamas was certain that Iran, Syria, or Hezbollah would come to its rescue and open up a second front, none did. Its final mistake was misreading the Palestinian "street." Aman believes that many Palestinians became disenchanted with Hamas, blaming it for what they considered an unnecessary war and its subsequent devastation in Gaza.

By the beginning of 2012, however, Hamas had replenished its rocket quantities and obtained new and more advanced rockets, such as Iran's Fajr-5 artillery rocket capable of striking Tel Aviv. The Islamic Jihad terrorist group had also grown in size and, according to some intelligence estimates in Israel, was believed to have missile arsenals that competed with that of Hamas in their quantity and quality. While the Hamas and Islamic Jihad arsenals paled in comparison to Hezbollah's stockpile in Lebanon, in the IDF Gaza was considered Israel's most volatile front and one that could erupt at a moment's notice.

Iran, Israel understood, continued to help both organizations. Iran's strategy was simple: it wanted to duplicate the success it had in creating and building up Hezbollah in Lebanon and assist with fortifying Hamas and Islamic Jihad in the Gaza Strip. In the event that Israel attacked Iran's nuclear facilities, Hamas and Islamic Jihad were supposed to light up Israel's southern front as Hezbollah did the same in the north.

With Iran controlling the action from behind the scenes in Gaza and with Israel considering military action to stop the Iranians' nuclear program, by 2012 the possibility of a large-scale confrontation in southern Israel seemed to be not a question of if but simply of when.

NEPTUNE'S WAR

The navy commandos on the speedboats appeared exhausted even though the operation had yet to begin. It was November 4, 2009, and as the waves of the Mediterranean Sea crashed against their boats, the commandos hunkered down and held on tight. Their target was still ahead.

Despite their vast experience at sea, even the more seasoned commandos found it hard to sail waters with waves that were three to five meters high. The boats rocked back and forth under the force of the waves. The soldiers standing over the radar systems kept wiping off the splashing water to ensure their boats would not collide with any of the other vessels participating in the operation. They later said that it felt as if a giant hand had been pouring buckets of water all over them.

Lieutenant Colonel G., the commander of the mission,[1] chewed on something nervously. This mission was his first as the commander since returning to the navy from the "greens," the term used for the IDF's army or ground forces. For close to three years G. had commanded one of the IDF's most elite infantry battalions, the Givati Brigade's Reconnaissance Battalion. Toward the end of his term in late 2008, his men were sent into the Gaza Strip and fought against Hamas in Operation Cast Lead. He had barely had time to return to the navy and clean off the infantry dust, as they called it in the commando unit, before he was assigned to lead an operation that the top IDF brass defined as critical and urgent.

The purpose of the operation was to prevent smuggled Iranian arms from reaching Lebanon. G. was fully aware of the dangers involved in sailing at sea under such conditions and knew that waves only a few centimeters higher could capsize the ships. As an old seaman he knew that the forces of nature were stronger than any human enemy.

But the weather was not the only challenge on the commando's mind. His greatest worry was the uncertainty surrounding the commandos' mission and particularly the cargo aboard the *Francop* cargo ship, their target.

The young fighters knew the rules of the intelligence game well. On one side of the playing field Iran was working to strengthen its forward bases in Lebanon and the Gaza Strip that are manned by its proxies, Hezbollah and Hamas, respectively. On the other side of the field the entire Western world, with efforts spearheaded by Israel, was trying to stop this smuggling industry. Though the whole world was concerned about the transfer of weaponry to these terrorist organizations, when it came down to it, the real threat was to Israel—the only democracy in the Middle East and where the smuggled missiles would eventually fall.

The two small wars that Israel had fought since the summer of 2006—the Second Lebanon War that year and the Gaza War in December 2008—showed the political establishment in Israel that time was not on its side. Iran and the terrorist organizations had an endless supply of weaponry, and the terrorists were arming at an alarming rate with the majority of the weapons arriving by sea.

The Iranian smuggling industry, which Israel's intelligence establishment described as a "kingdom without laws," encompassed the Persian Gulf, the Red Sea, and the Mediterranean Sea. This range ensured that it could both safely import into Iran the components it required for its nuclear program and export advanced conventional weaponry to terrorist organizations prepared to lead the fight against Israel.

As far as the Iranians were concerned, the sea was the perfect platform for smuggling. Despite the organized registration of incoming and outgoing cargos at various ports, once a ship is at sea, its activity is easy to conceal. Additionally, a large freighter can carry equipment that no fleet of airplanes can. As opposed to the set flight routes and the increased worldwide aviation security since the 9/11 attacks, maritime regulations and laws are mostly seen as recommendations. The International Ship and Port Facility Security Code to regulate these matters went into effect in 2004, but most countries do not enforce it. This lack of enforcement leaves the seas wide open and almost completely unsupervised. The Iranian Revolutionary Guard Corps understood this laxity well.

The Iranians' smuggling method is quite simple. They hoist a foreign flag, preferably from a third world country with no organized record of freighter routes, over a large commercial freighter; hire a foreign crew for it; load it; and send it on its way. The ship's crew can usually estimate what the hold's contents are based on the ship's final destination, although sometimes they do not know even that information. The ship's captain, in some cases a confidant of the Iranian regime, is responsible for ensuring that no crate is opened during the voyage. Sometimes, to hide the trip's true purpose, real goods are stored in other compartments of the ship and unloaded along the way. The IRGC is responsible for providing this smokescreen. Greedy merchants, mainly from Eastern Europe and Africa, who are aware that dealing with Iran is problematic choose not to think too much about it and provide the ships and crews for a hefty fee.

In April 2010, Rear Adm. Rani Ben-Yehuda, chief of the Israel Naval Staff, reported on the navy's method of dealing with Iranian maritime smuggling. "It has been clear to us for quite some time that there are supply channels between Iran and the terrorist organizations in our region, mainly Hezbollah, but those in Gaza as well. It is also clear to us that large amounts of weapons reach the region, among other ways, by sea. Since we know who supplies the weapons and what their destinations are, we have increased our sea patrols as well as inquiries and inspections of suspicious sea vessels," Ben-Yehuda said.[2]

"But how do we know which of the hundreds of passing vessels is suspicious?" one of Ben-Yehuda's soldiers asked during that meeting.

Ben-Yehuda, who had led a number of successful missions to capture arms boats on their way from Iran to the Middle East, hesitated before answering. In his mind he pictured Iranian intelligence personnel reading his response in an intelligence briefing and modifying Iran's smuggling tactics accordingly. After a moment, he answered carefully: "On a regular basis we follow the routine: which ships sail, their ports of origin and destinations. Based on regular surveillance combined with intelligence, we identify potentially suspicious vessels and focus our attention on them."

Using civilian ships to transport military cargo has been a source of major concern throughout Western navies and intelligence agencies for years. International law makes it difficult for a navy to seize a ship carrying another country's flag. A clear and present danger must exist in order to allow for the takeover and confiscation of foreign equipment, whether it is food or Katyusha rockets. The only territory in which it is really possible for a country to stop a ship is in that country's own sovereign waters or its port, which, under international law, holds supreme authority.

Lawyers for the IDF, however, found a convincing argument to allow raids on foreign ships in the middle of the ocean. Weapons smuggling to Hamas and Hezbollah constitutes a clear and present danger to the citizens of the State of Israel; therefore, Israeli security forces are permitted to carry out searches while at sea and even confiscate such cargo. Israel makes a similar argument to justify its sea blockade of the Gaza Strip.[3]

The Israeli defense establishment first experienced this dilemma during Operation Noah's Ark in 2002. The Israelis boarded the *Karine A* in the middle of the Red Sea, between Saudi Arabia and Sudan, and far from the Gulf of Eilat and its naval bases. Israeli naval commandos approached the ship via small boats and helicopters. As speedboats came close to the side of the ship and helicopters hovered over the top deck, armed fighters simultaneously climbed aboard from their speedboats as others fast-roped onto the deck from the helicopters above. The ship's crew was taken by surprise and did not respond. Within seconds the entire ship was under the control of the Israeli naval commandos, who still had to prove that they had just cause for the violent takeover.

The intelligence that led to the operation was based on satellite images and from HUMINT. Information transmitted in December 2001 said that several tons of advanced weaponry had been loaded onto the ship at the Iranian port of Kish. The crew intended to deliver the cargo to Arafat's "unofficial" gangs of Hamas and Islamic Jihad, the main perpetrators of terrorist attacks during the ongoing Second Intifada.

Immediately after boarding the ship, the commandos began searching the cargo hold but at first found nothing, not even a shell. "Look in the containers," IDF chief of staff at the time, Lt. Gen. Shaul Mofaz, ordered the commandos via radio while relying on his counterpart from the Mossad who had provided the intelligence. The faces of everyone sitting around the table in the IDF command center were drained of color. Then they heard the voice of R., the raid commander. "We found it," he said, allowing all the generals to let out a sigh of relief.

While approaching the *Francop* in the Mediterranean Sea, Lieutenant Colonel G. and Vice Adm. Eliezer Marom recalled those stressful moments during Operation Noah's Ark seven years earlier. That mission had ended successfully and revealed Arafat's true intentions to the entire world. Until the weapons were found, however, the commandos encountered a similar dilemma to the one they were about to face as they continued to speed toward the cargo ship.

"Think about the implications of mistaken identity and go explain to the international community why the IDF intercepted an innocent ship in the middle of the night with helicopters, boats, and battleships," a senior navy officer who had participated in the operation explained in 2010.[4]

The IDF received its primary information about the *Francop* shortly before Yom Kippur, the holy Jewish Day of Atonement, in September 2008. When navy operations was choosing a name for the mission, the computer first suggested "Kol Nidrei," the name of the opening prayer of the fast day. Later on, after the operation was postponed, its name was changed to Four Species, symbolizing the Jewish harvest festival of Sukkot when Jews traditionally pray with the *etrog* (Hebrew for citron) and a palm branch.

The preliminary information that had arrived through the Mossad and Unit 8200, Aman's SIGINT branch, was incomplete. A senior Aman officer involved in the mission had defined it as "crumbs of information." In an attempt to obtain as much concrete data as possible, Rear Adm. Ram Rothberg, chief of navy intelligence who was appointed commander of the navy in October 2011, assembled a special team to oversee the intelligence efforts. Including representatives from Aman's Research Division, from the Mossad, and from Unit 8200, the team met once a week with Admiral Marom, the commander of the navy, and discussed the status of the intelligence and its veracity. An officer who had participated in the meetings compared it to "detective work—adding tiny pieces of information together in an attempt to complete the entire picture."

Among the participants in the discussion, an expert in international law stood out. Despite the air conditioners that whirred inside the room, all of the participants were sweating. The intelligence was scarce. While there was still a real chance that the ship was empty, the team needed to make a recommendation. All of those present understood the great risk Israel would be taking if it decided to carry out a military raid on a foreign ship.

Israeli newspapers at the time were full of speculations about the relationship between Israeli prime minister Binyamin Netanyahu and U.S. president Barack Obama, and the world had taken a cool approach toward Netanyahu's policies, particularly his aggressive stance on Iran's nuclear program. Israelis once again felt isolated in a hostile world. A military operation against an innocent ship would only add fuel to the flame that Israel's detractors had already ignited.

The final recommendation of those meeting with Admiral Marom could end up impacting Israel's diplomatic status in the near future. They made the recommendation to proceed, but the fear that they were committing a grave error hung in the air.

As late as fifteen minutes before the commandos boarded the *Francop* to inspect its cargo, senior Aman officials were still recommending that IDF chief of the General Staff Lt. Gen. Gabi Ashkenazi abort the mission. For them, the information was not conclusive enough to take such a huge risk. The chief of staff and his team listened to their arguments but decided to move forward. Their own experiences as soldiers and commanders taking part in navigation exercises had taught them that the greatest obstacle to succeeding in a mission was doubt. If the commander hesitated, then the soldiers also would begin to question their own capabilities. By now, the mission could no longer be stopped. Later on, Lieutenant Colonel S., one of the navy's intelligence officers, would recall: "There were a lot of suspicious indicators regarding the boat but not 100 percent certainty. The certainty only arrived after the commandos opened the containers. . . ."

A decision to abort the mission because of insufficient intelligence or to postpone it because of the weather conditions would have meant allowing the purported Iranian weapons to be smuggled right under Israel's nose. The ship was close to Lebanese territory, and an Israeli incursion into Lebanon would have been interpreted as an act of aggression that could have led to war. In a reality in which Israel and Hezbollah exchanged mutual threats at least once every few months, it seemed Israel could not afford to take this risk.

Ashkenazi once again opened the brown file on his desk. The top of the first page had big, bright red Hebrew letters on it reading Top Secret. On the dossier's first few pages were the bits and pieces of intelligence that had led to the operation and detailed the ship's course.

The weaponry was first loaded onto the *Visea* cargo ship at southern Iran's Bandar Abbas Port, which is also home to one of the IRGC's main bases. On October 9, 2009, the *Visea* left the port, carrying thirty-six containers and headed toward Latakia's port in Syria. On October 26, after crossing the Suez Canal, the *Visea* docked at the transit port of Damietta, Egypt, west of Port Said. The cargo was unloaded onto the Damietta dock, and on November 2 the German freighter *Francop* arrived at the port, loaded all the containers, and informed the port that its final destination was Syria.

At that point, the interagency intelligence team contacted Ashkenazi's office and requested his approval of a mission to seize the ship and its contents. While the intelligence fog was beginning to disperse, real rain clouds were beginning to form, the likes of which the Israel Navy had not seen in years.

The navy soldiers who presented the boarding plan had a measured sketch of the distances the commandos would need to travel to intercept the ship in time. According to the map, the *Francop* would have to pass through the Mediterranean Sea off Israel's coast to reach Syria. They explained to the chief of staff that as opposed to other raid operations in the past, this time the navy would have to sail west and then wait until the ship reached the area. Several more days would pass before they would receive word from Aman indicating that the *Francop* had left the Egyptian port and was beginning to head north. Navy commanders remained patient as the weather turned unstable.

On Monday, November 2, 2009, the team conducted one final review of the mission and the available intelligence at a navy base near the city of Atlit in northern Israel. Located on the Mediterranean coast, the base is overshadowed by an old Crusader's castle that juts out into the sea and is home to the navy's Shayetet 13, or the navy's commandos.

It was now or never, explained the operation's intelligence officer. One night remained to carry out the mission.

G., the commander of the force, walked into an office where the navy's commanding officer, Marom, was working. "The time has come to make a decision," G. said.

Admiral Marom looked out the window. Outside the skies were dark and gloomy. The rain was not letting up, and the short trees on the commando base looked as though they might be knocked over by the wind. "You're crazy," he said, "but I grant you permission to go out to sea."

"Call Lieutenant Colonel A. and we'll conduct a final briefing on how to handle the weather," he added.

"The storm had not yet reached its peak," Lieutenant Colonel A., deputy commander of a missile boat flotilla, recalled after the operation.[5]

Everything was very vague. We did not know exactly when the *Francop* would leave Egypt, how long it would take until we finished all our preparations or where we would meet up with it. We had taken into account all of the small details. In those water conditions, with waves five meters high, ships move slowly. Generally, sailing is not even permitted under such conditions. The *Francop* weighs 8,500 tons and is much more stable on the water than the Sa'ar-5-class missile ships, which weigh about 1,200 tons. As far as the direction of the wind as well, the *Francop*'s conditions

were better. According to our estimate, we would have to travel 110 miles
in order to meet up with it.

But the navy's problems did not end there. While the intelligence team was
trying to put together a final assessment of the situation, most of the navy's commando teams had been rushed to another mission. The only ones left were cadets
in the middle of their training—without any operational experience—and a small
number of commanders, who were supervising their training.

Later on Lieutenant Colonel G. would tell the press: "I had concerns. We
always prepare for the worst-case scenario: that the ship's crew would resist and
we would have to take over using force. The cadets were prepared to fight. In the
final briefing I stressed to them that this was not another exercise but was real
combat."

As the commandos walked out of their last briefing, they passed the memorial room where a plaque and picture hang for every commando killed in the line
of duty. About to embark on their first real operation, the commandos stole quick
glances into the room.

At 3 a.m., after completing their final preparations, they received the green
light to move ahead with the mission. Admiral Marom was still walking around
the Atlit base. He ordered Lieutenant Colonel G. to tell everyone to "go to sleep"
as they were set to leave the next day at dawn.

On Tuesday, November 3, 2009, two ships set out in the direction of the
Francop. Lieutenant Colonel G. was aboard the ship carrying the flotilla's sailing
gear, and A. was on the INS *Eilat*, a Sa'ar 5-class missile ship. At Shayetet 13's
command post at the base in Atlit, Admiral Marom and his deputy, Admiral Ben-
Yehuda, used two separate radio systems to oversee the two different operations
that were taking place simultaneously.

The voyage took almost ten hours. Under normal weather conditions it
would have taken three. The navy already had concerns that the commandos
would reach the cargo ship too late. But then the weather calmed down a bit, and
the navy's ships were able to reach the rendezvous point near Cyprus's territorial
waters, an area where it would still be possible to prepare for combat without
being discovered by any of the other countries in the region. A maritime patrol
plane with a powerful radar spotted the *Francop* sailing north. The pilot, who had
vast experience working with the navy, contacted the leading missile ship and
transmitted the *Francop*'s precise coordinates.

The soldiers put on their combat gear and stood ready for their first encounter with the enemy. No one really knew what awaited them on the ship and who would be there to greet them—civilians, terrorists, or IRGC officers. Everyone did know, though, that if they had been sent out on a mission under such bad weather conditions, there must have been a pretty good reason for it. The missile ships moved closer until they could make out the ship's profile with their surveillance gear.

At this point, representatives of the Foreign Ministry were brought into navy headquarters in Tel Aviv. They were available to put out any diplomatic fires that the operation might set. It would be their job to call the ambassadors of the relevant countries and calm them in case an error occurred during the operation or an innocent civilian or seaman was killed.

The lead missile ship was the first to make contact with the *Francop* on Channel 16, the international frequency. In contrast to Operation Noah's Ark, there was no point in sending the soldiers in the dark to surprise the *Francop*'s crew. This time they were close enough to Israel to take over the ship and receive support from the coast if needed.

The missile ship's commander called over the radio in fluent English: "This is the Israel Navy. I am requesting details about your destination and your crew." The captain of the *Francop* was an old Pole, a hired seaman. He had been through many similar ordeals over the course of his years at sea. He immediately asked: "Do you want to board?"

At this point the Shayetet 13 commandos were getting closer to the side of the ship on their speedboats. For the *Francop*'s crew, they must have been a frightening sight. The soldiers had painted their faces black, and they were aiming their guns at the ship. These men were not the type of inspectors the captain had encountered in the past. Though he had worked in Arab countries before, he had never come into contact with Israeli naval commandos.

On Lieutenant Colonel G's order, the commandos boarded the *Francop*, herded its crew in the ship's stern, and began searching for weapons. As during Operation Noah's Ark in 2002, all of the Israeli officers in the command centers in Tel Aviv and Atlit were standing by, biting their nails.

From the captain, the soldiers received a list of the ship's contents and bills of lading that documented the contents. The soldiers began opening various containers, especially the ones that originated in Iran and were destined for Syria. Lieutenant Colonel G. supervised the search. According to prior intelligence, the containers they were looking for were supposed to be in the ship's belly, deep in the storage rooms.

"I saw how the soldiers were opening the container, and that it was filled with sacks of polyethylene [a plastic material]," Lieutenant Colonel G. later recalled.[6]

> I stopped breathing for a moment. I thought to myself that there was nothing in them. The soldiers began taking apart the sacks, and then suddenly military crates appeared behind them, removing all doubt of what was in the containers. I opened the crates. Inside were munitions shells. I had been aware of the enormous pressure at Navy headquarters the night before. I had overheard the commander of the Navy on the phone with the decision makers, calming them down and supporting the operation. I knew that he had everything riding on this and I understood that I had better find something, that there had better be weapons on the ship. As soon as I opened the crate and saw the shells, I called headquarters using my satellite phone, and said to him: "Bingo."

Senior officials in the defense establishment, some of whom had been hesitant to approve the mission until the very last moment, were amazed at its great success. The scope of ammunitions and weapons found on the *Francop* was enormous, more than five hundred tons. This haul was more than ten times the amount that the Israelis had intercepted in January 2002 from the *Karine A*.

In the summer of 2010, after a number of similar top secret operations, the Shayetet 13 naval commando unit received two Medals of Honor from Chief of Staff Ashkenazi in a closed ceremony. The IDF awarded the medals as a result of the war against the Iranian smuggling industry, but the IDF did not allow the media to cover the event. "We may have been successful in some cases," a senior officer said, "but the cards are stacked against us. Hezbollah has turned from a guerrilla force into an Iranian-controlled guerrilla superpower."[7]

Israel conducted counter-smuggling operations not only against Hezbollah. They were as concerned with developments in southern Israel, where another Iranian proxy in the form of Hamas was quietly growing into a major threat in the Gaza Strip. Similar to what occurred immediately after the Second Lebanon War, the IDF's withdrawal from Gaza in 2005 was the signal the IRGC had been waiting for to rush inside the small strip of coastal territory wedged between Israel and Egypt.

Since Israel controls the coastline, weapons are smuggled into Gaza via tunnels underneath its border with Egypt. According to Israeli intelligence estimates, at least five hundred tunnels line the Rafah border at the southern end of the Strip. Each tunnel costs roughly $15,000 to build, but the investment pays off. The diggers own the license to the tunnel and rent it out for weeks, days, or even hours at a time. Everyone in the Strip—from those who simply want to visit Egypt to those who wish to start an independent terrorist organization—rents the tunnels.

Out of the approximately 1.7 million inhabitants of the Gaza Strip, 70,000 work in the tunnel industry. They work as diggers, organizers, smugglers, or traffic police on behalf of the Rafah clans, or *hamulas*. The Hamas representation in the south grants the licenses to the diggers, who are mostly children under the management of a Palestinian tunnels expert. It takes seven months to produce a kilometer-long tunnel. The more the network branches out, the longer the tunnel needs to be. Successful tunnels can generate tens of thousands of dollars in revenue on a single workday, but that tunnel's mining must be good, with lighting and sufficient infrastructure.

Israel tried to convince the Egyptians to crack down on the smuggling industry in the Sinai but to no avail. Eventually, the U.S. military donated advanced engineering equipment to Egypt, but the Egyptians put it in storage.

December 2008 was a turning point. Israel Navy ships captured on thermal cameras Palestinian smugglers transferring packages along the coastline, while Egyptian soldiers stood nearby, watching and smoking, and in some cases even assisting the smugglers. The IDF chief of the General Staff Ashkenazi decided to take action. He inserted the tapes into the Foreign Ministry's diplomatic pouch and sent them to the Israeli Embassy in Washington, D.C. The tapes' final destination was to have been the Congressional Committee on Appropriations. Ashkenazi knew some of the committee members personally from his previous job as director general of the Israeli Ministry of Defense, when he oversaw Israeli budget requests to the United States. His objective was to make the U.S. administration aware of Egypt's role in the smuggling. He had hoped it would use the foreign military funding that Cairo received from the United States—Egypt received about $1.3 billion annually since the 1979 peace treaty with Israel—as leverage.

The Israeli Foreign Ministry, however, learned of Ashkenazi's plot and stopped the tapes from reaching the Appropriations Committee; instead, they stored them in a safe in the Washington office of the IDF military attaché. The fear in Israeli diplomatic circles was that if the tapes were released, Israel's ties with Egypt would go from bad to worse.

The Israelis, however, were helpless. The politicians felt it was impossible to argue with a third world country to use its limited capabilities to stop smuggling. IDF officers countered, however, that if weapons were being smuggled into Egypt to be used to overthrow then-president Hosni Mubarak, the entire Egyptian Army would be stationed at the ports and on the outskirts of the Sinai, and the peninsula would be closed to travelers. Why did these capabilities disappear when it came to preventing smuggling into Israel?

After Operation Cast Lead, Western countries and Egypt changed their approach. Israel had created too much noise throughout the Arab world. It became impossible to ignore the need to stop the smuggling into the Strip.

Against the backdrop of Israel's thundering cannons in Gaza, the American administration and some European countries finally reached a number of understandings with the Israeli government about the assistance it required to stop the smuggling—understandings that should have been implemented years earlier. In December 2010, the IDF's Public Affairs Office revealed what the IDF had unearthed during Operation Cast Lead about the scope of Iranian smuggling to Hamas. Close to ten thousand rockets and missiles had traveled a complex route, the officers told the press, beginning in an Iranian factory and ending in a tunnel in Rafah or in one of the 160 villages in southern Lebanon.

Immediately after the Islamic Revolution in 1979, the West officially cut its commercial and military ties with Iran.[8] For the first time in years, Iran became completely dependent on its internal resources and production capabilities. Iran had abundant Western-made weapons systems, but spare parts were scarce and dwindling. Similar to other countries facing commercial sanctions, Iran developed an impressive weapons industry. Its purpose was to reduce its dependence on outside sources, or those countries that were willing to sign a deal one day but might dismiss it the next day.

This perception was proven correct particularly in 2010, when Russia froze the sale of its S-300 surface-to-air defense system to Tehran. When it was signed in 2007, the agreement seemed as if it was a clear act of Russian defiance of the Bush administration's policies on the one hand, and a good deal for Russia's economy on the other. In between, senior Israeli officials made countless visits to Russia. Prime Minister Binyamin Netanyahu and his Russian-born foreign minister, Avigdor Lieberman, tried to convince Russian prime minister Vladimir Putin and President Dmitry Medvedev in 2010 of the dangers in dealing with Iran, but it was actually the Obama administration that successfully convinced them to freeze the deal.[9]

By April 2010 it had become clear to the Iranians that the Russian defense system would not arrive. In response they revealed a new, domestically developed and produced air defense system called Mersad later that month.[10] The IDF, which had firsthand experience in dealing with the Iranian industries' weaponry during the Second Lebanon War, did not need to see the Mersad's unveiling. The war had amply demonstrated the advances that the Iranian industries had made in their antitank and land-to-sea missiles and antiaircraft weapons.[11]

The main problem Iran and particularly the Revolutionary Guards' al-Quds Force faced was how to export their successful products to their peripheral bases— that is, Iran's forward bases manned by Hezbollah in Lebanon and Hamas in Gaza—and to others. How could it export contraband materials when Western satellites photographed every suspicious crate leaving its seaports, airports, storage houses, and containers?

Gen. Qassem Suleimani, commander of the IRGC al-Quds Force since 1998, was entrusted with the task. Not much is known about Suleimani, other than he was born in 1957 in the town of Qom, but he is believed to have helped transfer long-range missiles to Hezbollah before the 2006 Second Lebanon War.

The IRGC had established al-Quds Force in the early 1990s to operate covertly outside Iran. The IRGC built the elite unit as an executing mechanism, that is, to export the Islamic Revolution outside of Iran. The revolution's ultimate goal is to abolish the evil of the West and of both its great Satan—the United States—and its ally, or the small Satan, Israel. Since this effort was a primary ideological interest in Iran, Iran's supreme leader appointed the force's commander and handed down the force's orders directly.[12] According to Western intelligence agencies, several thousand agents operate under General Suleimani. Most are Iranian, and the remainder are from other nations. The fighters' common traits were their knowledge of Arabic and their uncompromising devotion to the revolution.[13]

The first commander of al-Quds Force, Gen. Ahmed Vahidi, won Iran's greatest success thus far and exported the revolution to Hezbollah. According to a senior Israeli official, Vahidi assumed his job in 1990, parallel to the transformation of Hezbollah into an effective guerrilla organization, and ensured that nearly $200 million a year was transferred to Beirut to support the forces on the ground. In August 2009, Vahidi became Iran's defense minister shortly after Interpol issued an international extradition order against him for his involvement in the 1994 AMIA center bombing in Buenos Aires.

Hezbollah was and remains al-Quds Force's greatest investment, but General Suleimani directed the revolution and the smuggling networks to other areas as well. A report in the London-based *Asharq al-Awsat* Arabic newspaper claimed that Muqtada al-Sadr, an Iraqi Shia militia leader, visited Iran in 2003 and met with Suleimani. According to the report, al-Quds Force had set up training camps throughout southern Iran and along the border with Iraq to train the radical cleric's Mahdi Army. It also provided funding to the tune of millions of dollars.[14] On December 22, 2006, during the Coalition's Iraq War, U.S. forces arrested two of the al-Quds Force's most senior operatives—Gen. Mahsan Shizri and Col. Ahmed Dori—in Iraq.[15] Although both men were walking founts of intelligence information and their presence in Iraq should have been sufficient cause for alarm, the Americans decided to release them shortly after their capture.

At the end of February 2007, Adm. Michael McConnell, director of the U.S. National Intelligence Office, stood before the Senate and declared that Iran was producing weapons and that al-Quds was in charge of delivering them to Iraq. He estimated that smuggled Iranian weapons in Iraq had killed 170 American soldiers. A month later, in March 2007, two senior commanders from Muqtada al-Sadr's Shi'ite al-Mahdi army reported that hundreds of Iraqi operatives were being sent to Iran to train at al-Quds bases.[16] The Iranian mechanism that had successfully established Hezbollah had begun working fervently inside Iraq, preparing the ground for the day after an American withdrawal.

The Gaza Strip and the Palestinian terrorist organizations also featured prominently on General Suleimani's list of priorities. Since the end of the Second Lebanon War, Iran began sending assistance there, too, on a regular basis. In October 2006, Iran transferred $250 million to Hamas and set up al-Quds training camps in the Gaza Strip. They served as an alternative to the Revolutionary Guards' training centers in Iran, where jihadists from all over the world had been sent until then.[17]

Already in 2002, at the height of the al-Aqsa Intifada and the suicide terror campaign against Israel, Ayatollah Ali Khamenei—Iran's supreme leader and the man who had connected General Suleimani with Ramadan Shallah, leader of Syrian-based Islamic Jihad—said he would increase his investment in the organization and cover all of the costs of its suicide bombers. After the 2005 elections in Iran and Ahmadinejad's rise to power, Iran increased the amount of money it sent to Gaza. At that point Israeli Shin Bet chief Yuval Diskin, speaking before the Knesset's Foreign Affairs and Defence Committee, called the smuggling into Gaza a strategic threat to Israel.

Suleimani maintains, however, that the Islamic regime in Tehran requires Hezbollah, the Palestinians, and Iraqi insurgents as necessary defenses to protect Iran from an Israeli or Western attack.

At the same time, exporting the revolution remains a top priority for al-Quds Force. In 2008, there were signs of al-Quds activity in Afghanistan, Pakistan, Jordan, Egypt, Turkey, Chechnya, the Caucasus, and Bosnia-Herzegovina. With financial and training assistance, al-Quds Force made sure that the Islamic terrorist organizations worldwide would enjoy the close support of the Revolutionary Guards. The money and weapons that General Suleimani has sent to each organization was an expression of that unofficial covenant. But the more an organization became dependent on Iran, the stronger became its duty to obey Iran's orders in times of need.

In July 2010, Lt. Gen. Gabi Ashkenazi stood at the IDF's intelligence surveillance post on Mount Hermon, the northernmost point in Israel. Syria was sprawled out before him. Ashkenazi had arrived via a helicopter with an entourage to brief the soldiers stationed at the fort and to oversee the switching of forces there. The company commander, a twenty-five-year-old from the Golani Brigade, tried to answer the questions that the top IDF officer posed. Holding a cigarette and carrying a long rifle, Ashkenazi spent a lot of his week out in the field and served as a role model for the soldiers for how a combat soldier must carry himself twenty-four hours a day.

From afar, he could make out the outskirts of Damascus and a tall structure only 35 kilometers from where he stood. "Do you see that?" Ashkenazi asked the young commander. "That is the Damascus Airport, right under our noses."

Ever since the IDF withdrew from Lebanon in 2000, this airport has served as a central stopover in the smuggling route. Al-Quds Force loaded planes in Iran, landed them in Damascus, and from there smuggled the weapons in trucks across the border and into Lebanon. Gen. Qassem Suleimani, who enjoyed free access to the top Iranian command, was well aware of the Israeli surveillance and so from time to time he tried to trick the West and change the smuggling routes.

For example, after the earthquake in the city of Bam in southeastern Iran in December 2003, Suleimani secretly loaded some of the Syrian planes that had brought aid to Iran with advanced weaponry to take back to Syria. But the many flights could not continue without attracting attention. As Suleimani searched for a new land route, Recep Tayyip Erdogan's ascent as prime minister in Turkey signaled an opportunity. Although Erdogan came from an extreme Islamic background, he appeared to continue his predecessors' secular policies and strengthened Turkey's commercial ties with Israel. At the time, Iran was more of an enemy than a friend. Further, in May 2007, the Turks even reported that they had intercepted a shipment of Iranian arms intended for Syria that contained more than three hundred rockets. The cargo had been disguised as building materials and sent in a freight train. This smuggling method had been tried on at least two occasions before. The Turkish success, however, did not compensate for an earlier failure. Israel had supplied Turkey with intelligence information that Iranian cargo planes during the Second Lebanon War carried weapons. The Turks forced them to land in Turkey during the war; however, a search of the planes revealed nothing.

For the Israeli defense establishment this development was a surprise. The Israelis discovered the details later. Instead of carrying out a surprise takeover of the planes and confiscating the weapons, the Turks had sent Iran the message that they did not wish to be embarrassed. In other words, they asked Iran either to refrain from flying weapons or to change its flight routes. The Iranians understood and emptied the contents of their planes before they flew over Turkey.

This deception was the first sign that Turkey was becoming an important part of the smuggling route. A significant portion of the long-range rockets that arrived in Lebanon immediately after the 2006 war made their way through Turkey under the guise of civilian cargo. Instead of packed trains, the Iranians used innocent-looking trucks. Turkish intelligence, for its part, preferred to turn a blind eye to the problem. If it did not ask, then it would not know.

Another land-based smuggling route sets out from Iran to either Sudan or Eritrea by air or sea, and from there it continues by land to the Sinai Peninsula. In January 2009, Israeli Hermes 450 attack drones bombed weapons convoys in Sudan that were carrying long-range rockets to Egypt. The final destination of these rockets was Rafah. In the first convoy, seventeen trucks trucks contained dismantled Fajr-3 rockets.[18]

For Israel, these weapons were a breach of the balance of power in the region. Sources in Israel pointed out that Iranian al-Quds officers were waiting in Gaza for the shipment alongside fresh Hamas recruits who had recently returned from training in Iran. They were supposed to assemble the rockets, which were to be smuggled into Gaza in several pieces and would have been capable of reaching Israel's nuclear reactor in Dimona.

In February 2009, Suleimani reportedly tried again. As before, the cargo was unloaded in Sudan, where locals handled the smugglings. Arabic-speaking al-Quds officers oversaw the operation. According to Suleimani's plan, the Sudanese were supposed to hand the cargo over to Egyptian smugglers at the Egyptian border. The Iranians assumed that Israel would never attack there because of its fragile relations with the Egyptian regime; so from that point until Rafah, they thought the convoy would be secure.

Thus the second and third convoys set out under the surveillance of the Israeli drones. In this attack as well, Israel never officially admitted it had been involved. However, the defense establishment supplied the Israeli media with enough information for journalists to surmise that it was the case. A senior security official explained a month after the attacks that the main reason for choosing unmanned aerial vehicles for this type of mission was that vehicle convoys are usually "slippery" targets.

"When you attack a fixed target, especially a big one, you are better off using jet aircraft. But with a moving target with no definite time for the move, UAVs are best, as they can hover extremely high and remain unseen until the target is on the move," the senior official was quoted as saying.[19]

Additional bombings occurred in Sudan in December, 2011. They, too, were attributed in the Sudanese press to the IAF. The events in Sudan exposed the increasing scope of the various routes in the smuggling effort. Suleimani understood that every time his cargo touched land, it was in danger. The sea was and remained an ideal solution.

In the IDF, the navy has always been viewed as something of a "stepchild" to the rest of the military. Despite Israel's large sea border and its being a Mediterranean country, IDF commanders have always invested more in the ground forces and the air force than in the navy. The navy, in the meantime, developed slowly and not as dramatically as the other military branches.

On October 7, 1973, the navy took part in the first ever naval battle in which sea-to-sea missiles were used. The small army force aboard battleships arrived at the Syrian port of Latakia, positioned itself alongside the Syrian ships, and through the use of innovative tactics and electronic deception measures, wreaked havoc on the opposing Syrian forces. The sea battle proved to the world that the Israel Navy was up to par with the other branches in the IDF.[20]

While the navy attained its highest glory during the Yom Kippur War, nothing changed in the IDF, and the navy continued to receive a relatively tiny budget. It was the only branch in the military that had stronger competitors in the
surrounding Arab countries. It was not until Operation Cast Lead against Hamas
in Gaza that the navy was able to position itself as an integral partner in a land
battle. The navy not only laid siege to Gaza and prevented weapons smuggling,
but at the same time it also exercised sea-ground support while demonstrating a
close level of interoperability with IDF infantry units ashore. Finally, in 2010, the
IDF significantly increased its budget by tens of millions of dollars.

The Israel Navy is also undergoing an unprecedented procurement phase. By
2013, the navy is slated to receive two new Dolphin class attack submarines that
are being built in Germany to join the three it currently has. In December 2011,
Israel signed the contract for a sixth submarine that will arrive towards the end of
the decade. The navy was also looking to secure a budget for the procurement of
two new, next-generation missile ships, which, navy officers said, would put the
branch on another level in the Middle East.

While it took time for Israel's top defense brass to realize it, a strong navy is
integral for Israel's defense. Israel's sea lines of communication are a strategic asset for the small country and span the length of the Mediterranean and around the
Maghreb region of North Africa. Some 99 percent of all goods arriving in Israel
come by sea as well as more than 90 percent of its security-related supplies and
military hardware. Israel's coast is also lined with strategic installations, such as
power plants, ports, and oil refineries, and a significant percentage of Israel's 7
million people live on the coastal strip.

"The State of Israel is an island and our job is to ensure that everything that
needs to get in can get in and everything that needs to get out can get out during times of peace and also at times of war," Rear Admiral Ben-Yehuda said in
2010.[21]

The IDF only began to understand how valuable its sea-based platforms could be
after the Second Lebanon War in 2006. Until then, both the General Staff and the
Israel Navy perpetuated the problem by continuing to view the navy as a kind of
upgraded coast guard responsible for ensuring that terrorists did not succeed in
smuggling illicit goods by way of the sea.

The data that navy intelligence collected prior to the Second Lebanon War
supported this approach. Other than Egypt, which possesses a modern and ad-

vanced navy that is quantitatively larger than Israel's, Lebanon and Syria had small naval forces. Their glorious ships of the past were rusty. Further, intelligence assessed the Syrians' detection equipment, which was mainly land-based radars, to be only partially active because of poor maintenance and would not pose a real threat to Israel in case of war.

As a result, Israel's navy force was perceived as important only within a civilian-commercial context. Most international commerce is transported by sea. The volume of goods shipped by air remains negligible for strictly economical reasons. First, one medium-size ship can carry the contents of ten cargo planes. From a military context, if a country is interested in shipping weapons from one place to another, it will usually do so by sea rather than by assembling an airlift. For example, the *Francop* freighter's smuggled cargo of weaponry and explosives would have required nearly twenty Galaxy cargo planes to ship by air. The same is true for commercial goods.

Another component is the cost. Hiring a ship's crew is less expensive than a flight crew. Whereas flight crews consist of expensive manpower because of the prestige attributed to the profession, most commercial ships around the world employ citizens from third world countries who usually accept wages lower than what is accepted in Western economies but is still more than they would make at home.

Finally, as noted previously, those people interested in smuggling contraband goods have another reason to favor maritime shipping: while the 9/11 attacks led to a revolution in air traffic control and security, no critical event has occurred at sea that has led to radical changes in maritime shipping rules. A ship sailing for days waving the flag of a third world country and with a signed bill of lading has a small chance of being caught if committing illegal activity.

The first group to capitalize on this situation was the modern-day pirates, who understood that to generate large profits from small investments they could hijack ships, hide them, and collect money without the Western world being able to clamp down on them. This activity occurs around the Horn of Africa, a particularly crowded sea route, and has made piracy a problematic international phenomenon that the United Nations is trying to address.[22] The second group that learned to take advantage of the sea routes consists of elite terrorist organizations that receive support from General Suleimani, commander of the Iranian al-Quds Force. The Israel Navy, which in January of 2009 received compliments for its integration into the fighting in Gaza, now found itself facing a new and complex challenge: it must track down and stop Iranian weapons shipments to Hezbollah and Hamas.

Now a major player in the covert war against Iran, the Israel Navy serves as the long arm of the IDF. Far from the headlines of the Israeli media, the navy soldiers have become welcome guests in the hallways of General Staff Headquarters in the Kirya.

Tracking down arms shipments from Iran requires patience and endurance. Mistaken identity could lead to a raid on an innocent ship and cause a diplomatic incident, thereby escalating tensions throughout the entire Middle East. The key to tracking down suspicious ships and making correct identifications has always depended on intelligence, but who could take responsibility for civilian ships coming from Iran, bearing foreign flags, and sailing in the direction of Iranian allied countries while carrying suspicious cargo? How could anyone verify that the cargo was indeed prohibited?

Intelligence agencies devised several methods for working out this issue. The Mossad and the IDF's Aman had already accumulated more than a decade of experience collecting information on Suleimani and al-Quds Force. As far as they were concerned, they only needed to sharpen the focus of the intelligence gathering directed at southern Iran's Bandar Abbas Port, an IRGC base from which most of the weapons ships set sail.

Navy intelligence requested and received a direct communications line to the specific departments that dealt with Iran. Now all it had to do was fish for information. But it quickly became clear that this task was not simple. The air force, despite its enormous resources, could not simply stay in the air to conduct long surveillance over suspicious ships. The satellite department, which worked in conjunction with Aman, the IAF, and the IDF's C4I Directorate, was already busy with planned missions for the coming couple of years. So, as far as Israel was concerned, following freighters along a sea route was impossible. Thus the navy was left following the Mossad's sources along with anything that Western intelligence agencies chose to share from information they had already accumulated on Iran's illicit activities.

Meanwhile, as the Obama administration tried to hold talks with Iran and the United Nations tried to impose sanctions, General Suleimani was constructing the largest shadow fleet in naval history. General Suleimani's rationale was simple. If the rest of the world was watching Iranian cargo ships because of sanctions, he needed to transform these ships into other ones. All it took was to hoist a different flag on them—preferably from a third world country—and hire foreign crews and send them on their way. To coordinate this naval smuggling effort, Suleimani needed vast knowledge of the seas and enough ships that could transport the cargo under other countries' flags. The solution he found was the Iran Shipping Lines (IRISL), the national shipping company, which served as an excellent platform for smuggling materials in and out of Iran. But Suleimani went too far, and in 2008 the United States blacklisted IRISL and all of its 123 ships.

Britain also joined the boycott of the IRISL, prompting the Iranians in the port of Bandar Abbas to search for ways to bypass the West's sanctions. In the autumn of 2008, Iranian ships began sailing with German, Hong Kong, and Maltese flags. From there the path to working with third world countries that had no maritime regulations was short. They changed the names of most of their ships —at least 90 out of the 123—thinking it would be the perfect cover to fool the average sea official. Thus the freighter *Mufateh* became the *Diplomat* and afterward the *Amplify*. When this tactic did not help, the Iranians changed the ownership over the ships. German and Maltese shell companies replaced the IRISL. Out of 123 ships only 46 officially remained under the ownership of the IRISL, and in January 2009, the IRISL transferred the ships to three new Iranian companies in an effort to fool the West.

A comprehensive *New York Times* study revealed that all of these companies were closely tied to the IRISL. Some were owned by the same shareholders, and some even used IRISL employees. The companies' data showed that they were simply fronts, but the countries that had imposed the sanctions were fooled. The aliases prevented the world from stopping the new/old ships.[23]

In March 2011 Suleimani tried his luck again, this time with the MV *Victoria*, a 179-meter-long cargo ship flying a Liberian flag. The ship had departed from Mersin Port in southern Turkey and set a course for Alexandria, Egypt. The Israel Navy then seized the ship as it sailed near Cyprus. According to intelligence the Mossad and Aman had received, the ship was carrying containers on its deck that had been loaded at Latakia, Syria, the week before. Latakia is one of Syria's primary ports and is also the site of a newly built Russian navy base. Although Israel had tried to stop the deal, the Russians were scheduled to bring supersonic P-800 Yakount cruise missiles there in mid-2011 to upgrade Syria's antiship missile capabilities.

When the navy commandos boarded the *Victoria*, they were looking for three of the shipping containers that had been loaded aboard in Latakia and were supposed to be delivered in Alexandria. Their cargo certificates said they held lentils and cotton, but when the commandos located them on the upper deck, they were sealed with heavy locks. After breaking them open and pulling out a few rows of sacks, the commandos discovered a number of crates that had "Made in Britain" stickers pasted to them.

The first few crates contained mortar shells of various sizes and regular ammunition. After pushing deeper into the containers, the commandos found the real jackpot—six Iranian-made Nasr-1 antiship radar-guided missiles, with a range of 35 kilometers and a 130-kilogram explosive warhead, and two of the British-made radars that are used to guide them. Had Hamas been able to use these missiles in the Gaza Strip, they would have forced the Israel Navy to move its operations, which are only a few kilometers from shore.[24]

Finding such missiles en route to Gaza clearly demonstrated Hamas's and Iran's nerve. This Syria to Egypt route also raised the IDF's concerns about how the Sinai Peninsula will play into Iran's smuggling schemes. In the past, Israel tracked ships as they sailed through the Red Sea and unloaded weaponry in Sudan or Eritrea that then went by land to the Egyptian-Gaza border. In this case, the ship was loaded in Syria, sailed north to Turkey, and then went south again to Egypt. This new route led Israeli intelligence officials to believe that the stopover at Mersin was a ploy to draw attention away from the ship.

The battle against Iranian arms shipments to Syria, Hezbollah, and Hamas is made possible by an unprecedented level of coordination between Israel and its allies, primarily the United States. Israel is also a member of Operation Active Endeavor, a NATO counterterrorism mission based in Naples, Italy. There, at an international command center, officers share intelligence information on ships possibly involved in terrorism and weapons proliferation that are sailing through the Mediterranean Sea. In 2009, Israel asked NATO also to send a missile ship to participate full time in the mission. By the beginning of 2012, the request had yet to be answered, mainly due to Turkish opposition.

While in recent years the different players in the Middle East have boarded thousands of ships traversing the Mediterranean and questioned their crews, Israel ultimately only trusts its own forces when it comes to carrying out such operations. In January 2009, the U.S. Navy boarded the *Monchegorsk*, a ship carrying a Cypriot flag sailing in the Red Sea. It discovered illicit material aboard the ship but could not detain it owing to a loophole in international maritime law.

Cyprus decided to intervene, and as the ship passed the country, the Cypriot Navy detained the ship and brought it to port. There, officials discovered that the IRISL had chartered the *Monchegorsk*, which was carrying artillery and tank shells and raw materials to manufacture rockets. Its final destination was Syria.

In October 2009, the *Hansa India* ship left Iran flying a German flag. U.S. soldiers discovered it was carrying eight containers filled with bullets and industrial equipment that could be used to manufacture weapons. These containers were also intended for Syria.

Since early 2009 the Israel Navy has intercepted hundreds of suspicious vessels. Even if the successful interceptions do not significantly alter the next battle in Lebanon or Gaza, they serve to embarrass Iran and expose its intentions. For instance, Hezbollah and Hamas are not the only organizations that Iran supports. In October 2009, Yemen announced it had seized an Iranian ship, the *Mahan 1*, carrying a wide range of ammunition intended for Shiite rebels in the country.

Despite these successes, the Israel Navy's chances of stopping the giant smuggling machine were slim. Beyond the direct military activity at sea, it needed to establish a deterrent. To that end, in 2009 and 2010 Israel began to publicize its naval presence in the Red Sea. In June 2009, the navy leaked to the press that its submarines and Sa'ar 5-class missile ships had crossed the Suez Canal into the Red Sea. The purpose of the exercise was to demonstrate regional cooperation as well as an Israeli presence in areas where Iranian ships were active.

The passage of submarines held another meaning as far as the Iranians were concerned. Israeli submarines are reported to have the capability to carry cruise missiles with nuclear warheads and represent Israel's second-strike weapons. Israel's message was that it could reach any place where Iran was operating, including, if necessary, the port of Bandar Abbas in southern Iran.

7

ATTACKING IRAN

The briefing room will be packed when the prime minister takes his position at the podium and asks everyone to sit down. As the young pilots stare up at their nation's leader, the prime minister will gaze into their eyes, searching for one more confirmation that he has made the right decision.

While clearly nervous, the pilots are ready. They have prepared for this day for the past few years, some of them from the beginning of their Israel Defense Force service. The prime minister does not have much to say.

"This is a historic day for our small nation," he will announce. "Some seventy years ago Nazi Germany tried to destroy our people, but we survived and succeeded in establishing the State of Israel. It is now up to you to ensure that we will continue to survive and live here."

Then the rabbi for the Israeli Air Force will stand up at the podium, and all of the pilots will cover their heads. Together they will say the Traveler's Prayer, a short plea to God written at the time of the Talmud, to ask that they make it to their destination and return safely.

At once, the pilots stand and salute the prime minister, the defense minister, and the IAF commander. Minutes later, they climb inside their aircraft and begin lining them up along the runway.

The prime minister had actually made up his mind to attack Iran several months earlier but had waited, hoping to coordinate the operation with the White House. While the president tried to persuade Israel to back down and even threatened to cut military aid, the Israeli leader explained that he was not asking for his permission. Instead, the prime minister asserted, he was doing what allies do and

informing the president of his government's decision ahead of time. The Israeli
cabinet had spoken: Iran's nuclear program had to be stopped.

When and if Israel makes such a decision, nothing will ever be the same for Israel. While some Israelis hope that Iran would follow the Syrian and Iraqi model
and restrain itself as those two countries did after Israel bombed their nuclear
reactors in 1981 and 2007, respectively, the chances of Iran's not retaliating are
understood to be slim. Instead, Iran likely would unleash its full wrath against
Israel and call on Hezbollah, Hamas, and possibly even Syria to join the fray.

There is another alternative: Israel does not attack and allows Iran to become
a nuclear power. This option would spell the end of the Nonproliferation Treaty,
paving the way for other countries to break their agreement and forever altering
the balance of power in the region and possibly throughout the entire world. Israel would live under a constant threat of nuclear annihilation. Other countries—
Turkey, Saudi Arabia, and Egypt—would also pursue a nuclear capability.[1]

While Iran in 2012 was the gravest threat to the Jewish state, that situation
wasn't always the case. Until Mohammad Rezā Shāh Pahlavi was overthrown in
1979, Israel had diplomatic ties with Iran and even sold the Iranians weapons.
Had it not been for Ayatollah Ruhollah Khomeini's Islamic Revolution, Israel
might have sold Iran its most advanced long-range Jericho ballistic missile.[2]

Iran's nuclear ambitions, however, are not new. The shah started the program
in the 1950s, but when Khomeini took control of the country, it turned from
peaceful to dangerous. The facilities were severely damaged during the Iran-Iraq
War in the 1980s, but the Iranians worked quickly to rebuild them. Most notable
among Iran's leaders involved in the nuclear program was Akbar Hashemi Rafsanjani, the president of Iran from 1989 until 1997, who is sometimes described
as the "atomic ayatollah."

After becoming president, Rafsanjani openly appealed to Iranian nuclear
scientists who had fled the country following the revolution to return home. Before the revolution, the Atomic Energy Organization of Iran had employed more
than forty-five hundred scientists. After the revolution, barely eight hundred were
left.[3] When Rafsanjani's appeal did not have the desired effect, he was forced to
look elsewhere for nuclear assistance. His quest eventually involved China and
Russia, but possibly his most important contact was the founder of Pakistan's
nuclear program, Dr. Abdul Qadeer Khan. Rafsanjani and Khan met on two occasions and worked out agreements that allowed Iranian scientists to undergo

training in Pakistan and to procure advanced centrifuge designs and equipment needed for Iran's uranium enrichment.[4]

In a 2009 television interview, Khan openly admitted to assisting Iran's nuclear program. As noted in chapter 4, he also explained why Iran wanted nuclear weapons—to develop a strong regional bloc and to "neutralize Israel's power."[5]

Khomeini's death in 1989 heralded a new era in Iran's pursuit of nuclear weapons under his successor as supreme leader, Ayatollah Ali Khamenei. According to U.S. intelligence analysts, Khamenei plays a key role in Iran's nuclear program and is intimately familiar with technological developments sometimes down to the fine details. One Iranian scientist who defected to the West told of a secret meeting he had with Khamenei who asked questions about the production of Natanz's centrifuges to such detail that left no doubt regarding the mullah's direct involvement in the nuclear program that he officially heads.[6] An extreme radical, Khamenei also has called Israel a "cancerous tumor that should be cut" from the Middle East.[7] When Iran begins building a bomb, it will be after Kahmenei makes the decision to do so.

Israel throughout the 1980s was focused on a completely different country in the Middle East. Back home, the IDF was busy putting out the flames of a Palestinian uprising called the First Intifada and had its eye on Saddam Hussein's Iraq. During the 1991 Gulf War, Hussein had made no secret that if the Coalition invaded his country, he would respond by attacking Israel.

In response to the dangers Iraq posed to Israel, the Israeli government invested in preparing the country for possible missile attacks. In 1992, a year after the Gulf War ended, Israel was still focused on Iraq and even hatched a plot to kill the Iraqi leader, planning to send its elite Sayeret Matkal to infiltrate the funeral of Saddam Hussein's uncle. (A mishap during preparations for the mission, which killed five soldiers, eventually led to its cancellation.)[8]

At the same time, some Israelis began to sense a new threat, greater than Hussein's, brewing in Iran. One of the Israelis raising the alarm was Ephraim Sneh, in 1992 a new Knesset member with the Labor Party. Sneh had retired from the IDF following a thirty-year career during which he had served as the commander of the Israeli Air Force's 669 Search and Rescue Unit and was one of the commanders of the medical team during the legendary Sayeret Matkal's rescue operation in Entebbe, Uganda, in 1976. After only a few months in the Israeli parliament, Sneh says he "discovered" the Iranian nuclear threat.[9] Thus he submitted the Iranian question as an issue to be raised during debates in the plenum. A few weeks later, on January 26, 1993, Prime Minister Yitzhak Rabin himself approached the Knesset podium and for the first time in Israeli history declared that contrary to popular thinking at the time, Iran was a greater strategic threat to the State of Israel than Iraq was.

Aside from a handful of defense officials, most of the Israeli defense establishment had difficulty coming to terms with this new development, according to Sneh. Seven years later, Sneh, who had become the deputy defense minister, asked Prime Minister Ehud Barak for permission to oversee Israeli efforts to stop Iran's nuclear program. Barak granted his request.

In this new role, Sneh assembled a forum of senior intelligence analysts from the Mossad, the Shin Bet, the Foreign Ministry, and Aman to begin drafting operational plans for how to stop Iran. Some of the recommendations were of a diplomatic nature; others included plans for military and covert action. One of the officials on the team was Uri Lubrani, the former Israeli ambassador to Iran and a longtime advocate for supporting opposition groups in Iran as a way to overthrow the regime.

In January 2000, the forum submitted a large dossier to Prime Minister Barak with detailed plans for stopping Iran. Shortly thereafter, Barak was ousted in elections, and Sneh was replaced at the Defense Ministry. The fate of the dossier remains unknown.

Six years later, Sneh was again appointed deputy defense minister under Amir Peretz, the union leader turned defense minister. One of the first things Sneh did was to determine what had become of the plans for stopping Iran that he had submitted in 2000. He found that some of the operations had been set in motion right away and were still under way, but others had not been launched. For this reason in late 2007 when he announced his decision to leave politics, Sneh issued a stern warning for the people of Israel: "I am not satisfied with the funding that is being allocated to the defense establishment and the IDF to deal with the Iranian threat. We do not have all the resources needed to deal with the Iranian threat."

Sneh felt the Israeli government was neglecting both offensive and defensive capabilities. He thought systems such as the Arrow should have been higher on the government's list of priorities, and he believed it should have procured long-range ballistic missiles such as the LORA, which an Israeli company developed for strategic penetration of enemy territory. Under pressure from the air force, the IDF decided not to purchase the LORA. Apparently the Israeli Air Force felt that the IDF's general use of long-range accurate missiles would make the air force's capabilities irrelevant.[10]

In the nearly two decades since Rabin's declaration about Iran, the Iranian threat has continued to grow. Sneh has become an outspoken pessimist and a self-declared alarmist regarding a nuclear Iran. If Iran is allowed to go nuclear, Sneh warned, "most Israelis would prefer not to live here; most Jews would prefer not to come here with their families; and Israelis who can live abroad will. People are not enthusiastic about being scorched."[11] Thus the danger, Sneh continued, was that Iran would "be able to kill the Zionist dream without pushing a button. That's why we must prevent this regime from obtaining nuclear capability at all costs."

A military option was a last resort, he said, adding that a "last resort is sometimes the only resort."[12] Israel, he says, cautiously, is capable independently of striking Iran's nuclear facilities and causing significant enough damage to set back the program by a number of years.

"When Israel wants to do something it knows how to get it done," he said.

Many perceive Israel—the only country in the world to have successfully destroyed two nuclear reactors—as abiding by the Begin Doctrine. Named for Menachem Begin, prime minister during the 1981 strike on the Osirak reactor in Iraq, the comprehensive policy calls for using military force to deny its enemies nuclear weapons.[13] With its bombing of Osirak and Syria's al-Kibar reactor in 2007, Israel showed the world that it was not dependent on international support when considering launching a military action to stop a rogue state from obtaining WMD. Following the 1981 bombing, Israel came under harsh criticism, including from its closest ally, the United States. While Israel discussed its intentions and plans with the White House ahead of the 2007 strike, neither the United Nations nor the International Atomic Energy Agency in Vienna spared Israel from criticism.[14]

"The real issue is what is at stake and is it worth international condemnation. It seems that, in many cases, [Israeli] leaders are willing to take the risks," according to IDF Gen. Shlomo Brom (Ret.). He was one of the authors of Israel's revised national security doctrine that was compiled in 2007.[15]

Born in postwar Switzerland in 1945 to a pair of Austrian refugees who had fled Vienna on their wedding night in 1938, Louis René Beres is a professor of political science at Purdue University and an expert on international law. He is also one of the first academics to conduct a thorough review of Israeli nuclear policy.

Zalman Shoval, a former Knesset member who became ambassador to the United States, came across his work and invited him to the embassy in Washington, D.C. Shoval later took Beres to Jerusalem and Tel Aviv and set up lectures for him before the IDF's top brass and members of the Likud Party.

In 2000, only months before Shoval left Washington, Beres suggested putting together a "brain trust" to study the dangers Israel faces from weapons of mass destruction and to make recommendations for the policies Israel should set particularly in face of a nuclear Iran. "If you create it, I will support it," Shoval told Beres.[16]

With Beres serving as chairman, the group consisted of Israeli and American scholars and former military officers. It included Isaac Ben-Israel, a former Israeli general who served as the head of the IDF's research and development directorate, and Dr. Adir Pridor, head of the Hebrew University's Institute for Industrial Mathematics and a founder of the IAF's Operations Research Branch.

They called their project Project Daniel. The name "Daniel" was an interesting choice. The name of one of the later books in the Hebrew Bible, Daniel was a Jewish leader during the exile in Babylon following the destruction of the First Temple in Jerusalem. He is famous for being thrown into a lion's den and surviving. An Israel in the midst of a lion's den was on the authors' minds when choosing the name for their project, but they also could not ignore the believed location of Daniel's tomb, near the city of Shush in western Iran.

After two years of meetings, mostly in hotel conference rooms in New York and Washington, the team had completed its report and submitted it to Prime Minister Sharon in 2003. A grand strategy for how Israel should defend itself and prevent its enemies from obtaining nuclear weapons, the report's basic conclusion was that a policy of mutually assured destruction, which had prevailed between the United States and the Soviet Union during the Cold War, would never work between Israel and Iran. Nor would economic sanctions work against Iran. Instead, the group recommended that Israel needed either to adopt a policy of preemption, which basically calls for using military force to stop Iran's pursuit of a nuclear weapon, or to let Iran go nuclear.

According to Beres, "Recognizing the dangers of relying too heavily upon active defenses such as anti-ballistic missile systems . . . Project Daniel had advised that Israel take certain prompt initiatives in removing existential threats. These initiatives included striking first (preemption) against enemy WMD development, manufacturing, storage, control and deployment centers."[17]

Sharon approved of the recommendations, which were later presented to his successor, Ehud Olmert, and the IDF chief of staff at the time, Moshe Ya'alon.[18] The Israeli government, however, never officially codified or adopted the report.

Such a policy may exist in practice, as demonstrated by Olmert's decision in 2007 to bomb the Syrian reactor at al-Kibar. After taking office, Olmert set up a special forum of former Israeli prime ministers to discuss existential threats such as Iran and Syria. The forum recommended that he discuss each threat individually with the president of the United States in private. As shown in chapter 4, Olmert followed this advice before bombing the Syrian reactor. Clearly it was an act of preemption even though on a much smaller scale, particularly with regard to its regional ramifications and potential fallout, than a proposed attack on Iran.

But even if a policy as outlined in Project Daniel exists, it does not always mean that Israel will be capable of implementing it. An attack on Iran's nuclear facilities is not a simple operation and is not comparable to Israel's two previous strikes against the Syrian reactor in 2007 and the Iraqi reactor in 1981. In those two cases, the reactors consisted of one main facility that was above ground and lacked advanced air defenses. The same cannot be said of the nuclear facilities in Iran, which has learned from Iraq and Syria and has carefully concealed its facilities and spread them extensively throughout the country.

The feasibility of attacking Iran, if one ignores political considerations, is based on two primary military questions: First, does the military have the required intelligence to locate and identify its targets? Second, does the military have the operational capabilities required to carry out the mission? Operational capabilities have to take into account not only the ability to reach, bomb and destroy the targets but also the ability to overcome the resistance that the strike package will encounter, such as enemy aircraft and surface-to-air missiles

Assessments in Israel are split regarding these two questions and whether Israel can live with a nuclear Iran. One school of thought believes that Iran is bent on destroying Israel and that once it obtains a nuclear weapon, it will not hesitate to use it against the Jewish state. Iran's pursuit of the weapons is all about destroying Israel, according to this line of thinking.

The other school of thought believes that Iran is as it seems—a complicated, convoluted nation with varying and sometimes conflicting interests. While Supreme Leader Ayatollah Ali Khamenei may call for Israel's destruction, he is believed to be more rational and pragmatic than President Ahmadinejad and to have a more global perspective. Ultimately, this school of thought argues that Iran's program is motivated by national interests aimed at increasing its influence in the Middle East and not simply about destroying the Jewish state.

During his confirmation hearings in the U.S. Senate in 2006, Secretary of Defense Robert Gates gave his explanation for why Iran is pursuing nuclear weapons. While Ahmadinejad's denial of the Holocaust and calls for Israel's destruction should not be ignored, he said other elements in Iran, more senior than the president, wanted a nuclear capability for deterrence and not offensive purposes. "While they are certainly pressing, in my opinion, for nuclear capability, I think that they would see it in the first instance as a deterrent," Gates said. "They are surrounded by powers with nuclear weapons: Pakistan to their east, the Russians to the north, the Israelis to the west and us in the Persian Gulf."[19]

Israel's intelligence assessments regarding Iran's nuclear program have evolved over the years. In 2005, when Maj. Gen. Amos Yadlin was appointed head of Aman, its Research Division's assessment was that the moment Iran had obtained enough low-enriched uranium to turn it into the high-enriched uranium required for a single bomb, it would do so. In 2008 the assessment changed after Israel obtained new intelligence that indicated Iran first was working to obtain a significant amount of LEU—possibly close to ten tons—and then planned to go to the breakout stage and start enriching to the higher levels required for numerous nuclear weapons. By 2012, Iran had installed close to ten thousand centrifuges in its main uranium enrichment center in Natanz, although only about half were being fed uranium hexafluoride.

"They do not want to have just one bomb," explained a senior Aman officer in mid-2010. "They want to be able to create a number of bombs so they can test one, flaunt one, and claim to have several more in the storage room."

Israel again updated its intelligence assessment in late 2011. In interviews, senior Aman officers said that Khamenei was the man who would make the decision when and if Iran would move to the breakout stage of its fuel enrichment and enrich uranium to military-grade levels. When and if that stage happens, Iran will be able to make a crude nuclear device in anywhere from six months to a year.

Iran has always paced the growth of its nuclear program based on the effect that dramatic developments would have on the international community. In 2003, for example, when the United States invaded Iraq, Iran suspended its enrichment of uranium, but it restarted some two years later out of fear that it was next in line after Iraq and Afghanistan.

In 2010, Iran agreed in principle to transfer about half its stockpile of LEU—twelve hundred tons, or approximately the amount from which one can extract the twenty-five kilograms of HEU needed for a bomb—to Turkey. While the transfer never took place, its initial acceptance came as the world increased its pressure on Iran. The UN Security Council that June had passed a fourth round of sanctions pertaining to Iran. It imposed new restrictions on Iran's import of conventional arms, banned activities related to ballistic missiles, imposed a framework for inspecting suspicious cargo and aircraft, increased pressure on banks to sever ties with companies connected to Iran's nuclear program, and expanded the list of Iranian individuals and entities whose assets would be frozen.

Meanwhile, that same month, CIA director Leon Panetta estimated that it would take Iran about two years to build a nuclear bomb if it decided to do so. Panetta touched upon a point of disagreement between Washington and Jerusalem at the time. While the United States believed Iran had yet to make a political decision to make the bomb, Israel argued that it already had.[20] By early 2012, though, the Israeli intelligence community fell in line with the American assessment, agreeing that Iran had yet to make the decision to build the bomb but that once it did it would take about a year to have an operational device.

"The consensus is that, if they decided to do it, it would probably take them about a year to be able to produce a bomb, and then possibly another one to two years in order to put it on a deliverable vehicle of some sort in order to deliver that weapon," Panetta said in an interview with CBS's *60 Minutes* in January 2012.

One senior Israeli defense official warned that Iran could actually follow in the footsteps of Israel, which maintains a strong policy of ambiguity regarding its own nuclear capability, neither denying nor confirming that it has the weapon. "Ambiguity could be what they are really after," the official said in late 2011.[21] "They will build the bomb without making any announcements and then one day, when it is comfortable for them, they will present it to the world."

A major turning point in the world's assessment of the Iranians' nuclear program had come in February 2008 during a meeting that IAEA deputy director general Olli Heinonen convened at the agency's headquarters in Vienna.[22] At the meeting, Heinonen, a Finnish nuclear scientist who had monitored the Iranian nuclear program for decades, presented a small group of diplomats with images, diagrams, and copies of Iranian manuscripts that all showed Iran had lied. Its nuclear program was not purely for peaceful purposes.

Heinonen had saved the highlight of his three-hour presentation for last, a three-minute film produced in Tehran, likely for senior political leaders. Similar to a trailer for a Hollywood feature film, it used the theme music from the 1982 Oscar-winning *Chariots of Fire* to accompany footage of a computer-simulated explosion of a missile warhead. Heinonen pointed out that the explosion in the film, carried out at an altitude of six hundred meters, had no purpose unless it was nuclear.

The diplomats were speechless for several moments,. Then they began pounding Heinonen with questions. One was regarding the leadership of the Iranian program. The Helsinki-born scientist had expected the question and presented his audience with an organizational chart. At the top was the name Mohsen Fakhrizadeh-Mahabadi, whom he identified as Iran's equivalent of Robert Oppenheimer, the director of the Manhattan Project in the United States.

Mohsen Fakhrizadeh-Mahabadi is not simply an Iranian scientist. According to the CIA, he is a physics professor who also serves as an officer in the Iranian Revolutionary Guard Corps and is believed to be in charge of Iran's military nuclear program, also known as Project 111. According to the *London Times*, Iran's Project 111 was attempting to produce a nuclear warhead capable of exploding at two thousand feet and causing devastation over a vast area.[23]

Fakhrizadeh is essentially the Iranian equivalent of Pakistan's A. Q. Kahn. In 2006 and 2007 the UN Security Council passed resolutions that froze scientists' overseas assets, including those of Fakhrizadeh, and imposed a travel ban. The annex to United Nations Security Council Resolution 1747 declared, "The IAEA have asked to interview him about the activities of the PHRC [Physics Research Center] over the period he was head but Iran has refused."[24]

In December 2009, the world had another look at what Iran was really up to, and Fakhrizadeh may have been at the center of the activity. A memo leaked to the British press showed that Iranian scientists were conducting tests on a neutron initiator, one of the final technical steps in manufacturing a nuclear weapon.[25] Dated 2007, the document comes from the Field of Expansion of Deployment of Advance Technology, the organization that is responsible, according to Western intelligence agencies, for Iran's nuclear weapons program. Fakhrizadeh is believed to be at its helm.

In general, three main components are required for a nuclear weapon. The first stage is mining uranium and turning it into "yellowcake," a kind of yellow uranium powder. The powder is then turned into UF6 gas, which then runs through centrifuges to attain different levels of enrichment. The Iranians were successful in these different endeavors. The next stage involves taking the enriched uranium and inserting it into a device that can be used as a weapon. By early 2012 the Iranians were believed not to have reached that stage but to be working hard at it.

Even after creating HEU and accumulating enough of it, Iran would still need time to weaponize it, according to U.S. and Israeli military assessments. Having the uranium, it would take "another two to three, potentially out to five years" to move from the idea of having the material to a "deliverable weapon that is usable," Vice Chairman of the U.S. Joint Chiefs of Staff Gen. James Cartwright told the Senate Armed Services Committee in April 2010.[26]

The accumulating evidence led to a global consensus in 2010 that Iran was definitely working covertly on making a nuclear weapon. For most of the world this assessment was not new. For the United States, however, this determination was a sharp break from the official National Intelligence Estimate of late 2007 that had concluded Iran had suspended its nuclear weapons program in 2003 and likely had not renewed it. But by 2010, even the United States had backed away from its earlier intelligence assessments. Ahead of the vote on the fourth round of UN sanctions in June, it provided foreign diplomats with intelligence briefings that stated clearly, for the first time, that Iran was in fact pursuing a nuclear weapon. Part of the new intelligence it presented came from Shahram Amiri, the Iranian scientist who had disappeared in 2009 while on the Hajj in Saudi Arabia.[27]

"The U.S. is much closer to our assessments today," Israeli defense minister Ehud Barak said in a private meeting in Tel Aviv in April 2010. "Everyone understands that the materials that Iran is hoarding have no other purpose than making a bomb."

Barak's next observation was not surprising. "While we share the same assessments regarding the threat, there is still no agreement on how to deal with it," he said, alluding to the Obama administration's failed attempts to engage in talks with Iran.[28]

Barak's role in the U.S.-Israel relationship has shifted repeatedly in the years since he was appointed defense minister in 2007. First, after taking office he advocated that government ministers and IDF officers refrain from speaking publicly about Iran and that the rhetoric be saved for the diplomats and their closed-door meetings. In 2011, though, Barak began to change his strategy and became the most outspoken Israeli official on the possibility of a strike against Iran. Comments about the feasibility of a strike, the government's considerations, and even the potential fallout and number of Israeli casualties were made weekly by Barak.

If in 2008 Barak had said that Iran was not an existential threat to Israel, in 2012 he claimed that the Iranians "have set themselves a strategic goal of wiping Israel off the map."[29] The change was understood as part of an Israeli government strategy to get the world—and particularly the U.S.—to increase sanctions on Iran and possibly even to use military force to stop the ayatollahs from getting the bomb. "Barak has become the government's attack dog," a senior government official said in 2012. "He is out there to wave the big stick to warn the world that if action is not taken Israel will use military force."[30]

Two months before Obama took office in January 2009, Israeli foreign minister Tzipi Livni warned that his talking to Iran would "project weakness."[31] After the talks fell through, the Obama administration then advocated that the United Nations begin to push through more rounds of sanctions. Here, too, Israel warned that if the sanctions were not tough enough and if they did not pertain to the energy sector in Iran, they would not succeed. Further, after the UN passed sanctions in June 2010, Israel's ambassador to the United States Michael Oren hinted that on their own they would not suffice. "[The sanctions] can serve as a viable platform for launching very far-reaching sanctions by the United States or like-minded nations against Iran," Oren said.[32]

In the run-up to the sanctions in 2010 and amid concern that Israel would take unilateral action against Iran, the United States sent a parade of officials to Israel to reassure Israelis that their security interests would not be ignored. In a span of about six weeks, Vice President Joe Biden, CIA director Leon Panetta, National Security adviser Jim Jones, National Security Council strategist Dennis Ross, Deputy Secretaries of State Jim Steinberg and Jack Lew, head of the Senate's Foreign Relations Committee senator John Kerry, and Chairman of the Joint Chiefs of Staff Adm. Michael Mullen all passed through the gates of Ben-Gurion Airport south of Tel Aviv. This parade prompted some Israeli officials to joke that Israel had finally become the fifty-first state of the United States of America. Similar parades took place in 2012 as Israel again appeared close to launching a strike.

Israel's strategy during this period was to support America's use of diplomacy and sanctions while warning that sanctions, in order to be effective, needed to hit Iran where it hurts—namely, in the energy sector. Iran has loads of crude oil, but in 2012 it still did not have the necessary domestic infrastructure to refine the oil and turn it into fuel. As a result, curtailing its access to gasoline and diesel fuel would likely have a real impact on Iran's economy and would force the regime to make a decision about whether to continue its development of nuclear weapons at the risk of economic ruin or to stop the enrichment of uranium and open the door to economic relief.

"Sanctions can genuinely work," explained former Israeli deputy defense minister Sneh. "The key though is that they would need to be harsh and painful and the world doesn't seem to want to go there."[33]

The massive street protests that broke out in Iran following its 2009 rigged presidential elections demonstrated the growing rift in Iranian society. Tough sanctions imposed on Iran's economy could have potentially widened that gulf. But Iran's brutal suppression of dissent did not allow much room for optimism regarding the possibility of regime change.

In Israel, only a handful of senior defense officials believed in the possibility of regime change in Iran. While many openly expressed their hope that the ayatollahs would fall, they did nothing to make that happen.

One official was Israel's former ambassador to Iran Uri Lubrani. During his years in Tehran, he had cultivated close ties with the shah and other top Iranian officials, giving him unparalleled access to and an understanding of Iranian society. One memorable incident occurred in 1977, when Lubrani was summoned to the shah's private resort island of Kish, where he saw, for the first time, the decadence and corruption of the top Iranian leadership. Kish, for example, had a landing strip built especially for a Concorde jet that airlifted supplies from Parisian boutiques on a daily basis.[34]

Lubrani sensed the Iranians' growing discontent with the shah and his frivolous lifestyle. At a meeting with Israel's foreign minister at the time, Moshe Dayan, Lubrani warned that the shah's days were numbered. His prediction made its way to Washington, but the State Department completely dismissed it.

Lubrani turned out to be correct. After returning to Israel, he was appointed the coordinator of government activities in Lebanon following the First Lebanon War in 1982. By the late 1990s he had established a small unit in an office in the Defense Ministry and operated under the title of special adviser to the defense minister.

Officially Lubrani was the minister's eyes and ears in Iran. He closely followed Iranian society and maintained good contacts with Iranian exiles and dissidents. Over the years, Lubrani tried to get the government to allocate funds needed to support opposition groups in Iran and undermine the Islamic regime. He also looked for Iranian officials that could serve as potential candidates to lead a new government, holding periodic meetings in hotel rooms throughout European capitals. Lubrani's long-standing claim is that Israel needs to distinguish between Iran and the Iranians. "The Iranian people are our friends and allies," he says. "The problem is the Islamic regime which is in control of the country." No one in the Israeli government, however, was willing to listen. Instead of embracing Lubrani's ideas, Israeli defense ministers sidelined him and eventually ran him out of the Defense Ministry and into another government branch.

While the 2009 postelection protests vindicated Lubrani, the governments in Washington and Jerusalem again failed to make full use of the opportunity. President Barack Obama hesitated to speak out against the election fraud. When he finally did after several days of violence, Obama voiced concern over the way the elections were conducted but fell short of denouncing the vote. It was, however, too late.

Israel's policy in 2011 and early 2012 of cooperating with the international community's approach to Iran was conducted with the awareness that if the sanctions failed, the chances of the Obama administration's attacking Iran were slim. But by backing the international efforts and not working to undermine them, Israel has increased the likelihood of garnering international support for using unilateral military force against Iran's nuclear facilities in the event that all else failed. This way Israel would be able to say to the world, "We let you try everything, and now we don't have a choice."

Given the precedents of Israel's bombing of the Syrian and Iraqi reactors, Israel will be best served not asking Washington for permission to attack Iran. As noted previously, Israel was universally criticized for the Osirak attack, and the United States even delayed its shipment of fighter jets that had already been authorized.

The criticism later turned into praise, though. By 1991, during a visit to Israel, then-secretary of defense Dick Cheney gave Maj. Gen. David Ivry, who had been the IAF commander at the time of the Osirak strike, a satellite photograph of the destroyed reactor. At the bottom of the framed photo, Cheney had written: "For General David Ivry, with thanks and appreciation for the outstanding job he did on the Iraqi Nuclear Program in 1981, which made our job much easier in Desert Storm."[35]

In 2007, unprecedented and intimate coordination between President George W. Bush and Prime Minister Ehud Olmert preceded the attack on the Syrian reactor. Even so, at no point did Olmert ask Bush for permission to attack Syria.[36]

As a result, when Israel makes its decision on Iran it will likely be best off copying the two previous models and refraining from asking for permission.

It is important to note, however, that as policy choices, sanctions and the military option are not necessarily polar opposites. According to one senior cabinet minister, sanctions can only work if the Iranians believe that a "credible military option" is on the table.[37] "They need to fear that the military option is real and could be used," he explained. "Otherwise, there is no reason for them to stop." To support his argument, the minister cited Iran's decision in 2003 to suspend its enrichment of uranium and weapons program because it feared Coalition forces might invade it after Iraq. "When faced with survival or destruction, the Iranians chose survival, and that is what they would do again if faced with the same dilemma," the minister said.[38]

Embarking on the military option also entails many risks. Among some of the questions planners must consider are: Will the Israeli Air Force planes reach their targets? Will any jets be shot down? Will the bombs penetrate the fortified underground nuclear facilities?

Israel will likely not be able to strike Iran, though, without some sort of coordination with the United States, even if the U.S. government does so solely to ensure that Israel has the necessary weapons to win the subsequent war against Hezbollah, Hamas, and possibly Syria. During the Second Lebanon War in 2006, for example, the United States sent Israel emergency shipments of GBU-28 laser-guided bunker buster bombs so that the IAF would be able to bomb Hezbollah underground command and control centers more effectively. It also received joint direct attack munitions (JDAM) kits which turn regular bombs into guided weapons. These capabilities would be needed in a future war as well.

Not many Israelis can testify to having watched from the front lines the Islamic Revolution and Iran's rise to regional dominance. One of them is Israel's former IDF chief of General Staff Lt. Gen. Moshe "Bogie" Ya'alon, whose military and political career—spanning more that forty years—has been shaped by Israel's war against terrorism and efforts to prevent Iran from going nuclear. In 2009 Ya'alon was elected to the Knesset and appointed Israel's vice prime minister and minister of strategic affairs in the Netanyahu government.

Born in 1950, Ya'alon enlisted in the IDF in 1968. During the Yom Kippur War of 1973, he served as a reserve paratrooper. The heavy losses to Israel convinced him to return to active duty and go to officer training school. In 1979 he joined Sayeret Matkal and remained with the unit for a number of years. Eventually he became its commander, directing Israel's global war on terrorism in operations that remain top secret.

His first run-in with Iran was in 1982 when he served as a commander of the 890th Battalion of the Paratrooper's Brigade. Fighting against Palestinian terrorists in southern Lebanon during the First Lebanon War, Ya'alon encountered a number of imams in the scattered villages. He stopped and spoke to one imam who had returned to Lebanon recently from the city of Qom in Iran, the largest center for Shia Muslim scholarship in the world." These Imams were already undergoing indoctrination by the Iranians immediately after the revolution in 1979," Ya'alon said.[39] "This was part of Khomeini's strategy—to send out tentacles to other countries in the region and to export the revolution elsewhere." At the time, though, the thirty-two-year-old battalion commander had heard of Iran but did not yet understand the regional and strategic impact the revolution was having and how it would later touch his own country.

In 1995, when he was appointed head of the IDF's Aman, Ya'alon recalled the run-in with the imams in southern Lebanon. It was the period after the signing of the Oslo Accords and shortly before the assassination of Yitzhak Rabin, Israel's prime minister at the time. While the IDF's main focus was on stabilizing the Palestinian front, combating terrorism, and working to create viable conditions for peace, Ya'alon was also spending a significant percentage of his day gathering intelligence on Iran and its developing nuclear program. Iran, Ya'alon says, made the strategic decision to begin fast-forwarding its nuclear program following the Gulf War in 1991. It feared that without a nuclear capability, it too could one day be run over as Iraq had.

About a year later, Aman and the Mossad began picking up tidbits about Iran's nuclear and missile programs. By 1995, the IDF had already compiled a thick dossier on Iran's nuclear program with evidence that, Ya'alon recalls, left no doubt regarding Tehran's real goals.

Ya'alon crisscrossed the globe, meeting with his counterparts in the United States, France, England, and Germany. To each intelligence official, he presented the dossier, albeit without revealing sources. "Everyone listened, but no one was willing to accept our assessment that Iran's nuclear program was actually of a military nature," he recalled.

Ya'alon's work as head of Aman also took him to Russia, where he had high-level discussions with officials at Russia's Foreign Intelligence Service and met its director and later the Russian foreign minister, Yevgeny Primakov. Ya'alon tried to convince the Russians to stop selling missile technology to Iran. While the talks were substantial, Primakov was mostly interested in who Israel's sources were and how Ya'alon knew what he knew.

By 1997, the United States came around and officially accepted Israel's assessment of Iran's nuclear program. It took the Europeans another three years.

In 1998, toward the end of his term as head of Aman, Ya'alon issued a secret memo to the government warning that if Iran was not stopped, it would be capable of manufacturing an operational nuclear bomb within a decade. He was not that far off. By 2010, all Western intelligence agencies agreed that Iran was fully capable of making the bomb. Their difference of opinion was over whether Iran had made the political decision to do so.

By the time Ya'alon was appointed the IDF's chief of General Staff, Israel already perceived Iran as an existential threat. While his three-year tenure was marked mostly by combating Palestinian terrorism in the West Bank and Gaza Strip, he also spent a great deal of time strategizing and planning for possible military action against Iran. Eighteen months into his term as chief of staff, he said, "We believe that there is a chance of success talking about the elimination of the Iranian capabilities of weapons of mass destruction, first of all using political and economic resolutions. From my point of view and my recommendation, this has to be used first of all. If not we have to be prepared, and I am talking about the Western community, to use other options in order to eliminate the Iranian capabilities."[40]

One example of preparing for a nuclear Iran under Ya'alon's leadership was the delivery in 2004 of the 102 F-16I fighter jets that Israel had purchased in a massive $4.5 billion deal in 1999. The jets' arrival brought Israel's total to 362 F-16s, giving it the largest fleet in any country in the world behind the United States.[41] The backbone of the IAF, the new "I" models provided Israel with greater long-range capabilities and complemented the squadron of F-15Is that Israel had received at the end of the 1990s.

A few months after the planes began arriving, the air force again made headlines when it successfully conducted the first test of the Arrow 2. Israel is banking on this advanced version of the missile defense system to protect the Jewish state in the event that Iran succeeds, despite all of the world's efforts, in building a bomb.

By the time Ya'alon had stepped down as chief of General Staff, Iran was still moving full speed ahead with its nuclear program. On the day his successor, Maj. Gen. Dan Halutz, took over, Iran announced it had successfully tested a solid-fuel engine for its Shahab-3 long-range ballistic missile, which is capable of hitting anywhere inside Israel. As noted in chapter 2, the upgrade to solid fuel gives the Iranian missiles greater accuracy and a longer shelf life, allowing them to be stored in underground missile silos, hidden far away from Israeli spy satellites.

At their core, Ya'alon says, Iranians are open and moderate people who actually are fond of Israel and the United States. The problem is with the regime. To explain, he recalls how as head of Aman in 1995 he was part of the decision to allow Kish Air Flight 707—an Iranian Boeing airliner that had been hijacked by a flight attendant—to land in the IAF's Uvda Air Base in southern Israel. The women passengers, Ya'alon recalled, removed their headscarves, took off their long chadors and revealed their jeans underneath, and began speaking to their Israeli hosts in fluent English. Once they discovered they were close to Eilat, they asked if they could go there.

After a four-year hiatus from the public sphere, Ya'alon returned to the spotlight in March 2009 as a newly elected member of the Knesset on the hawkish Likud Party ticket. Immediately he was appointed the vice prime minister and the minister of strategic affairs, a job specially created for him. Ya'alon's office is located inside the Prime Minister's Office in Jerusalem, only a few floors above where the prime minister sits, a place called the "Aquarium" owing to its large glass doors and walls. Ya'alon's bare office has two pictures. One is of a sickle, a reminder of his days as a farmer on a small kibbutz in southern Israel. The other picture is of the railroad tracks leading to the Auschwitz-Birkenau concentration camp as a trio of Israeli F-15 fighter jets flew over it in September 2003. The picture includes former IAF commander Maj. Gen. Eliezer Shkedy's written dedication: "To remember and never forget that we can only rely on ourselves."

Ya'alon strongly follows Shkedy's dictum. He also often uses another line attributed to the ancient Jewish sage Hillel the Elder when talking about Iran: "If I am not for myself, who will be for me?"

Israel had always hoped that the United States would stop Iran's nuclear program, either with diplomatic or military means. Many Israeli officials had been certain that President George W. Bush would not leave office in January 2009 without having stopped Iran, but they were wrong. They had thought that the National Intelligence Estimate of 2007, which claimed that Iran was not developing a nuclear weapon, was simply a stumbling block in Bush's way but nothing more.

In 2006 Prime Minister Olmert had even optimistically and publicly declared that Bush would stop Iran. "First of all I think President Bush has the courage," Olmert said. "This is something that is very important. There is no one in the world today who has greater courage and determination, and a sense of mission about these issues, than President Bush, and I admire his determination and sense of mission."[42]

Two years later, by the end of Bush's term, that assessment seemed hopelessly naive. Bush had not only refused to order an attack against Iran, but he also had rejected the Israelis' requests for bunker-busting bombs, refueling tankers, and rights to fly over Iraq.[43] Instead, as noted in chapter 2, in late 2008 Bush gave Israel a defensive capability in the form of the X-Band radar. Located deep in the Negev Desert, the cube-shaped X-Band radar is manned completely by American soldiers. The radar's significance, however, cannot be overstated. Hooked up to Israel's Arrow missile defense system—said to be capable of intercepting Iranian missiles—the X-Band radar gives Israel advance warning after a missile is launched from Iran toward the Jewish state. These five to seven minutes are more than enough time to order the public into bomb shelters.

But the radar's deployment also sent a clear message to Israel: while America was willing to invest heavily in Israel's defense, it was not willing to provide offensive capabilities that Israel could use to attack Iran.

By the summer of 2010 almost everyone agreed that President Barack Obama was unlikely to order an attack against Iran, particularly in light of his decision to withdraw American troops from Iraq by the end of 2011. In October 2011, Leon Panetta, the U.S. secretary of defense, visited Israel to pass on a message from the Obama administration to the effect that Washington expected Israel not to take unilateral military action. Panetta said that preventing Iran from becoming a threat "depends on countries working together." Panetta's visit came amid speculation that Prime Minister Binyamin Netanyahu and Defense Minister Ehud Barak were pushing for a strike and going against the recommendations of the chiefs of Israel's military and intelligence agencies.

But this stance did not mean that the IAF had not already been preparing for an assault against Iran. In what the world viewed as a practice run for such a strike, a hundred Israeli aircraft—fighter jets, helicopters, refueling tankers—

flew nine hundred miles and participated in an aerial exercise over Greece in June 2008. A few months later, IAF jets flew more than two thousand miles to Gibraltar.

During Israel's offensive against Hamas in the Gaza Strip in January 2009, Israeli fighter jets and attack drones flew a thousand miles to the Sudanese desert to attack a convoy of trucks carrying long-range missiles for Hamas. This foray, too, was considered preparation for a long-range strike against Iran's nuclear facilities.

But the question still remained—could Israel do it?

The answer depends on whom you ask. The general assessment in the IDF is that Israel has the ability to knock out some of Iran's key facilities and set back the Iranian nuclear program by a couple of years, although it could not completely destroy it. One IDF general called such an attack a "bridge loan," in reference to a bank loan that covers a debt until more permanent financing is secured, meaning that Israel could delay the Iranian's program but not obliterate it.

Because Iran has already mastered the technology, some in the IDF point out that even if Israel causes significant damage to key facilities in the nuclear production line, it will be only a matter of time before Iran makes the necessary repairs and has the facilities up and running again.

Thus, a top IDF general said in April 2010, it is important to note that even if Israel attacks Iran, a diplomatic process would need to be in place to prevent Iran from rebuilding the nuclear facilities. The United States would be the likely candidate to lead such a process; however, if Israel were to attack Iran against President Barack Obama's wishes, the United States might not fill the role.

Ultimately, Israel faces four major questions in considering a strike against Iran. First is the intelligence question. Does Israel know the locations of all the various nuclear facilities that would need to be destroyed, particularly those next to large population centers? Second, can the IAF's F-15 and F-16 fighter jets reach those targets and return home safely considering the limited midair refueling capability it has? Third, can the IAF overcome Iranian air defenses—its air force and Russian-made surface-to-air-missile systems? Fourth is determining the hardening of the facilities. Some have been built in heavily fortified underground bunkers and cannot be easily penetrated. As one senior government official who participated in strategic forums on Iran said: "To attack [these] facilities we would need to know what the exact specification are of the bunkers and whether

they are made of steel, concrete, or a mixture of both. This defines the requirements for the type of bomb that would need to be used."[44]

Without question, the IAF would take on a large part of a potential Israeli
military operation against Iran's nuclear facilities. When former Israel Defense
Force chief of staff Dan Halutz was asked once how far Israel would go to stop
Iran, he quipped, "Two thousand kilometers"—roughly the distance to Iran.

What would its potential targets be?

Of the known Iranian nuclear sites, approximately five key nuclear facilities
would likely be targeted in a preemptive strike. The first target could be Bushehr,
the light water reactor built along the coast of the Persian Gulf in southwestern
Iran. Iran began constructing the power station in the 1970s with German assistance. It stopped after the revolution in 1979 but reactivated the plan in the
summer of 2010 under a new agreement with Russia.

The next facility would be the heavy water plant near the town of Arak. In
addition, the IAEA has seen designs for the construction of two heavy water
nuclear reactors at the Arak plant that the Iranians claim will be used for medical and research isotope production, but in reality they could have the ability to
produce plutonium for nuclear weapons.

Next is Iran's Uranium Conversion Facility located at the Esfahan Nuclear
Technology Center. Based on satellite imagery, the facility is above ground, although some reports have suggested the presence of tunnels near the complex.[45]

Another target is the Fordow uranium enrichment facility, which Iran officially
revealed to the IAEA in September 2009 even though the major Western intelligence agencies already knew about it. The facility, which was expected to hold
about three thousand centrifuges, was being built near the city of Qom and not
far from the Caspian Sea. Built into a mountain, the hardened facility—estimated
to be located under 100 meters of earth—would be difficult to penetrate. Israeli
defense minister Ehud Barak noted in 2010 that the facility was "immune to
standard bombs."[46]

In June 2011, Iran announced that it was planning to move centrifuges to
Qom from its main uranium enrichment facility at Natanz, which would be one
of the most difficult targets to strike. The Natanz complex consists of two large
halls, roughly 300,000 square feet each, dug somewhere between eight and twenty-
three feet below ground and covered with several layers of concrete and metal.
The walls of each hall are estimated to be two feet thick. Short-range Russian-
made Tor-M surface-to-air missiles surround the facility.

Razing Natanz, Arak, Fordow, and Esfahan alone is believed to be be enough to set back the ayatollahs' dream of obtaining the bomb, but Israeli military planners would also likely feel compelled to attack Iran's centrifuge fabrication sites. Their destruction would make it extremely difficult for Iran to reestablish its program. In addition to these key targets, the attacker would probably want to bomb Iranian radar stations, missile bases, silos, launchers—estimated to number around a hundred—and air bases and knock out Iran's ability to strike back with its long-range missiles or combat aircraft.

Some Israeli officials have also called for bombing Iran's energy infrastructure and vulnerable oil fields, which lack surface-to-air missile protection. Such strikes could have a demoralizing effect on Iran and influence the regime's decision-making process. Oil revenues provide at least 75 percent of the government's income and at least 80 percent of its export revenues. The political shock of losing its main source of income could also cause the regime to rethink its nuclear stance and make it difficult to finance the rebuilding of the destroyed facilities.[47]

One former IDF general claimed that in total, Israel would have to strike more than fifty different targets in sorties possibly lasting two days. But can Israel do it?

The first line of Iran's defense is its fleet of approximately 160 operational combat aircraft, most of which are outdated American and French planes purchased during the days of the shah, or before the Islamic Revolution of 1979. While a challenge, the outdated planes will not pose a direct threat to Israeli (or American) pilots flying in the most advanced aircraft in the world today. Then Iran's second line of defense is its surface-to-air missiles. It significantly upgraded its system throughout the 2000s, mostly by purchasing Russian-made air defense systems.

The main problem Israel would encounter in attacking Iran's nuclear facilities is the distance involved. The nearest installation is more than seven hundred miles from Israel. Top targets are even farther, at distances ranging between a thousand and fifteen hundred miles from Israel.

According to most estimates, with its F-16 and F-15 aircraft Israel is capable of unilaterally attacking Iran's nuclear facilities. Israel's vaunted twenty-five F-15I Ra'ams (Thunder), based in the Negev and with a combat range of more than two thousand miles, are believed capable of striking Iran in a nonstop operation. Israel in 2010 also received the last of the F-16I Sufas it procured in the late 1990s. The Sufas can also fly long-range missions but have a combat radius of a thousand miles.

Israeli fighter jets have carried out long-range missions, some with refueling support and some without. In 1981, without mid-air refueling support, Israeli F-16 jets bombed the Osirak reactor near Baghdad and returned to Israel on their last drops of fuel. In 1985, Squadron 120—the IAF's refueling tanker unit—was activated for Israel's longest-range air strike to date, when fighter jets flew more than fifteen hundred miles to bomb the PLO's headquarters in Tunis. Israel again demonstrated its long-range capabilities in 2003 when three F-15 jets flew to Poland, or sixteen hundred miles, for the famous Auschwitz flyover.

The IAF could increase the combat radius of these aircraft by using the IAF's limited fleet of Boeing 707 air-to-air refueling tankers to nurse attack planes as they make the flight to Iran and back. Since every drop of fuel will count, the IAF in 2009 instituted a new training regimen that included fueling planes while sitting on the runway with their engines running. The fuel nozzles are disconnected seconds before takeoff. The IAF is believed to be capable of launching and refueling two to three full squadrons of combat aircraft for a single set of strikes against Iran. Other escort jets would shoot down enemy aircraft and use Israel's advanced electronic warfare systems to suppress Iran's air defenses.[48]

Israeli Air Force jets could take three possible routes to Iran. The northern route skirts along the Turkish-Syrian border into Iran and is estimated to be about thirteen hundred miles. This route entails several risks and needs to take into account Syrian air defenses and Turkish opposition to violating its airspace. Israel flew over Turkey in 2007 when it bombed the Syrian reactor in al-Kibar and even dropped fuel tanks in Turkish territory. However, Turkey's deteriorated relationship with Israel could nix that route.

The central route—flying directly over Jordan and Iraq—is the most direct and would bring the distance from Israel's Hatzerim Air Force Base to Natanz down to about a thousand miles. It would require hurdling serious diplomatic obstacles, however. While Israel has a peace deal with Jordan, it is unlikely that Amman will want to be perceived as cooperating with an Israeli military action against Iran and possibly face the brunt of an Iranian reprisal. The same could happen to Iraq.

Finally, the southern route would take Israeli planes over Saudi Arabia and into Iran. While this path is longer than the one over Jordan and Iraq, Israel, according to a number of media reports, has received permission from the Saudis to use their airspace for such an operation.[49] Riyadh, one report claimed, had in 2010 conducted tests on its air defense systems to ensure that they would not engage Israeli fighter jets if such an operation were to take place.

In reviewing the IDF's offensive capabilities, the IAF also has the necessary munitions to destroy the Iranian facilities and penetrate the fortified bunker in Natanz. Israel developed some domestically and purchased others over the years from the United States. Examples of the latter include the GBU-27 and GBU-28 bombs, which can carry anywhere from one thousand to three thousand pounds of explosives.[50] While Natanz and Fordow are the most difficult targets and the missiles might not succeed in penetrating them on their own, Israeli pilots could guide them as former IAF commander Maj. Gen. Eitan Ben-Eliyahu, who participated in the strike on Osirak in 1981, has explained: "Even if one bomb would not suffice to penetrate, we could guide other bombs directly to the hole created by the previous ones and eventually destroy any target"[51] In contrast to the 1981 strike, when the Israeli pilots needed to fly directly over the target before dropping their bombs, today's standoff technology allows pilots to fly at high altitudes and safe distances when releasing satellite or laser-guided missiles toward their targets.

Israel also potentially could use the Jericho road-mobile, two-stage solid-propellant missile, whose range is reportedly between twelve hundred to more than three thousand miles and is capable of carrying a one-ton conventional or nonconventional warhead. Various accounts indicate that Israel tested the latest version of the missile, called Jericho III, in early 2008. Its enhanced accuracy and range put every Arab capital, including Tehran, within striking distance of Israel.

Israel also has three Dolphin class German-made submarines, which, according to unconfirmed reports, can carry surface-to-surface Harpoon missiles capable of delivering a 227-kilogram warhead to a range of 130 kilometers and at high subsonic speed. Some suggest that the subs might be capable of carrying nuclear-armed Popeye Turbo cruise missiles, granting Israel clear second-strike capabilities. Moreover, the submarines represent Israel's other long-arm capabilities, as was demonstrated in June 2009 when one of Israel's submarines openly passed through the Suez Canal. News of the passage, conducted under tight Egyptian security, was a closely guarded secret in the IDF.[52] The submarine's presence in the Red Sea and possibly elsewhere in the region showed that Israel had a maritime attack option in addition to air strikes, and that Israel could even count on Egypt to enable the passage of its vessels to the Red Sea and then on to the Persian Gulf.[53]

Not everyone agrees about Israel's offensive capabilities. One former brigadier general in the IAF, for instance, said he was not certain that the air force was capable of dealing Iran the powerful blow necessary even to delay the program. "If we send the air force there, we run the risk of losing a third of our fleet," he said. "And if we return without fulfilling the mission, then what did we achieve?"[54] Michael V. Hayden, director of the CIA from 2006 to 2009, said in January 2011 that an attack against Iran was "beyond the capacity" of Israel, in part because of the distance the aircraft would need to travel.[55]

More optimistic assessments are that Israel is capable of causing extensive enough damage to delay the program. This effort might be enough. Before the 1981 strike on the Osirak reactor outside Baghdad, then too the IDF's assessment was that the operation would only succeed in delaying Saddam Hussein's nuclear program by a few years. In reality, though, Iraq never rebuilt it.

Other questions remain about the effect of a strike on Iran. First, the world witnessed media accounts of Iranian protestors demonstrating for democratic freedoms after the June 2009 elections. Will a strike unite the Iranian public with the regime of President Mahmoud Ahmadinejad and Supreme Leader Ali Khamenei, or will it be met by cheers on the streets of Tehran? This would likely depend on how surgical the strikes are. If there is no collateral damage then the Iranian people might not be disturbed, but if the fallout affects them they will likely rally behind the embattled regime.

Next, estimates in Israel vary regarding the losses the IAF might suffer during such an operation. Some claim that with its advanced Russian-supplied air defense systems, Iran might be able to succeed in shooting down a small albeit significant percentage of Israel's strike package. Iran's shooting down and capturing even a few IAF pilots would be devastating for Israeli morale. While any Israeli strike package would include search-and-rescue teams needed to retrieve downed pilots, the possibility of failure definitely exists. As a result, in 2009, the IAF began increasing its mental training regimen for its airmen with an emphasis on survival skills.

A final consideration for Israeli military planners would be the effect that bombing the Bushehr reactor, the uranium conversion facility at Esfahan, and the enrichment facility at Natanz would have on the Iranian civilian population. These three facilities possess uranium hexafluoride and even some low-enriched uranium. The release of uranium into the environment would raise public health concerns.

What would happen the day after an Israeli strike? One possible scenario is based on Israel's past experiences. In 1991, during the Gulf War, Iraq fired thirty-nine

Scud missiles into Israel, causing extensive damage, injuring dozens of people, and directly killing one person. A year later, in 1992, a car bomb went off outside the Israeli Embassy in Buenos Aires, killing twenty-nine people. In 1994, another car bomb went off outside the AMIA center in Buenos Aires, killing eighty-five. Both attacks were attributed to Hezbollah terror cells, directed and financed by Iran. In 2006, during the Second Lebanon War, Hezbollah fired more than four thousand short-to-medium-range rockets into Israel, again causing extensive damage in northern Israel and killing forty-four civilians. Now, multiply these attacks and their consequences threefold, and the product will approximate the IDF's prediction for the fallout that Israelis can expect from a military strike against Iran's nuclear facilities.

Hezbollah, Iran's primary proxy, would most certainly be activated to ignite hostilities along the Lebanese-Israeli border. Although during the 2006 war Hezbollah failed to fire its long-range Iranian-made Fajr and Zelzal missiles, which can reach Israeli cities south of Tel Aviv, it would most probably launch these missiles following an attack on Iran. Hamas in Gaza would also attack Israel from the south with various rockets. In addition, Iran has developed an extensive terrorist infrastructure overseas cultivated in conjunction with Hezbollah that could be activated. During the 2006 war in Lebanon, the IDF held a press conference at military headquarters in Tel Aviv. Afterward, Aman's director General Yadlin warned that Iran had "awakened" its sleeper Hezbollah cells abroad and were preparing plans to launch attacks on Jewish and Israeli sites worldwide in retaliation for the IDF operations in Lebanon. An example of this was provided in February 2012, when alleged Iranian plots to attack Israeli targets were uncovered in India, Georgia, Thailand, and Azerbaijan.

This strike could ultimately start World War III. An attack against Iran's nuclear facilities is essentially the day the Iranians have been preparing their proxies for, and Israel could find itself fighting a war on three fronts: in the north, in the south, and on the home front, which would be pounded with missiles. Syrian involvement was also possible as well as the possibility that Iran would send its own ground troops to Lebanon or Syria to fight against Israel.

Such a war would have a great chance of spreading to other parts of the Middle East with Iran potentially attacking American forces based in the Persian Gulf and Saudi oil fields. In this case, the question of what the United States would do is unclear. Would it become actively engaged militarily, or would it confine its response to engaging in diplomatic endeavors, to recruiting allies to retaliate, and to watching from the sidelines?

In preparation for this war, Israel in 2010 had renewed its distribution of gas masks to help protect the public in the event that Syria or Iran uses chemical or biological weapons. The IDF's Home Front Command received an increased budget to prepare bomb shelters and to teach the public what to do during an emergency. C4I systems were improved with early warning missile detection systems and air sirens, including specially designed radars that can accurately predict the exact landing site of a missile launched at Israel.

Iran would not need to rely solely on Hezbollah's weaponry to attack Israel. The Iranians have developed their own array of ballistic missiles such as the Shahab and the Sajil with ranges of more than a thousand miles, giving Iran the capability to strike directly at targets in Israel. Because some of these missiles could reach Israel's nuclear reactor in Dimona, Israel in 2008 beefed up air defenses in the area and implemented safeguards to shut down the reactor in the event of a conflict. In mid-December 2005, Iran had acquired eighteen longer-range BM25 missiles from North Korea. Iran is also said to be working on the development of intercontinental ballistic missiles, indicating that Tehran has its sights not only on Israel but also on European countries and possibly even on U.S. military bases in Germany.

Even though the aerial operation against Iran would have been completed at this stage, Israel would find it hard to sit back and allow Hamas and Hezbollah to bomb its cities mercilessly. Owing to limited resources, it would likely need to focus its attention on Lebanon rather than on Gaza. If Syria were to attack Israel as well, the war would be of a different scale.

How long would such a war last? It would mostly depend on the Iranians. Judging by the Iran-Iraq War, which lasted eight years, Iran is determined and driven by radical ideology and religion and feels almost nothing can stop it. Therefore, it is possible that Iran will continue fighting until it believes it has caused Israel enough pain.[56]

Either way, in making a decision, Israel still faces two options—either launching a large-scale war that could escalate to other parts of the region or allowing Iran to go nuclear. "The fallout of a preemptive attack would be painful," Defense Minister Ehud Barak said in 2011. "But we need to think of the tradeoff: A nuclear bomb could be devastating for the State of Israel."[57]

8

ARMAGEDDON: THE DAY AFTER

In 2007, Iran and Venezuela made a surprise announcement: Iran Air was establishing a route from Tehran to Caracas, the Venezuelan capital. Several weeks later, the weekly sixteen-hour flights began taking off in Iran, stopping for a short layover in the Syrian capital of Damascus, and then continuing to Caracas.

When the announcement about the new route was made, alarms went off at Mossad headquarters near Tel Aviv. The Israeli espionage agency immediately began investigating the real nature of the route, looking to discover who and what was really being ferried inside Iran Air's Boeing 747 passenger planes. What they found amazed even some of Israel's most veteran intelligence analysts: Iran and Venezuela had established a secret terrorist pipeline into South America, essentially into the United States' backyard.

Israel was not the only country interested in the planes and the thriving relationship between Iran and Venezuela. Although Israel was concerned that Iran was establishing the terror infrastructure for attacks against Israeli sites such as the ones it launched in 1992 and 1994 in Buenos Aires, the United States had taken notice of the unusual relationship between Venezuela and Iran and their two presidents—Mahmoud Ahmadinejad and Hugo Chávez. In 2008, in its country report on Venezuela, the U.S. State Department also cited the flights as a cause of concern. It singled out the airline's lists of passengers as being especially worrisome. "Passengers on these flights were not subject to immigration and customs controls at Simon Bolivar International Airport," the report claimed, noting one specific passenger that year by the name of Abdul Kadir.[1] A citizen of Guyana, a small country on the northern coast of South America, Kadir had served in his country's parliament and was the mayor of the country's second-largest city, Linden, in the mid-1990s. In August 2010, he was convicted in a Brooklyn court for plotting to blow up fuel storage tanks at New York's John F. Kennedy International Airport. According to U.S. authorities, Kadir had conducted surveillance of a transportation facility at the airport. He was arrested in Trinidad while en route to Caracas for the weekly flight to Tehran, where he claimed he was going to attend an Islamic conference. He had already purchased the ticket.

In court, Kadir had a slip of tongue. He revealed that on numerous occasions he had been in touch with an Iranian national named Mohsen Rabbani, the so-called cultural attaché at the Iranian Embassy in Buenos Aires in the 1990s. According to Israel and Argentinean prosecutors, Rabbani was directly involved in the 1994 bombing of the AMIA center in the city. He still appears on Interpol's most-wanted list.[2]

The flights between Iran and Venezuela are believed to be run out of the office of Gen. Qassem Suleimani, the commander of Iranian Revolutionary Guard Corps' al-Quds Force. His predecessor, Ahmad Vahidi, is wanted by Interpol for his involvement in the AMIA bombing and is now Iran's defense minister. A decorated veteran of the Iran-Iraq War, Suleimani has become omnipresent, representing the interests of the Revolutionary Guards in Lebanon, Afghanistan, Iraq, Asia, and, of course, South America. In 2007 the U.S. State Department designated Suleimani as a terrorist supporter. That same year, he was named in United Nations Security Council Resolution 1747 as an Iranian official targeted for international sanctions. His level of influence in Iran cannot be overestimated. Suleimani reports directly to Supreme Leader Ayatollah Ali Khamenei and is a key player in the support Iran provides its proxies—Hezbollah, Hamas, and other Shiite terror groups—around the world.

Hezbollah, with Suleimani's assistance, has succeeded in establishing strongholds in South America. Particularly in Venezuela and the tri-border area that connects Brazil, Argentina, and Paraguay, Hezbollah supporters are actively involved in drug smuggling, arms trafficking, money laundering, fraud, and intellectual property piracy.[3]

Iran has found a convenient ally in Venezuelan president Chávez who, like Iranian president Mahmoud Ahmadinejad, despises the United States. Between 2000 and 2009, Chavez had been to Iran seven times for talks that are estimated to have produced more than $20 billion in deals.[4]

Assessments vary as to what the Iran Air planes might have carried. Some intelligence analysts have raised the possibility that the planes are transporting raw uranium from Venezuela's vast untapped reserves back to Iran, where the material is used for its illicit nuclear uranium enrichment program. According to a classified Israeli Foreign Ministry report from 2009, Venezuela is not alone in supplying Iran with uranium. Bolivia was also accused of supplying Iran with the key nuclear material.[5]

Israeli government officials also theorized that planes were actually carrying Iranian weaponry and military officers to Venezuela to help solidify Chávez's regime and potentially one day threaten the United States. The planes reminded one top Israeli security official of the planes Israel sees land periodically at Beirut International Airport that also transport weaponry destined for Hezbollah. "This is the Cuban Missile Crisis all over again," a senior Israeli cabinet minister said in 2010, referring to the 1962 standoff between Washington and Moscow over a Russian attempt to deploy long-range missiles in Cuba. "The only difference is that the United States does not appear to be doing anything about it."[6]

In November 2010, a report in the German newspaper *Die Welt* reinforced the Israeli intelligence assessment. According to the report, Iran was planning on deploying its long-range ballistic missiles in Venezuela, and from there it would be able to threaten the United States directly.[7]

A few days later, Israeli deputy foreign minister Danny Ayalon met with a group of Latin American journalists at the Foreign Ministry in Jerusalem and warned that Venezuela was becoming Iran's "advance outpost" in Latin America. "The two countries have joined together to create an axis of conventional and nuclear terror [that threatens] not only the Middle East, but also the continent of America, and the United States in particular," Ayalon told the journalists.[8]

To counter the growing Iranian influence in South America, Israel had decided in 2009 to launch a massive diplomatic push throughout the region to warn other moderate countries of the potential lurking dangers from the new Iranian-Venezuelan axis. That summer, Israeli foreign minister Avigdor Lieberman flew to Brazil, Argentina, Peru, and Colombia. In early 2010, Israeli strategic affairs minister Moshe Ya'alon flew to Panama, Mexico, and Guatemala. Both Israeli ministers returned with similar conclusions: Iran's power and presence in South America is growing, and the United States is not doing enough to stop it.

What should alarm the United States when looking to the Southern Hemisphere is the possibility that Iran could use the route it has established between Tehran, Damascus, and Caracas as a way to smuggle explosives or even a crude nuclear weapon one day into South America. From there, it could threaten Chicago, Dallas, or Miami.

"The routes already exist for drug smuggling," the Israeli cabinet minister said. "What is the problem using these routes to also smuggle in explosives or even a dirty bomb?"

Some have even claimed that an attack against the United States would be easy to execute. In 2009 at a conference aired on Al-Jazeera television, a Kuwaiti professor named Abdallah Nafisi explained how smuggling tunnels could be used in an attack on the United States. "Four pounds of anthrax carried in a suitcase this big," he said, using his hands to represent a small suitcase, "carried by a fighter through tunnels from Mexico into the United States is guaranteed to kill 330,000 Americans within a single hour if it is properly spread in population centers there."[9] According to Nafisi, following this scenario precludes any need for attacks similar to 9/11, which, he said, would be "small change" in comparison to the attack he envisions. "There is no need for airplanes, conspiracies, timings and so on. Just one person with courage to carry four pounds of anthrax will go to the White House lawn and will spread this confetti all over. . . . It will turn into a real celebration," he said.

While dismissing Nafisi as another crazy anti-American radical would have been easy, many observers took his remarks seriously. One was Ronald K. Knoble, secretary-general of Interpol, who in February 2009 mentioned the professor's televised speech in a letter he issued in commemoration of the 1993 World Trade Center bombing. Interpol's continuing pursuit of the Iranian masterminds behind the Buenos Aires bombings in the 1990s is a further demonstration of its concern with such terrorist acts. "If we add to these global security gaps the devastation that could follow a nuclear or biological terrorist attack within the next five years . . . then we must conclude that now is no time for complacency," Knoble wrote.[10]

From the Israelis' point of view, Iran's increased activity in Latin America needs to be regarded as part of its overall strategy to achieve hegemony not only in the Middle East but also in the United States' backyard. A reminder of this threat was provided in October 2011 when the FBI announced that it had thwarted an Iranian plot to assassinate Saudi Arabia's ambassador to the United States. According to the FBI, an Iranian-born U.S. citizen and car salesman Mansour Arbabsiar was working as an agent for the Iranian Revolutionary Guard Corps and had been recruited to hire a Mexican drug cartel to assassinate Saudi ambassador Adel al-Jubeir. A second man, named Gholam Shakuri, was also charged but was not apprehended. The FBI described him as being a senior official in al-Quds Force. Why al-Quds would operate so openly in the United States was unclear, but some Israeli officials speculated that it could have been an indication that Iran was feeling strong and confident and was therefore willing to act on American soil.

The Iranians' interests in Latin America are varied. They appear to be making an effort to improve Iran's strategic position vis-à-vis the United States by posing a clear and present security threat to America while simultaneously creating a new balance of power by collaborating with revolutionary Latin American countries like Venezuela. Iran can do so by creating intelligence and terrorist networks throughout South America that can serve as the basis for future Iranian-led attacks against Israel and the United States, depending on international developments on the nuclear front. As early as 2000, a new group calling itself Hezbollah Venezuela claimed to possess "jihad warriors" willing to die in the war against the West.

Iran is also considering the economic factor. Facing growing sanctions to its energy and banking sectors and runaway inflation in 2012, its ties with Latin American states essentially undermine the sanctions and their effect. For example, it can coordinate prices with major oil-exporting countries like Venezuela, which is one of the top exporters of oil in the world.

Iran also looks to damage Israel's relations with Latin American countries. During Operation Cast Lead in the Gaza Strip, for example, both Venezuela and Bolivia cut off diplomatic ties with Israel.

Thus, when discussing the dangers involved in the prospect of a nuclear Iran, the threat is not only to Israel but rather to the entire free world. While the possibility exists that Iran would transfer a nuclear device to one of its proxies, Hezbollah or Hamas, now there is also the chance that it could do the same in South America. This latter gambit, however, would only be possible if Iran succeeds in obtaining a nuclear weapon, something Israeli leaders have claimed for years they would not allow to happen.

Nevertheless, besides making those declarations, Israel has also been preparing for years for two distinctly different options—that it would have to use military force to stop Iran (discussed in chapter 7) or that Iran would succeed in going nuclear. Some Israeli officials have warned that if and when Iran goes nuclear, it will use its nuclear weapon against Israel, possibly even by fitting a nuclear warhead on one of its long-range missiles and firing it into downtown Tel Aviv. While this scenario is considered possible, Aman analysts believe that

Iran is more likely to give the weapon to one of its proxies—maybe Hezbollah in Lebanon, Shiite terror groups in Iraq, or even Latin American organizations—to use. This way Iran will be able to maintain some level of plausible deniability.

Becoming a nuclear power will also embolden its proxies, particularly Hezbollah, to take greater risks and act as if they are untouchable by Israel. What would Israel do, for example, if Iran becomes a nuclear power and Hezbollah decided to launch missiles into downtown Tel Aviv or the Dimona nuclear reactor, causing extensive damage and casualties? How would Israel respond if its intelligence apparatuses learned that Iran had transferred radioactive material to Hezbollah or another one of its many terror proxies?

The issue of nuclear terrorism is one of Israel's primary concerns when considering the ramifications of a nuclear Iran. As Israeli defense minister Ehud Barak explained in 2008,

> I do not belong to those who think that if Iran has a nuclear weapon it will hurry to drop it on a neighbor. Iran well understands that an act of this sort would set her back thousands of years. The primary danger is that a nuclear weapon will reach a terrorist group that will not hesitate to use it immediately. They will send it in a container with a GPS to a leading port in the United States, Europe, or Israel.[11]

Already in the early 2000s, Western intelligence agencies began to warn of nuclear terrorism. In 2003, the U.S. government's "National Strategy for Combating Terrorism" warned that the risk of nuclear terrorism had increased significantly and posed one of the greatest threats to the national security of the United States and its allies.[12] In December 2008 the Commission on the Prevention of Weapons of Mass Destruction Proliferation and Terrorism, which the U.S. Congress established about a year earlier, issued its first earth-shattering report and warned that a nuclear or biological terrorist attack was likely to occur somewhere in the world by 2013. "Unless the world community acts decisively and with great urgency, it is more likely than not that a weapon of mass destruction will be used in a terrorist attack somewhere in the world by the end of 2013," the commission concluded.[13]

Possibly of more concern for Israel is the nuclear arms race that a nuclearized Iran will set off, turning the Middle East from an already volatile region into a nightmare. If Iran succeeds in defying the world and developing the bomb, then the Nonproliferation Treaty would be proven ineffective and could completely collapse, paving the way for additional countries to develop nuclear weapons.

The congressional committee on nuclear terrorism issued a warning about this possibility. "Failure to stop Iran and North Korea could result in a cascade of proliferation, which would dramatically increase the likelihood of the use of weapons of mass destruction," commission chairman Bob Graham wrote in early 2010.[14]

Fearing such a scenario, in 2012 Israel held its first ever civil defense exercise to prepare for a dirty bomb attack. The exercise centered in on the city of Haifa and set up roadblocks throughout the city to simulate how it would contain the fallout in the event that a radioactive device went off.

Meanwhile, in December 2006, a number of Gulf States announced at the end of the Twenty-seventh Gulf Cooperation Council (GCC) session in Riyadh, Saudi Arabia, that they were considering developing a shared civilian nuclear program. The member states of the GCC are oil-rich countries: Kuwait, Bahrain, the United Arab Emirates, Oman, Qatar, and Saudi Arabia. Egypt had also announced earlier that year that it too was renewing its nuclear program, and Turkey has also announced plans to build nuclear power reactors for electricity. Other countries in the region, such as Algeria and Morocco, already have limited nuclear infrastructure that could be expanded.

The congressional commission raised concern that should Iran become a nuclear power that some of these countries—possibly Saudi Arabia—may go as far as to buy a rogue nuclear weapon on the black market and skip the development process and its technological obstacles. The idea would be to create an immediate balance of power with Iran.

Egyptian leaders make no secret of the motivation for their costly decision to pursue nuclear technology. "A nuclear armed Iran with hegemonic ambitions is the greatest threat to Arab nations today," then Egyptian president Hosni Mubarak told the Arab summit in Riyadh in March 2009.[15]

Avigdor Lieberman, Israel's foreign minister, called the possibility that Saudi Arabia and Egypt would obtain nuclear weapons an "apocalyptic scenario."[16] He continued, "Their intentions should be taken seriously, and the declarations being made now are to prepare the world for when they decide to actually do it."

This possibility is all the more worrisome in light of the so-called Arab Spring and the subsequent upheaval that swept through the Middle East and North Africa in 2011 and led to the toppling of the Mubarak regime in Egypt, revolutions in

Libya and Tunisia, and unprecedented resistance to the Assad regime in Syria. Moreover, Saudi Arabia's King Abdullah, aligned with the United States, also faces threats from al Qaeda and Shiite elements that seek to undermine his regime. Regime changes could take place in the region in the coming years that would create even more uncertainty. "All of these countries have the potential of being led by radical Islamists," a senior Israeli defense official said in late 2011. "Now imagine that they had already developed a nuclear programs. Whose hands would it fall into?"[17]

Israeli president Shimon Peres made Israel's concern clear in a speech in early 2010. "Having imperialistic ambitions and a nuclear bomb is a very dangerous combination because a single bomb today is like a whole army in other times," Peres told a group of Jewish leaders who had gathered for a conference in Jerusalem. "The world will become ungovernable if every country in the Middle East will have a nuclear bomb without responsible people to govern it."[18]

For these reasons, the question of whether Israel can live with a nuclear Iran is not an easy one to answer and goes well beyond worries about the possible lone nuclear-tipped ballistic missile fired into downtown Tel Aviv. Officially, Israeli politicians or defense officials do not speak openly about the option of a nuclear Iran. That reticence doesn't mean, however, that they are not preparing for such an outcome.

In 2007, for example, a small team of senior analysts with Israel's National Security Council drafted a secret memorandum about "the day after" Iran obtains atomic weapons. The memo did not go into too much detail about what course of action Israel should take if it happened, but the memo's mere existence was an indication that not everyone in Israel believed in the preemption doctrine.[19]

A few years later, a prestigious Israeli think tank convened a group of former senior military officers and diplomats to participate in a day of war games that broke new ground by assuming the existence of what Israel had pledged it would prevent—namely, an Iranian bomb. Discomfort with the scenario of Iran having a nuclear weapon prompted the Defense Ministry to cancel its participation in the event. In the game, shortly after the announcement that Iran had gone nuclear, Hezbollah launched long-range missiles at Tel Aviv, striking the Defense Ministry and causing casualties and large-scale destruction. The next stage in the game was that Israel and the United States had obtained intelligence information indicating that Iran had transferred radioactive technology, which could be used to create a crude device, to Hezbollah. According to the simulation's findings, such a situation could lead the United States to form a multinational force—another so-called coalition of the willing—to enter Lebanon and dismantle Hezbollah.

Nevertheless, the overarching conclusions of the simulation were that nuclear weapons in Iranian hands would dramatically increase the Iranians' deterrence against an Israeli counterattack, as long as the means that Iran used were conventional, such as Hezbollah firing a missile into Tel Aviv. The moment the game changed and involved nonconventional weapons, the response by Israel and its allies escalated.

It came as no surprise that some of the top officials, when summing up the event, played down the impact a nuclearized Iran would have on the State of Israel. For instance, former IDF chief of staff Lt. Gen. Dan Halutz, who commanded the Israeli military during the 2006 war in Lebanon, said the world would not come to an end if Iran went nuclear. "I am not underestimating the significance of a nuclear Iran, but we should not give it Holocaust subtext like politicians try to do," said Halutz. Then he cast doubt that the United States and Israel could ever agree to cooperate on a military strike against Iran.[20]

Professor Yehezkel Dror, a leading Israeli academic who served on the panel that investigated Israel's failures during the 2006 war, also participated in the war games. In his briefing, he concluded his remarks by threatening Iran with annihilation: "The Israeli public cannot be allowed to live in fear of Iran. There is the same chance of an earthquake happening. If Israel is attacked by a nuclear weapon, Iran will not survive."

But in all likelihood, what would happen in Israel if Iran were to obtain a nuclear capability? Some analysts predict that Israel, which has for decades abided by a strict policy of ambiguity regarding its own purported nuclear capabilities, would go public with at least some of its capabilities to persuade a nuclear-armed Iran it was outgunned. Professor Louis René Beres, an expert on nuclear policy who chaired Project Daniel (see chapter 7), says that Israel would likely need to alter its policy of ambiguity in the event that Iran obtains a nuclear weapon.[21] Beres stresses that Israel would not necessarily need to open its nuclear facilities to inspectors from the International Atomic Energy Agency, but it could succeed in bolstering its deterrence by revealing more about the weapons it possesses. "Israel does not need to start disclosing secrets," he said. "It could be enough to lift the ambiguity by indicating the availability and the capability of the weapon."

In December 2006 it had seemed for a moment that Israel was on the verge of doing so. Israeli prime minister Ehud Olmert said in an interview with German

TV at his Jerusalem residence: "Iran openly, explicitly and publicly threatens to wipe Israel off the map. Can you say that this is the same [threat] level, when they are aspiring to have nuclear weapons, as [that posed by] America, France, Israel, Russia?"

The common denominator of both men's comments—confirmation of Israel's presumed nuclear capabilities.

While Olmert's comment caused quite the stir in the diplomatic and defense corridors in Israel, he was not the first Israeli leader to make a slip of the tongue when speaking about Israel's nuclear program. One of the first was Israeli president Ephraim Katzir, who in December 1974 said that Israel had "nuclear potential."[22] Katzir knew what he was talking about. Before becoming president, he worked as a scientist at the Weizmann Institute of Science on nuclear matters. In 1962, when American inspectors came to visit Dimona, Katzir was their escort.[23]

In another "slip," after Israel destroyed Saddam Hussein's Osirak reactor in 1981, former defense and foreign minister Moshe Dayan told the *New York Times*, "We do have the capacity to produce nuclear weapons."[24]

Shimon Peres, the man attributed with formulating Israel's policy of nuclear ambiguity, has also made some revealing comments over the years. In 1998 he said at a press conference in Jordan that Israel had "built a nuclear option, not in order to have a Hiroshima but an Oslo." Basically he was warning that Israel had such power in case peace talks failed.

In the early 1960s Peres and Prime Minister Levi Eshkol formulated the ambiguity policy, pledging that "Israel will not be the first nation to introduce nuclear weapons to the Middle East." Israel has neither admitted to having the weapon nor denied that it ever did.[25]

In 1969, the visits to Dimona came to an end after Israeli prime minister Golda Meir reached a tacit understanding regarding Israel's nuclear capability with U.S. president Richard Nixon. Under the agreement that Israel reportedly reached with the United States, Washington promised to stop pressuring Jerusalem on nuclear matters while Israel promised not to test a bomb, not to publicly declare a weapons capability, and not to threaten any state with the weapons. But that compromise did not mean that the world believed Israel lacked a nuclear weapon. The nuclear reactor known as the "textile factory" in Dimona has reportedly been the birthplace of hundreds of Israeli nuclear weapons, according to various media reports—easily found on the Internet—that also detail the location of Israel's ballistic missiles launch sites. It is also said that on two occasions, during the Six Day War and the Yom Kippur War, the Israeli leadership felt that the country's existence was in jeopardy and ordered nuclear bombs to be loaded onto attack jets for what has been dubbed "the Samson option."

So with all that information available, what difference would a change in Israel's policy of ambiguity make today? It would all depend on the timing of making an announcement of its nuclear abilities.

With Iran racing toward nuclear weapons, Israeli officials have debated the continued importance of nuclear ambiguity. Some have called for "nuclear transparency" or the relaxing of the ambiguity policy. It can come in the form of an official government announcement of Israel's nuclear capabilities or in the testing of a nuclear weapon—which it is believed to have—to show that its power is real and viable. The Israeli defense establishment, however, generally wants to retain the policy of ambiguity.

When Olmert was prime minister he held several long meetings with Dan Meridor, the author of Israel's newly formulated defense doctrine. Meridor briefed Olmert on the doctrine's main principles, including the recommendation that Israel retain the long-standing policy of nuclear ambiguity. When Meridor returned to the government in 2009 as minister in charge of intelligence affairs, he continued to push his argument that Israel needs to retain its policy of ambiguity.

Another believer in the policy is Ilan Mizrahi, an expert on Iran who served as head of the Israeli National Security Council under Olmert and before that as deputy head of the Mossad. "This policy scares our adversaries," he has said. "They are scared of us since they don't know anything for certain."[26]

The ambiguity policy allows Israel valuable flexibility based on the gap between presumption and certainty. By not declaring that it has nuclear weapons, Israel avoids the scrutiny of IAEA inspection teams at its nuclear facilities, but by occasionally hinting that it has capabilities, it can create an effective deterrent against its enemies. According to Israeli officials, their policy has paid off, first by preventing IAEA inspections of Israel's nuclear sites. In addition, until now the policy has warded off attempts by other Middle Eastern countries—except for Iran and Syria—to begin their own development of nuclear weapons under the excuse that Israel has nuclear weapons. The policy has also allowed Israel to continue receiving billions of dollars in annual foreign military aid from Washington, a deal that could come under major American and international criticism if Israel were to abandon its policy of ambiguity.

The most important reason to maintain ambiguity, however, is to preserve Israel's ability to act on its own if international diplomatic efforts fail to stop Tehran's race to obtain nuclear weapons. With Iran still moving forward in 2012 to obtain a bomb, this possibility was under greater consideration.

Epilogue

No matter which way Israel decides to go, there is no heroic Hollywood ending to this shadow war between Israel and Iran.

If Israel decides to try to stop Iran's nuclear program on its own, it can expect the outbreak of a painful war with Iran and its proxies—primarily Hezbollah and Hamas—and possibly even Syria. This type of war, with so many different actors, would likely have repercussions well beyond the Middle East.

If Israel does not attack, Iran could end up succeeding in developing nuclear weapons. Even as sanctions gained momentum in 2012, Iran remained steadfast in its determination to continue its program, and Israel warned that sanctions alone would not be enough to stop the regime. Iran, Israeli officials have stressed, had already crossed the point of no return in pursuing its weapons program.

Nuclear weapons in the hands of an Iranian regime that calls for Israel's destruction effectively means that Israelis would have to live under a constant threat of annihilation. Despite the impressive and advanced missile defense systems Israel has developed over the years, such as the Arrow, there is no such thing as a hermetic defense. Further, the significance of living in those conditions for Israel is critical. Israelis would lose their sense of security, the economy would likely weaken, and Israelis would begin considering the benefits of living in the Diaspora over the state of Israel, spelling an end to the Zionist dream of a Jewish homeland.

A nuclear weapon in Iran would also start an unprecedented nuclear arms race throughout the region, the beginning of which was already noticeable as early as 2007. As noted previously, moderate Arab countries such as Egypt, Saudi

Arabia, Jordan, and the United Arab Emirates have expressed an interest in creating their own nuclear insurance policies in the face of Iran's belligerence and regional ambitions. The Middle East is a already a volatile region. Nuclear proliferation would turn it into something of a nightmare.

Global terrorism will also grow. With the backing of a nuclear state, Iran's proxies will feel braver and empowered to take more aggressive action against Israel and the West. This irruption could span several continents from Venezuela in South America to Afghanistan in Asia.

Pinpointing exactly when Israel's shadow war with Iran began is difficult. Some would say in the early days of the Islamic Revolution of 1979. Others trace it to more recent times with the rise of Hezbollah and Hamas. No one, though, doubts that the shadow war has steadily intensified over the years.

We opened this book with a description of the war that erupted in 2006 between Israel and Hezbollah. Hezbollah's abduction of Israeli reservists placed a mirror in front of the Israel Defense Force, and it did not like its reflection. Shortly afterward, as in other rounds of the IDF's ongoing war with Iran and its proxies, it was difficult to tell who had won, but it was clear that the IDF had received a long-overdue wakeup call. By mid-2012, though, it was clear that the war had effectively deterred Hezbollah from attacking Israel; so the war has recently been cast in a different light.

Further, the Second Lebanon War also lifted the curtain that had obscured Iran's covert efforts to develop and foster foreign armies as its own contractors, or proxies. It became evident that Iran was creating a proxy army, and the IDF awoke from its slumber imposed by the Second Intifada and the war on Palestinian terrorism. For the first time, it directly witnessed how tight a grip Iran really had over Lebanon.

The IDF needed to undergo a major transformation with the understanding that the potential war with Iran would not only be fought a thousand miles away at Bushehr, Natanz, Fordow and Arak but also right along Israel's own borders. Further, it was not enough to develop advanced offensive and defensive technology; in addition, the IDF had to review the basics and prepare for the next war against Iran's proxy army. The appointment of Gabi Ashkenazi as the IDF's chief of the General Staff following the war signaled a change as he redirected the defense budget to the ground forces and the reserves corps. He did not do so at the expense of the Israeli Air Force, which continued to grow as well. Standing out was the IDF's decision in 2010 to purchase a first squadron of the F-35 stealth fighter jet.

When the story behind Israel's remarkable strike against the Syrians' nuclear reactor, which they were secretly building in September 2007, was disclosed, the world once again witnessed how close a rogue state and sponsor of terrorism was to obtaining a functioning nuclear reactor. The world also saw how such a rogue state can be stopped, if the decision to act is made in time.

While the Bush administration urged Israel to hold off on taking military action and instead to go through regular diplomatic channels, the Olmert government proved its decisiveness and courage by taking action with the risk of an all-out war erupting in the Golan Heights. Israel was lucky. Syria decided to contain the strike, likely owing to the embarrassment it felt from being caught developing an illicit nuclear program. And here, too, Israel once again revealed Iran's influence—both in the financial assistance and the technological cooperation it had provided Syria in building the reactor.

But the war with Iran goes far beyond the battlefields of Lebanon and Syria. Chapter 4 details the covert war Israel and the West are waging against Iran and its proxies, including countless acts of sabotage, assassinations, cyber warfare, and defections. This war is far from over. Furthermore, as Iran continues to pursue a nuclear capability and to support terror proxies in an increasingly wider network, this conflict will intensify.

Off the record, Israeli officials are willing to talk, albeit vaguely, about this covert war. Israeli finance minister Yuval Steinitz, during a visit to New York, met with a group of American Jews in September 2010. When someone asked him about the Stuxnet virus, he replied that "whatever you imagine Israel is doing, Israel is doing much more."

In Israel, people refer to Mossad agents as "Rain Men," imagining them standing on a street corner with their hands deep in their raincoat pockets, watching a suspect as the raindrops beat down on their heads. They walk inconspicuously and without being detected into places no Israeli would want to go. They could have been in Damascus that night when Imad Mughniyeh's car blew up, or they might have been walking through the Al Bustan Rotana Hotel in Dubai as Mahmoud al-Mabhouh died in his hotel room. Maybe the Mossad was on the beach in Syria when a lone sniper killed Assad's closest adviser, Gen. Mohammed Suleiman, or again agents may have been standing at the entrance to an Istanbul hotel when Brig. Gen. Ali-Reza Asgari turned himself over to the West. Terror and guerrilla groups cannot survive on their own. In the past decade, Iran has turned into the number one state sponsor of terrorism in the Middle East, with the aim of projecting its power not only throughout the region but also throughout the world. A demonstration of its efforts is identified in the war on smuggling that Israel has launched against Iranian attempts to arm its enemies. The geographical distance between Israel and Iran and its proxies requires safe and secret travel routes that can carry large loads but are not easily detected. Using an extensive list of straw companies, Iran has turned the sea into a smuggling highway.

Developing its proxies also has come at an unbelievable economic expense. Despite the millions of unemployed Iranians, the Islamic regime and its ayatollahs have preferred to invest their money not in their own people but in places such as Lebanon and the Gaza Strip.

Meanwhile, the increased range of Hamas's missiles in Gaza that can reach Israel's strategic installations—like the Dimona reactor—in the south led the IDF in late 2008 to launch Operation Cast Lead and curtail the military buildup there. It was the first experiment since the war in Lebanon, and the IDF went up against an Iranian proxy and came out victorious. At the same time, though, both sides learned valuable lessons and in the years since have been preparing for the next round. Shortly after the operation ended, Hamas already had more missiles than it did before, but with longer ranges and larger warheads.

The book's final section covered Israel's options as Iran has pursued a nuclear weapon. The Israeli Air Force has a small unit, whose personnel come from different scientific and operational backgrounds, that conducts risk analyses of operations and assesses the chances of success and failure. Its answer usually comes in the form of a number, dependent on various factors. One consideration when debating the use of military action in this showdown is without a doubt the chance of success between Israel's capabilities versus Iran's.

While Israeli officials are careful not to speak openly about it, the IAF has proven its capabilities and willingness to act twice before—in 1981 against Iraq and in 2007 against Syria. Iran is undoubtedly a far more formidable adversary, but a strike is perceived to be possible. In this scenario, Israel will need to prepare for the fallout from such a strike—that is, the war that would ensue with Hezbollah, Hamas, Iran, and possibly Syria.

But the alternative—Iran continues its current march toward the bomb without being stopped—would have catastrophic effects. The balance of power in the Middle East would be forever altered.

During the work on this book—the countless meetings, interviews, and research—

our feeling was that these are historic times. The mix of our routine of being reporters in Israel covering the daily aspects of the Israeli-Arab conflict alongside moving in the world of shadows, which is disconnected from daily life in the Western world, was complex but mostly fascinating. We wrote this book while skipping between continents and traveling through Israel, Europe, and the United States. On the one hand, in all of the different countries we visited, the average person is familiar with the Iranian threat but has more faith in the human race and in our ability to overcome this challenge as we have so many before it. On the other hand, the wrinkled foreheads and the circles under the eyes of the senior officials we met in these countries to discuss the Iranian threat demonstrated for us what is at stake and how grave the situation really is.

Nobody in Israel wants a war. As a country that has fought one every decade since its existence, however, it cannot afford to sit idle as its enemies actively seek its destruction. Time is unfortunately not on the Israelis' side.

In this book, we tried to describe not only the dilemma facing the decision makers who were gracious to share with us their time, but also, more important, their thoughts. We do not pretend to know the solution; instead, we have tried to help prepare for the future. We hope to be proven wrong.

Notes

Introduction

1. Binyamin Netanyahu, "Address by Prime Minister Benjamin Netanyahu at Yad Vashem Holocaust Museum," January 25, 2010.

2. Peter Hirschberg, "Netanyahu: It's 1938 and Iran Is Germany," *Haaretz*, November 14, 2006.

3. "Shavit (Israel), Space Launch Vehicles—Orbital," *Jane's Space Systems and Industry*, April 21, 2009.

4. Maj. Gen. Eliezer Shkedy, interview with one of the authors in Tel Aviv, January 2008.

5. Based on conversations with Israeli officials who were involved in the Israeli-U.S. dialogue at the time.

6. Allyn Fisher-Ilan, "Israel Defense Chief: Iran not an Existential Threat," Reuters, September 17, 2009.

7. Meeting with an IDF officer who asked not to be named, January 2010. The question of whether Iran should be defined as an existential threat is more rhetorical than substantial. See also Louis René Beres, *Israel, Iran and Project Daniel* (Herzliya, Israel: Interdisciplinary Center (IDC) Herzliya, Lauder School of Government, Diplomacy and Strategy, Institute for Policy and Strategy, 2009); Arie Idan, *The Iranian Nuclear Challenge: Present Situation and Confronting Strategies* (Herzliya, Israel: Interdisciplinary Center (IDC) Herzliya, Lauder School of Government, Diplomacy and Strategy, Institute for Policy and Strategy, 2004).

8. Speech at Tenth Annual Herzliya Conference, February 3, 2010, http://www .herzliyaconference.org/_Articles/Article.asp?CategoryID=347&Article ID=3029 (in Hebrew).

9. See cable 08RIYADH649 sent by the U.S. Embassy in Riyadh on April 20, 2008, http://www.cablegatesearch.net/search.php?q=08RIYADH649&qo=0& qc=0&qto=2010-02-28.
10. See cable 09MANAMA642 sent by the U.S. Embassy in Manama on November 4, 2009, http://www.cablegatesearch.net/search.php?q=09MANAMA642 &qo=0&qc=0&qto=2010-02-28.
11. See cable 07TELAVIV2652 sent by the U.S. Embassy in Tel Aviv on August 31, 2007, http://www.cablegatesearch.net/search.php?q=07TELAVIV2652&q o=0&qc=0&qto=2010-02-28.
12. "Mubarak, Sarkozy Agree on Need for Achieving Stability in Lebanon, Establishing Independent Palestinian State," *Egyptian State Information Service*, December 17, 2007.
13. This quest for nuclear energy is based on intelligence and diplomatic assessments in Israel and other countries in the world. See also Yoel Guzansky, "The Saudi Nuclear Option," *Insight* 176 (2010); and John Bolton, "Get Ready for a Nuclear Iran," *Wall Street Journal*, May 2, 2010.
14. See Chuck Freilich, *The Armageddon Scenario: Israel and the Threat of Nuclear Terrorism* (Center Perspectives Papers No. 104, Begin-Sadat Center for Strategic Studies, 2010).
15. Yossi Klein Halevi and Michael B. Oren, "Israel's Worst Nightmare," *New Republic*, January 26, 2007.
16. "Poll: More Fear Iran as Biggest Threat to U.S.," *Associated Press*, July 2, 2006.
17. See Pew Research Center, "Global Threats and Use of Military Force," http://people-press.org/2009/12/03/section-2-global-threats-and-use-of-military-force/ (accessed in 2010).
18. See Uzi Rubin, *New Developments in Iran's Missile Capabilities: Implications Beyond the Middle East* (Jerusalem, Israel: Jerusalem Center for Public Affairs, 2009).
19. See transcript of speech, http://www.examiner.com/us-headlines-in-national/mahmoud-ahmadinejad-president-of-iran-speech-at-u-n-general-assembly-full-text-and-video (accessed in 2010).

Chapter 1. The Wake-up Call

1. Moshe Tamir, *War Without Insignia* (Tel Aviv: Ma'arahot Publishing, 2005) (in Hebrew).
2. Based on a series of meetings one of the authors held with Erez Zuckerman and Egoz commanders in the summer of 2007.
3. Last name must be omitted owing to Israeli censorship laws.
4. Later, following the conclusions of an investigative panel led by Maj. Gen.

Doron Almog (Ret.), Gal Hirsch left the IDF and turned to the private business sector. See also Gal Hirsch, *A Story of War: A Story of Love* (Tel Aviv: Yediot Ahronot, 2009) (in Hebrew).

5. See "English Summary of the Winograd Commission Report," *New York Times*, January 30, 2008, http://www.nytimes.com/2008/01/30/world/middle east/31winograd-web.html. For more on Israeli failures during the war, see Amos Harel and Avi Issacharoff, *34 Days: Israel, Hezbollah and the War in Lebanon* (New York: Palgrave Macmillan, 2009).

6. Amos Harel, "Mossad Tip Led to Capture of Hezbollah Cell in Sinai," *Haaretz*, April 14, 2009.

7. See Yossi Kuperwasser, "Regional Implications: From Radicalism to Reform," in *The Second Lebanon War: Strategic Perspectives*, ed. Shlomo Brom and Mier Elran (Tel Aviv: Institute for National Security Studies, 2007).

8. Tal Russo, in interview with one of the authors in Tel Aviv in 2009.

9. On the process see Yehuda Wagman, *The Limited Conflict Catch* (Tel Aviv: Ma'arachot Publishing, 2002) (in Hebrew).

10. See Amir Rapaport, "The IDF and the Lessons of the Second Lebanon War" (Ramat Gan, Israel: Begin-Sadat Center for Strategic Studies, 2010) (in Hebrew).

11. Ron Tira, *The Limitations of Standoff Firepower–Based Operations: On Stand-off Warfare, Maneuver, and Decision* (Tel Aviv: Institute for National Security Studies, 2007).

12. Lecture attended by one of the authors in 2001 at a military base near Tel Aviv.

13. Interview with one of the authors in 2007.

14. See Israeli Ministry of Foreign Affairs, "Behind the Headlines: Hizbullah Weapons in Southern Lebanon," July 16, 2009, http://www.mfa.gov.il/MFA/About+the+Ministry/Behind+the+Headlines/Hizbullah-weapons-in-Southern-Lebanon-16-Jul-2009; and Yaakov Katz, "The IDF Intel," *Jerusalem Post*, July 8, 2010.

15. See cable RIYADH 000768 02 from May 14, 2008, http://www.cablegate search.net/search.php?q=RIYADH+000768+02+&qo=0&qc=0&qto=2010-02-28.

16. Interview with senior officer from the Northern Command in Safed in 2009.

17. Jonathon Lis, "Netanyahu: Today, Lebanon's Real Army Is Hezbollah," *Haaretz*, December 7, 2009.

18. Alex Fishman, "Pay Attention Nasrallah," *Yediot Ahronot*, October 2, 2008 (in Hebrew).

19. Interview with senior member of the IDF General Staff in 2008 in Tel Aviv.

20. Based on conversations authors held with participants at the meeting.

21. Roee Nahmias, "Report: Nasrallah Replaced as Head of Hizbullah Military Wing," *Ynetnews*, December 13, 2007.

22. Top IDF officer, in interview with one of the authors in Tel Aviv in 2009.

23. See cable S E C R E T STATE 017894 written on February 26, 2010.

24. Ronen Bergman, "How the Next Middle East War Could Start," *Wall Street Journal*, March 29, 2010.

25. Interview with senior Israeli defense official in Tel Aviv in 2010.

Chapter 2. Technology and Training

1. Yuval Steinitz, "The Growing Threat to Israel's Qualitative Military Edge," *Jerusalem Issue Brief* 3, no. 10 (2003).

2. Herb Keinon, "Livni Praises US Aid Package to Israel," *Jerusalem Post*, August 15, 2007.

3. Yaakov Katz, "Israel Anticipates Record Defence Sales in 2010," *Jane's Defence Weekly*, June 9, 2010.

4. Yaakov Katz, "Israeli Drones Take Over Skies of Afghanistan," *Jerusalem Post*, January 21, 2010.

5. See Israeli Ministry of Foreign Affairs, "Facets of the Israeli Economy—the Defense Industry," June 1, 2002.

6. Haim Eshed, in interview with one of the authors in Tel Aviv, April 2009.

7. Isaac Ben-Israel, in interview with one of the authors in Jerusalem in 2009.

8. Maj. Gen. Ido Nehushtan, in interview with one of the authors in Tel Aviv, September 2009.

9. See also Uri Bar-Joseph, ed., *Israel's National Security Towards the 21st Century* (London: Frank Cass Publishers, 2001).

10. Moti Basok, "NIS 5.5 Billion for the Air," *Haaretz*, March 13, 2008 (in Hebrew).

11. A senior IDF operations officer involved in planning the operation in August 2006, in interview with one of the authors in Tel Aviv in 2006.

12. William Rosenau, *Special Operations Forces and Elusive Enemy Ground Targets: Lessons from Vietnam and the Persian Gulf War* (Santa Monica, CA: RAND, 2000).

13. Speech by Military Intelligence chief Maj. Gen. Amos Yadlin at Institute for National Security Studies in Tel Aviv on December 15, 2009.

14. Robin Hughes, "Explosion Aborts CW Project Run by Iran and Syria," *Jane's Defence Weekly*, September 26, 2007.

15. See Lt. Gen. Michael D. Maples, *Annual Threat Assessment, Statement before the Committee on Armed Services United States Senate*, March 10, 2009, http://armed-services.senate.gov/statemnt/2009/March/Maples%2003-10-09 .pdf.

16. Ishaan Tharoor, "Unbowed, Ahmadinejad Shows Up in Russia," *Time*, June 16, 2009.

17. Nehushtan interview.
18. David Fulghum, "Israel Shows Electronic Prowess," *Aviation Week*, November 25, 2007.
19. A senior IDF intelligence officer, in interview with one of the authors in Tel Aviv in 2010.
20. David Horovitz, "Editor's Notes: A Nation Held Hostage," *Jerusalem Post*, December 24, 2009. "Families nationwide imagine themselves facing the same plight, with their child—one moment safely within Israel, protecting our border; the next dragged away into Gaza—kept tantalizingly just out of reach by murderous extortionists. Pay the ransom, we urge from our gut," Horovitz wrote.
21. An IAF base commander, in interview with one of the authors in Tel Aviv in 2010.
22. Nehushtan interview.
23. Recollection of the conversation with Ivry by Ehud Barak told to authors in Tel Aviv, 2009.
24. Speech by Barak at International Aerospace Conference near Tel Aviv on November 17, 2009.
25. Interview with one of the authors in 2009 in Tel Aviv.
26. See Uzi Rubin, "Hizballah's Rocket Campaign Against Northern Israel: A Preliminary Report," *Jerusalem Issue Brief* 6, no. 10 (August 31, 2006).
27. "Hezbollah Missile Stock Tripled," *BBC News*, November 24, 2008.
28. A senior officer from the IDF Northern Command, in interview with one of the authors in Tel Aviv in 2009.
29. Briefing with intelligence officers at Israel's Northern Command in July 2010.
30. Anthony H. Cordesman, *Israel and Syria: The Military Balance and Prospects of War* (Westport, CT: Praeger Security International, 2008).
31. David Horovitz, "Only a Drill?," *Jerusalem Post*, May 28, 2010.
32. Maples, *Annual Threat Assessment*.
33. Yiftah S. Shapir, "Iran's Ballistic Missiles," *Strategic Assessment* 12, no. 2 (2009).
34. Ibid.
35. Israeli missile analysts, in interviews with the authors in Tel Aviv in 2009.
36. Uzi Rubin, "New Developments in Iran's Missile Capabilities: Implications Beyond the Middle East," *Jerusalem Issue Brief* 9, no. 7 (August 25, 2009).
37. Colonel Aviram spoke at a conference in Tel Aviv in 2009.
38. Interview with one of the authors in 2009 in Tel Aviv.
39. For example, see Specialist Kristopher Regan, "Proper Planning Key to Success during Juniper Cobra 2010," October 30, 2009, the U.S. Military European Command's press release, http://www.eucom.mil/english/FullStory.asp?article=Proper-planning-key-success-Juniper-Cobra-2010.

40. Erez Zuckerman, in interview with one of the authors at the Elyakim Base in 2007.

41. See address to National Defense College, August 12, 1999, at http://www.mfa.gov.il/MFA/Government/Speeches+by+Israeli+leaders/1999/Prime%20Minister%20and%20Defense%20Minister%20Ehud%20Barak-s%20S.htm?DisplayMode=print.

42. Zvi Ganin, *An Uneasy Relationship: American Jewish Leadership and Israel* (Syracuse, NY: Syracuse University Press, 2005).

43. Interview one of the authors conducted with Ashkenazi in 2010.

44. Yaakov Katz, "Israeli Commando Missions Come Out of the Shadows," *USA Today*, August 13, 2006.

45. Yoaz Hendel, "IDF Special Units: Their Purpose and Operational Concept," *Strategic Assessment* 10, no. 2 (August 2007).

Chapter 3. Operation Orchard

1. Owing to rules of censorship and restrictions regarding the publication of classified material in Israel, this chapter is based on a mix of information from a variety of sources, including foreign news reports and dozens of interviews the authors conducted, particularly with IDF officers. (Israel destroyed the first nuclear reactor, an Iraqi facility, in 1981.)

2. Erich Follath and Holgar Stark, "The Story of 'Operation Orchard': How Israel Destroyed Syria's Al Kibar Nuclear Reactor," *Spiegel*, November 2, 2009.

3. See Gordon Thomas, *Gideon's Spies: The Secret History of the Mossad* (New York: St. Martin's Press, 1999).

4. Interviews with Israeli intelligence officials, Tel Aviv, 2008.

5. Follath and Stark, "Story of 'Operation Orchard.'"

6. Ibid.

7. On the Syrians' weapons development, see Cordesman, *Israel and Syria*.

8. On Meir Dagan see Yaakov Katz, "Why Is the Dagan Era Ending?," *Jerusalem Post*, July 3, 2010.

9. Information obtained from an Israeli intelligence officer in interview with one of the authors in Tel Aviv in 2009

10. Based on Israeli intelligence analysis of Bashar al-Assad following the discovery of the nuclear reactor and shared with one of the authors in 2010.

11. Philippe Naughton, "Elite Iranian General Defects with Hezbollah's Arms Secrets," *Sunday Times*, March 8, 2007.

12. Senior American administration officials who were involved in the dialogue Bush held with Olmert, in interview with the authors in Washington DC in 2009. See also David E. Sanger, *The Inheritance: The World Obama Confronts and the Challenges to American Power* (New York: Three Rivers Press, 2009).

13. Ibid.

14. Insight is based on interviews with U.S. and Israeli officials familiar with the content of Olmert's conversation with Bush in Tel Aviv and Washington DC in 2009.

15. Seymour Hersh, "A Strike in the Dark," *New Yorker*, February 11, 2008.

16. George W. Bush, *Decision Points* (New York: Crown, 2010).

17. See UN Security Council Resolution 487; and Anthony D'Amato, "Israel's Air Strike Against the Osiraq Reactor: A Retrospective," *Temple International and Comparative Law Journal* 259 (1996).

18. Follath and Stark, "Story of 'Operation Orchard.'"

19. Associated Press, "Syria's Assad Acknowledges Israel's Military Superiority," *Haaretz*, July 16, 2001, http://www.haaretz.com/news/syria-s-assad -acknowledges-israel-s-military-superiority-1.63667.

20. The following sequence of events is based on interviews with Israeli military planners on how similar, previous covert operations took place in Tel Aviv in 2009.

21. Mark Mazzetti and Helene Cooper, "An Israeli Strike on Syria Kindles Debate in the U.S.," *New York Times*, October 10, 2007.

22. "Israel Condemned for Intrusion into Syria's Territorial Air," Korean Central News Agency, September 11, 2007.

23. JPost.com staff, "USAF Struck Syrian Nuclear Site," *Jerusalem Post*, November 2, 2007, http://www.jpost.com/MiddleEast/Article.aspx?id=80642.

24. William J. Broad and Mark Mazzetti, "Photos Show Cleansing of Suspect Syrian Site," *New York Times*, October 25, 2007.

Chapter 4. The Shadow War

1. Ari Shavit, "Barak: It's Clear that the Calm Was Not a Mistake: We Have No Interest in War," *Haaretz*, December 18, 2008.

2. Shapira, in interview with one of the authors in Tel Aviv, early 2010. See also Robert Baer, *See No Evil: The True Story of a Ground Soldier in the CIA's War on Terrorism* (New York: Three Rivers Press, 2002).

3. Uri Lubrani, in interview with one of the authors in Tel Aviv in 2010.

4. Ronen Bergman, *The Secret War with Iran: The 30-Year Clandestine Struggle Against the World's Most Dangerous Terrorist Power* (New York: Simon & Schuster, 2008), 242.

5. Danny Yatom, in interview with one of the authors in Jerusalem, 2008.

6. Bergman, *The Secret War with Iran*, 239.

7. For a more comprehensive analysis of Unit 1800, see Michael Eisenstadt and Neri Zilber, "Hizballah, Iran, and the Prospects for a New Israeli-Palestinian

Peace Process," Peace Watch no. 486, Washington Institute for Near East Policy, 2004.

8. Col. Eitan Azani, in interview with one of the authors in Jerusalem in 2010.

9. See "Hezbollah's Global Reach," House Committee on International Relations, 109th Cong. (September 28, 2006), 23, http://democrats.foreignaffairs .house.gov/archives/109/30143.pdf.

10. Ibid., 19.

11. Ibid., 29.

12. This information is based on Israeli intelligence assessments as late as mid-2010.

13. Gordon Thomas, "Mossad's Most Wanted: A Deadly Vengeance," *Independent*, February 23, 2010.

14. Ibid.

15. Igra Ram, in interview with authors in Jerusalem in 2010.

16. Uzi Mahnaimi, "Meir Dagan: The Mastermind behind Mossad's Secret War," *Sunday Times*, February 21, 2010.

17. Interview with intelligence officer in Tel Aviv in 2009.

18. Aluf Benn, "Is Mossad Responsible for Delaying Iran's Attainment of Nuclear Capability?," *Haaretz*, September 26, 2008.

19. Richard Spencer, "Iranian Nuclear Scientist 'Killed by Mossad or the CIA,'" *Telegraph*, November 29, 2010.

20. Julian Borger, "Attack on Iranian Nuclear Scientists Prompts Hit Squad Claims," *Guardian*, November 29, 2010.

21. Interview with former AMAN officer in Tel Aviv in 2009.

22. Zaki Shalom, "Prepare for an Iranian Response," *Ynetnews*, September 17, 2007.

23. Shalom Yerushalmi, "Two Missiles in a Cemetery," *NRG Ma'ariv*, December 16, 2003

24. Yaakov Katz, "Understanding the Enemy," *Jerusalem Post*, April 2, 2010.

25. UPI, "Israel's New Strategic Arm: Cyberwarfare," March 19, 2010.

26. "Spymaster Sees Israel as World Cyberwar Leader," Reuters, December 15, 2009.

27. Ralph Langner, in interview with one of the authors by phone from Germany in December 2010.

28. David Albright, in interview by one of the authors by phone from Washington DC in January 2011.

29. Peter Beaumont, "Stuxnet Worm Heralds New Era of Global Cyberwar," *Guardian*, September 30, 2010.

30. William J. Broad, John Markoff, and David E. Sanger, "Israeli Test on Worm Called Crucial in Iran Nuclear Delay," *New York Times*, January 15, 2011.

31. Byres, in interview with the authors by phone from Canada in December 2010.

32. Aharon Farkash, Yaakov Amidror, and Yossi Kuperwasser, *The U.S. National Intelligence Estimate on Iran and Its Aftermath: A Roundtable of Israeli Experts* (Jerusalem: Jerusalem Center for Public Affairs, 2008).

33. Amos Yadlin, in an interview with one of the authors in Tel Aviv in November 2011.

34. Yaakov Katz, "10 Israelis Recruited as Spies by Iran," *Jerusalem Post*, April 17, 2007.

35. Frances Harrison, "Huge Cost of Iranian Brain Drain," *BBC*, January 8, 2007.

36. Information is based on interviews with former U.S. government officials involved in efforts to stop Iran's nuclear program in New York in 2010 See also Greg Miller, "CIA Has Recruited Iranians to Defect," *Los Angeles Times*, December 9, 2007.

37. David Albright, *Peddling Peril: How the Secret Nuclear Trade Arms America's Enemies* (New York: Simon & Schuster, 2010), 70–81.

38. See ibid., 116–53.

39. R. Jeffery Smith, "Pakistani Scientist Cites Help to Iran," *Washington Post,* September 9, 2009.

40. A former U.S. intelligence officer, in an interview with one of the authors in New York in February 2010.

41. See the Institute for Science and International Security (ISIS) for a more comprehensive analysis of the Qom facility: Paul Brannan, "Qom Gas Centrifuge Uranium Enrichment Site in Iran May Have Been Re-purposed Tunnel Facility," ISIS Reports, September 26, 2009.

42. Israeli intelligence officials, in interview with one of the authors in Tel Aviv in 2010.

43. Nima Gerami and James M. Acton, "What Else Is Iran Hiding?," *Foreign Policy*, September 28, 2009.

44. Uri Lubrani, in interview with one of the authors in Tel Aviv in 2010.

45. See Mike Herzog, "The Middle East Security Agenda: An Israeli Assessment" speech, Washington Institute for Near East Policy, April 2009.

46. Philip Sherwell, "Iranian Scientist Who Vanished 'Gave Nuclear Secrets' to UN Inspectors Sent to Qom Site," *Daily Telegraph*, December 12, 2009. In July 2010, Amiri returned to Iran, claiming the CIA had abducted him. The circumstances of his return were unclear. Reportedly he feared harm would befall to his family.

47. BBC, "Mystery over Missing Iranian Researcher," October 8, 2009.

48. BBC, "Full Text: Leaders' Comments on Iran," September 25, 2009.

49. Uzi Mahnaimi, "Defector Spied on Iran for Years," *Sunday Times*, March 11, 2007.

50. Ibid.; and Dafna Linzer, "Former Iranian Defense Official Talks to Western Intelligence," *Washington Post*, March 8, 2007.

51. Alexander G. Higgins, "Report: Iranian Defector Tipped Syrian Nuclear Plans," *Associated Press*, March 20, 2009.

52. Ronen Bergman, "US Closer to Tracking Iran's Nuclear Secrets," *Ynetnews*, August 7, 2007.

53. Former U.S. intelligence officer, in interview with one of the authors in New York in February 2010.

54. Ibid.

55. See Office of the Director of National Intelligence, "National Intelligence Estimate: Iran—Nuclear Intentions and Capabilities," November 2007, http://www.dni.gov/press_releases/20071203_release.pdf.

56. Former head of Aman, in interview with the authors in Tel Aviv in 2010.

57. Israeli diplomatic officials, who were involved in dialogue between Israel and the United States after the NIE's publication, in an interview with the authors in Jerusalem and Tel Aviv in 2010.

58. Ilan Mizrahi, in interview with authors in 2007 in Tel Aviv.

59. Maj. Gen. Benny Gantz, in interview with authors in Tel Aviv in 2007.

60. Barak Ravid, "Dichter Raps 'Misconception' of Iran Nukes," *Haaretz*, December 16, 2007.

61. Yadlin interview.

62. See U.S. diplomatic cable, "Israeli Intentions Regarding the Iranian Nuclear Program," 05TELAVIV1593, http://213.251.145.96/cable/2005/03/05TELAVIV1593.html.

63. Director General, "Implementation of the NPT Safeguards Agreement and Relevant Provisions of Security Council Resolutions in the Islamic Republic of Iran," IAEA Board of Governors, November 8, 2011, http://www.iaea.org/Publications/Documents/Board/2011/gov2011-65.pdf.

64. Yuval Steinitz, interview with the authors in 2008 in Tel Aviv.

Chapter 5. Hamas: Iran's Other Army

1. Israeli foreign minister Avigdor Lieberman made this claim. See "Abbas Wanted Hamas Toppled in Gaza War: Israeli Foreign Minister," Reuters, March 29, 2010.

2. See cable TELAVIV1732 sent by the U.S. Embassy in Tel Aviv on June 13, 2006.

3. See cable 07TELAVIV1733 sent by the U.S. Embassy in Tel Aviv on June 13, 2006.

4. Yaakov Amidror, *Winning Counterinsurgency War: The Israeli Experience* (Jerusalem: Jerusalem Center for Public Affairs, 2008).

5. See Mordechai Kedar, "The Brain behind the Shalit Kidnapping and Hamas's Takeover of Gaza," *Israel Hayom*, August 27, 2009.

6. Israeli intelligence official, in interview with one of the authors in early 2009 in Tel Aviv.
7. See "Iranian Support for Hamas," Intelligence and Terrorism Information Center, January 12, 2008, http://www.terrorism-info.org.il/malam_multimedia /English/eng_n/pdf/iran_e004.pdf.
8. William Westmorland, *A Soldier Reports* (Garden City, NY: Doubleday, 1976).
9. Yossi Baidatz, in interview with one of the authors in 2008 in Tel Aviv.
10. Reporters briefing after the Knesset meeting attended by authors.
11. The Shin Bet held a briefing with reporters following the operation in 2008 in Tel Aviv.
12. For a comprehensive analysis of the death toll, see "'Cast Lead' Casualties Report" (Herzliya, Israel: The International Institute for Counter-Terrorism–Interdisciplinary Center [IDC], April 2009), http://www.ict.org.il/Research Publications/CastLeadCasualties/tabid/325/Default.aspx.
13. On January 1, Nizar Rayan, a Hamas cleric and liaison between the group's military and political wings, was killed in an Israeli targeted killing. On January 15, Hamas interior minister Said Siam was killed. In total, Israel did not succeed in killing as many Hamas leaders as it had hoped to, and following the operation, the IDF's Southern Command and Shin Bet established joint teams to improve the coordination between intelligence and operations ahead of a future conflict.
14. Col. Yigal Slovik, in interview with one of the authors in August 2009 in Tel Aviv.
15. Marie Colvin, "Hamas Wages Iran's Proxy War on Israel," *Sunday Times*, March 9, 2008. The article is based on an interview the *Times*'s senior correspondent Marie Colvin had with a senior operative in the Izz ad-Din al-Kassam Brigade in the Gaza Strip. He was joined by an operative from Hamas's weapons production branch. Both terrorists mentioned the technological training Hamas received from Iran. The operatives said they had used Iranian technological know-how to develop IEDs and rockets from simple raw materials available in the Gaza Strip. The senior operative said that using Iranian technology, Hamas had developed the Shawaz 4, which was a new generation IED. The weapons production operative said, "Anything they [the Iranians] think will be useful [for us], our guys there e-mail it to us right away."
16. An IAF commander involved in planning for Operation Cast Lead, in an interview with one of the authors in Tel Aviv in 2010.
17. "Hamas and the Terrorist Threat from the Gaza Strip," Meir Amit Intelligence and Terrorism Information Center, March 2010, http://www.terrorism-info. org.il/site/content/t1.asp?Sid=13&Pid=334.

18. See Yaakov Lappin, "IDF Releases Cast Lead Casualty Numbers," *Jerusalem Post*, March 26, 2009.

19. Media briefing with Yadlin in Tel Aviv after Operation Cast Lead in February 2009.

Chapter 6. Neptune's War

1. Commander's name is classified in observance of Israeli military policy.

2. This section on the *Francop* is based on a series of interviews the authors conducted with IDF and Navy officers involved in the operation. See also Yossi Yehoshua, "The Story of Operation Four Species," *Yediot Ahronot*, March 29, 2010.

3. Ruth Lapidoth, "The Legal Basis of Israel's Naval Blockade of Gaza," *Jerusalem Issue Briefs* 10, no. 4 (July 2010). See also Yaakov Katz, "How Will Israel Deal with the Next Flotilla?," *Jerusalem Post*, June 3, 2011.

4. In interviews with one of the authors in Tel Aviv in 2010.

5. See Yehoshua, "Story of Operation Four Species."

6. Lieutenant Colonel G. in interview with one of the authors in Tel Aviv in 2010.

7. In an interview with one of the authors in mid-2010 in Tel Aviv.

8. Informally, the West, including Israel, continued to do business with Iran during the Iran-Iraq War in an effort to weaken Saddam Hussein.

9. See BBC, "Kremlin Bans Sale of S-300 Missile Systems to Iran," September 22, 2010.

10. Despite Iran's claims, Israeli weapons experts who viewed the pictures of the Mersad claimed that it was not an indigenous Iranian system but was a copy of a previously known Chinese-made air defense system. See Lauren Gelfand, "Skepticism Surrounds Iranian Air Defence System Claims," *Jane's Defence Weekly*, April 22, 2010.

11. For breakdown of Iran's military, see "Iran" in *Middle East Military Balance* (Tel Aviv: INSS, 2010).

12. See also Wilfried Buchta, *Who Rules Iran? The Structure of Power in the Islamic Republic* (Washington, DC: Washington Institute for Near East Policy, 2002); and Ray Takeyh, *Guardians of the Revolution: Iran and the World in the Age of the Ayatollahs* (Oxford, UK: Oxford University Press, 2009).

13. "Iran as a State Sponsoring and Operating Terror," Intelligence and Terrorism Information Center April 2003, http://www.terrorism-info.org.il/malam_multimedia/html/final/eng/iran.htm.

14. Ali Nouri Zadeh, "Iran's Secret Plan if Attacked by US Codenamed 'Judgement Day,'" *Asharq Al-Awsat,* April 27, 2006.

15. "Al Quds Force of IRGC," Intelligence and Terrorism Information Center, March 30, 2007. http://www.terrorism-info.org.il/malam_multimedia/English/eng_n/pdf/iran_e0307.pdf.

16. See Testimony, Annual Threat Assessment of the Director of National Intelligence, Hearings Before the Senate Armed Services Committee, 110th Cong., February 27, 2007 (Mike McConnell, Lt. Gen. Michael Maples, and Dr. Thomas Fingar), http://www.fas.org/irp/congress/2007_hr/022707transcript .pdf; and Phil Sands and Raymond Whitaker, "The Iranian Connection: From Tehran to Baghdad," *Independent*, April 15, 2007.

17. See Shimon Shapira and Daniel Diker, "Iran's Second Islamic Revolution: Its Challenge to the West," *Iran's Race for Regional Supremacy: Strategic Implications for the Middle East* (Tel Aviv: Jerusalem Center for Public Affairs, 2008).

18. Uzi Mahnaimi, "Israeli Drones Destroy Rocket-Smuggling Convoys in Sudan," *Sunday Times,* March 29, 2009.

19. Ibid.

20. Aryeh Rona, *The Latakia Battle of 1973: The First Modern Sea Battle* (Tel Aviv: Israeli Ministry of Defense, 2007).

21. Interview with Ben-Yehuda in Tel Aviv in 2010.

22. Yoaz Hendel, "Pirates: Not Only in the Caribbean," *Perspectives* 106 (April 2010).

23. Jo Becker, "Web of Shell Companies Veils Trade by Iran's Ships," *New York Times*, June 7, 2010.

24. Yaakov Katz, "Victoria's Secret: The Inside Story of an Arms-Laden Ship," *Jerusalem Post*, March 18, 2011.

Chapter 7. Attacking Iran

1. Libya was a signatory and ratifier of the Nonproliferation Treaty and was understood to have a clandestine nuclear program; however, it gave up the program in 2003 to renew its ties with the West. In one famous case, South Africa gave up its nuclear program to become a signatory of the treaty. For more on this treaty, see Emily Landau, "A Nuclear Iran: Implications for Arms Control in the Nuclear Realm," in *Israel and a Nuclear Iran: Implications for Arms Control, Deterrence, and Defense*, ed. Ephraim Kam, Memorandum No. 94 (Tel Aviv: Institute for National Security Studies, July 2008).

2. See Bergman, *The Secret War with Iran*.

3. Yossi Melman and Meir Javedanfar, *The Nuclear Sphinx of Tehran: Mahmoud Ahmadinejad and the State of Iran* (New York: Basic Books, 2007).

4. Ibid.; and Albright, *Peddling Peril*. See also Dore Gold, *The Rise of Nuclear Iran* (Washington, DC: Regnery Publishing, 2009).

5. Smith, "Pakistani Scientist Cites Help to Iran."

6. Interview one of the authors conducted with a former US intelligence official in New York in 2010.

7. Alex Spillius, "Khamenei Vows to Fight 'Cancerous Tumor' Israel," *Sydney Morning Herald*, February 5, 2012.

8. "How the IDF Tried Assassinating Saddam," *Yediot Ahronot*, December 16, 2003.

9. Ephraim Sneh, in an interview with one of the authors in 2010 in Tel Aviv.

10. Israeli Air Force commanders, in discussions with the authors in 2009 in Tel Aviv The core of the disagreement is over procurement budgets. See Yaakov Katz, "Ground Forces Aim for New Rocket System," *Jerusalem Post,* August 20, 2010.

11. Gil Hoffman and Sheera Claire Frenkel, "I Prefer Fewer Declarations and More Deeds," *Jerusalem Post*, November 10, 2006.

12. Ibid.

13. A few months after the Israeli bombing of Osirak, then-defense minister Ariel Sharon gave a major policy address in which he elaborated on Israel's new policy. "The third element in our defense policy for the 1980s is our determination to prevent confrontation states from gaining access to nuclear weapons. Israel cannot afford the introduction of the nuclear weapon. For us, it is not a question of balance of terror but a question of survival. We shall therefore have to prevent such a threat at its inception," Sharon said. Government Press Office, Jerusalem, December 15, 1981.

14. See Bush, *Decision Points*.

15. Shlomo Brom, "Is the Begin Doctrine Still a Viable Option for Israel?," in *Getting Ready for a Nuclear-Ready Iran*, ed. Henry Sokolski and Patrick Clawson (Carlisle, PA: Strategic Studies Institute, U.S. Army War College, 2005).

16. Louis René Beres, in interview with one of the authors in the summer of 2010 by phone from Indiana.

17. Louis René Beres, "Israel, Iran and Project Daniel: A Six-Year Retrospective" (Herzliya, Israel: The Institute for Policy and Strategy–IDC, 2009).

18. Beres interview.

19. "Gates on Iran," Carnegie Endowment for International Peace, December 5, 2006, http://www.carnegieendowment.org/publications/index.cfm?fa=view&id=18905.

20. Associated Press, "CIA's Panetta: Iran Has Enough Uranium for 2 Bombs," June 27, 2010.

21. Interview with senior Israeli defense official in Tel Aviv in 2011.

22. Erich Follath and Holgar Stark, "The Birth of a Bomb: A History of Iran's Nuclear Ambitions," *Spiegel*, June 17, 2010.

23. Michael Smith, "Father of Iran's Drive for Nuclear Warhead Named," *Sunday Times*, March 23, 2008.

24. "Individuals and Entities Designated as Subject to the Travel Notification Requirements and Assets Freeze Imposed by Resolutions 1737 (2006) and 1747 (2007)," Annex to Resolution 1747, http://www.un.org/sc/committees/1737 /desindv.shtml.

25. Catherine Philp, "Leaked Memo Identifies Man at Head of Iran's Nuclear Programme," *Sunday Times*, December 14, 2009.

26. Joseph Cirincione and Elise Connor, "How Iran Can Build a Bomb," *Foreign Policy*, July 1, 2010.

27. David E. Sanger, "U.S. Presses Its Case Against Iran Ahead of Sanctions Vote," *New York Times*, June 8, 2010.

28. After taking office in January 2009, President Barack Obama announced that his administration would attempt to engage Iran in a dialogue. Talks were held in Geneva but ended without an agreement of any kind. See Richard Wolf, "Obama: Talks with Iran 'No Substitute' for Action," *USA Today*, January 1, 2009.

29. Ronen Bergman, "Will Israel attack Iran?," *New York Times,* January 25, 2012.

30. Interview with senior government official in Jerusalem in 2012.

31. "Livni Urges Obama: Don't Broadcast 'Weakness' by Talking to Iran 'at This Time,'" *Jerusalem Post*, November 7, 2008.

32. Barak Ravid, "Netanyahu: Iran Nuclear Sanctions a 'Positive' Step," *Haaretz*, June 9, 2010.

33. Sneh interview. See also remarks by U.S. national security adviser James Jones: "These are very tough sanctions. A combination of those things could well trigger a regime change—it's possible." As reported by Reuters, February 14, 2010.

34. Charles Levinson, "Israeli Faith in Iran's Opposition Gains Favor," *Wall Street Journal*, March 10, 2010.

35. David Ivry, in interview with one of the authors in Tel Aviv in 2011.

36. See Bush, *Decision Points*.

37. Authors' interview with government minister in 2010 in Jerusalem.

38. Ibid.

39. Authors' interview with Ya'alon in 2010 in Jerusalem.

40. Arieh O'Sullivan, "Ya'alon: We Must Be Prepared to Strike Iran," *Jerusalem Post*, December 14, 2004.

41. See "F-16I Sufa (Storm)," Global Security, http://www.globalsecurity.org /military/world/israel/f-16i.htm.

42. Herb Keinon and David Horovitz, "PM: Bush Won't Allow Nuclear Iran," *Jerusalem Post*, September 26, 2006.

43. David E. Sanger, "U.S. Rejected Aid for Israeli Raid on Iranian Nuclear Site," *New York Times*, January 10, 2009.

44. Senior Israeli government official, in interview with one of the authors in Tel Aviv in 2010.

45. William J. Broad, "Iran Shielding Its Nuclear Efforts in Maze of Tunnels," *New York Times*, January 5, 2010.

46. Rebecca Anna Stoil, "Barak: Qom Plant Immune to Regular Strike," *Jerusalem Post*, December 28, 2009.

47. Patrick Clawson and Michael Eisenstadt, *The Last Resort: Consequences of Preventive Military Action Against Iran* (Washington, DC: Washington Institute for Near East Policy, 2008).

48. Anthony H. Cordesman, "The Iran Attack Plan," *Wall Street Journal*, September 25, 2009.

49. Hugh Tomlinson, "Saudi Arabia Gives Israel Clear Skies to Attack Iranian Nuclear Sites," *Sunday Times*, June 12, 2010.

50. See Cordesman, "Iran Attack Plan."

51. Alon Ben-David, "Paveway III Sale to Bolster Israeli Strike Capability," *Jane's Defence Weekly*, March 4, 2005.

52. Yaakov Katz, "In Possible Signal to Iran, Israel Sends Subs through Suez Canal," *Jerusalem Post*, July 3, 2009.

53. Steven Simon, "An Israeli Strike on Iran," CPA Contingency Planning Memorandum no. 5, Council on Foreign Relations, November 2009.

54. Former IAF general, in interview with one of the authors in 2009.

55. Elisabeth Bumiller, "Iran Raid Seen as a Huge Task for Israeli Jets," *New York Times*, February 19, 2012.

56. Moshe Vered, "Ending an Iranian-Israeli War" (in Hebrew), Begin-Sadat Center for Strategic Studies, September 2009.

57. Briefing with Defense Minister Ehud Barak in November 2011 in Tel Aviv.

Chapter 8. Armageddon: The Day After

1. Dugald McConnell and Brian Todd, "Venezuela Defends Controversial Flights to Iran and Syria," *CNN*, August 22, 2010.

2. "Target: New York: Trial Showed JFK Bomb Plotters Were a Deadly Threat," *New York Daily News*, August 4, 2010.

3. Based on a briefing authors had with Israeli intelligence officers in 2009 in Jerusalem.

4. Michael Rowan and Douglas E. Schoen, "Terror at Hugo Chavez's Hand," *Forbes*, January 21, 2009.

5. "Secret Document: Venezuela, Bolivia Supplying Iran with Uranium," Associated Press, May 25, 2009.

6. Interview with a senior Israeli cabinet minister in Jerusalem in 2010.

7. Anna Mahjar-Barducci, "Iran Placing Medium-Range Missiles in Venezuela; Can Reach the U.S.," *Hudson Institute–New York*, December 8, 2010.

8. "DFM Ayalon Briefs Foreign Journalists," Israel Ministry of Foreign Affairs, press release, December 13, 2010, http://www.mfa.gov.il/MFA/About+the +Ministry/MFA+Spokesman/2010/DFM_Ayalon_foreign_press_briefing _13_Dec_2010.htm.

9. Yaakov Katz, "Security and Defense: The Day After," *Jerusalem Post*, October 29, 2010.

10. Ronald K. Knoble, "INTERPOL Secretary General Shines Light on 'Other Global Crisis' on Anniversary of 1993 World Trade Center Terrorist Bombing," February 26, 2009, https://www.interpol.int/public/News/2009/OpEd 20090226.asp.

11. See Chuck Freilich, "The Armageddon Scenario: Israel and the Threat of Nuclear Terrorism," Center Perspectives Papers no. 104 (Ramat Gan, Israel: Begin-Sadat Center for Strategic Studies, April 2010).

12. See "National Strategy for Combating Terrorism," February 2003, https://www .cia.gov/news-information/cia-the-war-on-terrorism/Counter_Terrorism _Strategy.pdf.

13. Bob Graham, "Prevention of WMD Proliferation and Terrorism Report Card," Council on Foreign Relations, 2010.

14. Ibid.

15. Amir Taheri, "Iran Has Started a Mideast Arms Race," *Wall Street Journal*, March 23, 2009.

16. Avigdor Lieberman, in interview with one of the authors in 2007 in Jerusalem. See also Yaakov Katz, "'Apocalyptic Scenario' if Egypt, Saudis Start Nuclear Programs, Lieberman Warns," *Jerusalem Post*, November 9, 2007.

17. Interview with senior Israeli defense official in Tel Aviv in 2011.

18. Israel Government Press Office, February 21, 2010.

19. Dan Williams, "Israel Quietly Prepares for Iran Atomic Bomb," Reuters, November 15, 2007.

20. Briefing on simulation for reporters in Herziliya in 2009.

21. Louis René Beres, "Facing Existential Harm: Recommendations for Israel's Strategic Future," *Think-Israel* (blog of Department of Political Science, Purdue University), September 2010.

22. Avner Cohen, *Israel and the Bomb* (New York: Columbia University Press, 1998).

23. "Let the World Worry," *Post Global Blog, Washington Post*, December 14, 2006.

24. Ibid.

25. See Cohen, *Israel and the Bomb*.

26. Interview with Mizrahi in 2007.

Selected Bibliography

Books

Albright, David. *Peddling Peril: How the Secret Nuclear Trade Arms America's Enemies*. New York: Simon & Schuster, 2010.

Amidror, Yaakov. *Winning Counterinsurgency War: The Israeli Experience*. Jerusalem: Jerusalem Center for Public Affairs, 2008.

Baer, Robert. *See No Evil: The True Story of a Ground Soldier in the CIA's War on Terrorism*. New York: Three Rivers Press, 2002.

Bar-Joseph, Uri, ed. *Israel's National Security Towards the 21st Century*. London: Frank Cass Publishers, 2001.

Bergman, Ronen. *The Secret War with Iran: The 30-Year Clandestine Struggle against the World's Most Dangerous Terrorist Power*. New York: Simon & Schuster, 2008.

Brom, Shlomo, and Elran Meir. *The Second Lebanon War: Strategic Perspectives*. Tel Aviv: Yediot Books, 2007.

Buchta, Wilfried. *Who Rules Iran? The Structure of Power in the Islamic Republic*. Washington, DC: Washington Institute for Near East Policy, 2000.

Bush, George W. *Decision Points*. New York: Crown, 2010.

Clawson, Patrick, and Michael Eisenstadt. *The Last Resort: Consequences of Preventive Military Action Against Iran*. Washington, DC: Washington Institute for Near East Policy, 2008.

Cohen, Avner. *Israel and the Bomb*. New York: Colombia University Press, 1998.

Cordesman, Anthony H. *Israel and Syria: The Military Balance and Prospects of War*. Westport, CT: Praeger Security International, 2008.

Ganin, Zvi. *An Uneasy Relationship: American Jewish Leadership and Israel*. Syracuse, NY: Syracuse University Press, 2005.

Gold, Dore. *The Rise of Nuclear Iran: How Tehran Defies the West*. Washington, DC: Regnery Publishing, 2009.

Harel, Amos, and Avi Issacharoff. *34 Days: Israel, Hezbollah, and the War in Lebanon*. New York: Palgrave Macmillan, 2009.

Hirsch, Gal. *A Story of War: A Story of Love*. Tel Aviv: Yediot Ahronot, 2009 (in Hebrew).

Melman, Yossi, and Meir Javedanfar. *The Nuclear Sphinx of Tehran: Mahmoud Ahmadinejad and the State of Iran*. New York: Basic Books, 2007.

Rona, Aryeh. *The Latakia Battle of 1973: The First Modern Sea Battle*. Tel Aviv: Israeli Ministry of Defense, 2007.

Rosenau, William. *Special Operations Forces and Elusive Enemy Ground Targets: Lessons from Vietnam and the Persian Gulf War*. Santa Monica: RAND, 2000.

Sanger, David E. *The Inheritance: The World Obama Confronts and the Challenges to American Power*. New York: Three Rivers Press, 2009.

Spector, Iftach. *Loud and Clear: The Memoir of an Israeli Fighter Pilot*. Trans. Samuel Gorvine. Minneapolis: Zenith Press, 2009.

Takeyh, Ray. *Guardians of the Revolution: Iran and the World in the Age of the Ayatollahs*. Oxford, UK: Oxford University Press, 2009.

Tamir, Moshe. *War Without Insignia*. Tel Aviv: Ma'arahot Publishing, 2005 (in Hebrew).

Thomas, Gordon. *Gideon's Spies: The Secret History of the Mossad*. New York: St. Martin's Press, 1999.

Tira, Ron. *The Limitations of Standoff Firepower–Based Operations: On Standoff Warfare, Maneuver, and Decision*. Tel Aviv: Institute for National Security Studies, 2007.

Wagman, Yehuda. *The Limited Conflict Catch*. Tel Aviv: Ma'arachot Publishing, 2002.

Westmoreland, William C. *A Soldier Reports*. Garden City, NY: Doubleday, 1976.

Articles

Beres, Louis René. "Facing Existential Harm: Recommendations for Israel's Strategic Future." *Think-Israel*. Department of Political Science, Purdue University, September–October 2010.

———. "Israel, Iran and Project Daniel: A Six-Year Retrospective." Herzliya, Israel: The Institute for Policy and Strategy–Interdisciplinary Center (IDC), February 2009.

Brom, Shlomo. "Is the Begin Doctrine Still a Viable Option for Israel?" In *Getting Ready for a Nuclear-Ready Iran*, edited by Henry Sokolski and Patrick Clawson. Carlisle, PA: Strategic Studies Institute, U.S. Army War College, 2005.

Cirincione, Joseph, and Elise Connor. "How Iran Can Build a Bomb." *Foreign Policy*, July 1, 2010.

D'Amato, Anthony. "Israel's Air Strike Against the Osiraq Reactor: A Retrospective." *Temple International and Comparative Law Journal* 259 (1996).

Eisenstadt, Michael, and Neri Zilber. "Hizballah, Iran, and the Prospects for a New Israeli-Palestinian Peace Process." *Peace Watch* no. 486, Washington Institute for Near East Policy, December 22, 2004.

Farkash, Aharon, Yaakov Amidror, and Yossi Kuperwasser. *The U.S. National Intelligence Estimate on Iran and Its Aftermath: A Roundtable of Israeli Experts.* Jerusalem: Jerusalem Center for Public Affairs, March–April 2008.

Freilich, Chuck. "The Armageddon Scenario: Israel and the Threat of Nuclear Terrorism." Center Perspectives Papers No. 104. Ramat Gan, Israel: Begin-Sadat Center for Strategic Studies, April 2010.

Gerami, Nima, and James M. Acton. "What Else Is Iran Hiding?" *Foreign Policy*, September 28, 2009.

Graham, Bob. "Prevention of WMD Proliferation and Terrorism Report Card." Council on Foreign Relations, January 2010.

Guzansky, Yoel. "The Saudi Nuclear Option." *INSS Insight* 176, April 2010.

Hendel, Yoaz. "IDF Special Units: Their Purpose and Operational Concept." *Strategic Assessment* 10, no. 2 (August 2007).

———. "Pirates: Not Only in the Caribbean." *Perspectives* 106 (April 2010).

Idan, Arie. "The Iranian Nuclear Challenge: Present Situation and Confronting Strategies." Herzliya, Israel: The Institute for Policy and Strategy–IDC, December 2004.

Kulick, Amir. "The Assassination of General Mohammed Suleiman: Looking for the Motive." *INSS Insight* 67 (August 2008).

Kuperwasser, Yossi. "Regional Implications: From Radicalism to Reform." In *The Second Lebanon War: Strategic Perspectives*, edited by Shlomo Brom and Meir Elran. Tel Aviv: Institute for National Security Studies, 2007.

Rapaport, Amir. "The IDF and the Lessons of the Second Lebanon War." Ramat Gan, Israel: Begin-Sadat Center for Strategic Studies, December 2010.

Rubin, Uzi. "Hizballah's Rocket Campaign Against Northern Israel: A Preliminary Report," *Jerusalem Issue Brief* 6, no. 10 (August 31, 2006).

———. "New Developments in Iran's Missile Capabilities: Implications Beyond the Middle East." *Jerusalem Issue Brief* 9, no. 7 (August 25, 2009).

Shapir, Yiftah S. "Iran's Ballistic Missiles." *Strategic Assessment* 12, no. 2 (2009).

———. *Middle East Military Balance.* Edited by James Hackett. Tel Aviv: Institute for National Security Studies, 2010.

Shapira, Shimon, and Daniel Diker. "Iran's 'Second' Islamic Revolution: Its Challenge to the West." *Iran's Race for Regional Supremacy: Strategic Implications for the Middle East.* Tel Aviv: Jerusalem Center for Public Affairs, 2008.

Sher, Hanan. "Facets of the Israeli Economy: The Defense Industry," Israeli Ministry of Foreign Affairs, June 1, 2002.

Simon, Steven. "An Israeli Strike on Iran." CPA Contingency Planning Memorandum no. 5, Council on Foreign Relations, November 2009.

Steinitz, Yuval. "The Growing Threat to Israel's Qualitative Military Edge." *Jerusalem Issue Brief* 3, no. 10 (2003).

Vered, Moshe. "Ending an Iranian-Israeli War" (in Hebrew). Begin-Sadat Center for Strategic Studies, September 2009.

Other Print Publications

Egyptian State Information Service. "Mubarak, Sarkozy Agree on Need for Achieving Stability in Lebanon, Establishing Independent Palestinian State," December 17, 2007.

"Hezbollah's Global Reach," House Committee on International Relations, 109th Cong. (September 28, 2006), http://democrats.foreignaffairs.house.gov /archives/109/30143.pdf.

Israeli Ministry of Foreign Affairs. "Behind the Headlines: Hizbullah Weapons in Southern Lebanon," July 16, 2009, http://www.mfa.gov.il/MFA/About+the +Ministry/Behind+the+Headlines/Hizbullah-weapons-in-Southern-Lebanon -16-Jul-2009.

Knoble, Ronald K. "INTERPOL Secretary General Shines Light on 'Other Global Crisis' on Anniversary of 1993 World Trade Center Terrorist Bombing," February 26, 2009, https://www.interpol.int/public/News/2009/OpEd20090226.asp.

Korean News Service. "Israel Condemned for Intrusion into Syria's Territorial Air," September 11, 2007.

Office of the Director of National Intelligence. "National Intelligence Estimate: Iran—Nuclear Intentions and Capabilities," November 2007, http://www.dni .gov/press_releases/20071203_release.pdf.

Internet Sources

"Al Quds Force of IRGC." Intelligence and Terrorism Information Center, March 30, 2007, http://www.terrorism-info.org.il/malam_multimedia/English/eng _n/pdf/iran_e0307.pdf.

"Gates on Iran." Carnegie Endowment for International Peace, December 5, 2006. http://www.carnegieendowment.org/publications/index.cfm?fa=view& id=18905.

"Hamas and the Terrorist Threat from the Gaza Strip." Meir Amit Intelligence and Terrorism Information Center, March 2010. http://www.terrorism-info.org.il /site/content/t1.asp?Sid=13&Pid=334.

International Institute for Counter-Terrorism–IDC. "'Cast Lead' Casualties Report." Herzliya, Israel: International Institute for Counter-Terrorism–IDC, April 2009. http://www.ict.org.il/ResearchPublications/CastLeadCasualties/tabid /325/Default.aspx.

"Iran as a State Sponsoring and Operating Terror." Intelligence and Terrorism Information Center, April 2003. http://www.terrorism-info.org.il/malam _multimedia/html/final/eng/iran.htm.

"Iranian Support for Hamas." Intelligence and Terrorism Information Center, January 12, 2008. http://www.terrorism-info.org.il/malam_multimedia/English /eng_n/pdf/iran_e004.pdf.

Permanent Mission of Islamic Republic of Iran at the United Nations, New York. www.iran-un.org.

Speech at Tenth Annual Herzliya Conference, February 3, 2010, http://www.herzliya conference.org

Index

About the Authors

Yaakov Katz is the military correspondent and senior defense analyst for the *Jerusalem Post* and the Israeli correspondent for *Jane's Defence Weekly*. He has covered all of the major events in Israel since 2002 including the Second Intifada, the Second Lebanon War, and Operation Cast Lead in the Gaza Strip. A popular lecturer on military affairs and former correspondent for *USA Today*, Katz is a frequent contributor to numerous publications in the United States. He is a regular commentator on Israel Television, Sky News, Al Jazeera, and other networks.

Yoaz Hendel is a military historian, a lecturer at Bar-Ilan University, and chairman of the Institute for Zionist Strategies. He previously served as director of the Communications and Public Diplomacy Department in the office of Prime Minister Binyamin Netanyahu. Before that, he was a columnist on strategic and military affairs for *Yediot Ahronot*, Israel's largest news daily; the military commentator for the *Makor Rishon* newspaper; and a talk show host for Israel's Army Radio.